Inclusive Technology Enhanced Learning

Overcoming Cognitive, Physical, Emotional and Geographic Challenges

Inclusive Technology Enhanced Learning draws together a remarkable breadth of research findings from across the field, providing useful data on the power of technology to solve cognitive, physical, emotional or geographic challenges in education. A far-ranging assessment, this book combines research, policy, and practical evidence to show what digital technologies work best for which learners and why.

Inclusive Technology Enhanced Learning takes a number of unique perspectives, looking at uses of digital technologies through a detailed learning framework; considering different groups of users and how they can be individually supported through digital technologies; and exploring how those who support different categories of learners can apply technologies to their specific support needs. This powerful meta-analysis of research on technology enhanced learning will be invaluable reading for anyone concerned with the impacts of digital technologies on learning across subject areas, age ranges, and levels of ability.

Don Passey is a Professor of Technology Enhanced Learning in the Department of Educational Research at Lancaster University, UK.

Inclusive Technology Enhanced Learning

Overcoming Cognitive, Physical, Emotional and Geographic Challenges

Don Passey

Routledge
Taylor & Francis Group

NEW YORK AND LONDON

First published 2014
by Routledge
711 Third Avenue, New York, NY 10017

Simultaneously published in the UK
by Routledge
2 Park Square, Milton Park, Abingdon, Oxon OX14 4RN

Routledge is an imprint of the Taylor & Francis Group, an informa business

© 2014 Taylor & Francis

British Library Cataloguing in Publication Data
A Catalogue record for this book is available from the British Library
Library of Congress Cataloguing in Publication Data

ISBN: 978–0–415–52433–9 (hbk)
ISBN: 978–0–415–52434–6 (pbk)
ISBN: 978–0–203–07374–2 (ebk)

Typeset in Bembo
by RefineCatch Limited, Bungay, Suffolk

To
Alun, Christina and Petra

Contents

Illustrations

Figures

Tables

Preface

Do digital technologies overcome challenges and barriers for learners? This book considers this question, through a detailed exploration of learning, learners and mediator contexts. It considers challenges and barriers from different perspectives—including cognitive, physical, emotional and geographical—but does so from a learning landscape perspective, where digital technologies are an element (often common or crucial) within an integrated mix of resources that learners can draw upon and use to support and benefit their needs.

This book focuses on an aspect of education that is widely discussed, often highlighted, and sometimes of timely importance, by practitioners, policy makers and researchers: digital educational technologies and their relationships to learning. Digital technologies have been used for over 20 years in supporting learners and teachers in a wide variety of ways. While many learners and teachers talk about the ways that educational digital technologies offer them support, there is nevertheless variable and contested evidence about the extent of value or gains provided.

The contribution of educational digital technologies to learning, and particularly to learning viewed through different perspectives and in a variety of contexts, is the focus of this book. It looks at contributions to learning that arise from uses of digital technologies for young people, up to some 19 years of age (but some examples and sections of text take evidence about older learners up to 21 years of age in universities or colleges or adults in a few cases), although the emphasis is largely on learners who are of pre-school (kindergarten) through school age.

At the same time, the book takes a contemporary perspective on this debated field; it looks across the width of digital technologies used for learning, spanning not just hardware and devices, but more specifically on software and digital resources. It challenges the reader to consider this field in depth, rather than simplistically seeking an answer about the extent that educational digital technologies benefit learning and teaching. It details arguments as to why a wider contextual perspective should be taken, and begins to explore how it might be done. It asks the reader to question what appear to be widely-held assumptions—about the singularity of learning (and the role of learning theories and concepts in this respect), of learners (and how the learning of different learners might be dependent on differences arising from different digital technologies), of supporters (and the roles they play when educational digital technologies are used in different learning settings), and indeed of technologies themselves (and whether indeed they can be merely grouped together when studies seek to identify learning gains and benefits). The content argues and asks the reader to consider implications when these assumptions are questioned, and offers a framework through which to begin to explore this field through different lenses. As Bennett and Oliver (2011) said: "Research in learning technology has focused on practical, instrumental concerns, to the detriment of its ability to engage with theory. . . . We need to be able to develop theory, question it and even reject it if necessary" (p. 187). This book seeks to do this through complementary analytical approaches.

There is a strongly emerging literature in the field of educational digital technologies and how they enhance learning for young people. This literature can be grouped into four categories: literature focusing on conceptualising and framing the field (such as Luckin, 2010; Selwyn, 2011); literature looking at how to research the field (such as McDougall, Murnane, Jones, & Reynolds, 2010); literature available through a range of journals, in articles reporting studies about specific technologies and specific interventions with certain age groups or groups of students with certain attributes (such as the *Journal of Computer Assisted Learning; Learning, Media and Technology; Computers & Education; Computers in the Schools*; and the *British Journal of Educational Technology*); and literature from a variety of national and more local reports of uses and impacts of technologies on learning (such as Wenglinsky, 1998; Schachter & Fagnano, 1999; Harrison et al., 2002; Underwood et al., 2005; and Somekh et al., 2007). This text draws on evidence from across these categories, focuses on impacts of technologies on learning in detail, and on specific groups of learners, including vulnerable groups, and their supporters or mediators.

This book recognises that educational digital technologies are regularly being developed and emerging (see, for example, Becta, 2007; The New Media Consortium, 2010), and that research in this field has continued to keep pace with these emerging technologies. But it also highlights the fact that the developed evidence base forces us to question some of our concerns and approaches to this field. Do we take sufficient account of past research outcomes, or do we dismiss them in favour of exploring 'new' technologies? Have we reached the point of being able to consider an appropriate taxonomy of educational digital technologies so that emerging technologies can still fit into an existing framework?

Over the past 10 or more years, there has been a considerable investment in technologies (internationally, nationally, more locally at authority and school levels, and within homes) to support educational endeavour. While a continued investment in many countries as well as regionally and locally is likely, policy makers and educators currently raise concerns about learners being able to gain the most from existing and past investment and resources, while a current and future focus should be on efforts to ensure maximum benefits for learners and learning, minimising future investment. At the same time, economic concerns about the future organisation and structures of education are being raised internationally, nationally, regionally and locally. These concerns raise questions about the future nature of educational organisations and practices, and there are groups that argue that digital technologies can be used effectively to support more economic structures without organisational changes affecting learning outcomes. These concerns and questions will be discussed within this text, related to details concerned with learning and distinct learner groups.

This book adds to the current literature by drawing together outcomes and findings from across the field, but also by challenging some of the conceptions that are adopted and prevalent in some areas of the reported literature:

- It challenges the concepts that learning, learners and digital technologies are all singularities.
- It challenges the ways that impact reports tend to be over-generalised.

Acknowledgements

Almost all my research has involved collaborations between scholars, policy makers and practitioners, from a wide range of professional backgrounds. My work would not have been possible without the co-operation and willingness of, literally, hundreds of schools (and the very many head teachers, managers, teachers, learners and parents involved, not only in England, but in a number of countries around the world), tens of local authorities (and the many officers and consultants involved), dozens of policy makers, and dozens of scholars. I have been fortunate to receive a huge contribution in kind; those involved are unfortunately too numerous to mention individually, but their invaluable contributions are all recognised nonetheless, and I am indebted to them in so many ways. For their long-standing interest and support, I would particularly like to mention and thank sincerely: Steve Moss, initially at Cumbria LA; Dave Thomson, Worcestershire LA; Graham Fielden, Lancashire LA; Dr Dave Whyley, Jill Purcell and Gavin Hawkins, Wolverhampton LA; Dave Brodie, Mike Farmer and Chris Price, Birmingham LA; colleagues at Becta; Doug Brown, formerly at Birmingham LA and then at the DfES; David Moran and Phil Bourne then at the SSAT; and my many colleagues in IFIP. My thanks also to those many managers in corporations and companies who have supported and encouraged my work, particularly those in: Microsoft; RM Ltd.; the BBC; Espresso Education; Phase 6 and SAM Learning.

Within my own department and university, I have received continued support over many years, and I would like to thank Professor Jim Ridgway (who provided a great deal of stimulus in the early stages of my research career), Professors Murray Saunders, Colin Rogers, Paul Trowler, Mary Hamilton and Carolyn Jackson (heads of departments who have made my work possible), Professor David Hutchison, Dr Andrew Scott, Paul Davies, Dr Catherine Fritz, Dr Julia Gillen, Dr Joan Machell, Gilly McHugh and Dr Sadie Williams (colleagues directly involved in research studies), Shealagh Whytock (who supported my work through her remarkable administrative skills and qualities for 20 years), and the many administrative colleagues who have provided invaluable background support. Finally, my thanks go to Dr Paul Ashwin, my current Head of Department, who vitally supports my on-going work.

Chapter 1

An Overview of Approaches Taken in This Book

How Educational Digital Technologies Contribute to Learning

Fundamentally, this book looks at a key contemporary issue—the contributions educational digital technologies bring to learning. In exploring this issue, the educational digital technologies themselves (and how we classify or categorise them), how we identify or measure contribution, and how we define or describe learning, learners and those who support them, will be separately considered.

The question of contributions to learning from educational technologies has been debated for many years, and it is highly likely that the debate will continue as new and emerging technologies become accessible. This is particularly likely to be the case since methods to identify contribution cannot be placed outside the context of the digital technologies themselves; the digital technologies play a part not only in that contribution, but also, therefore, in how we measure that contribution.

Research Methodologies in the Context of Learning and Learner Differences

Although this book is not intended as a methodological text or a text centrally offering a methodological critique, it is important to note here that methodological issues need to be considered when looking at and exploring studies identifying learning outcomes, gains and impacts. Concerns currently are raised about research methods and their applicability to findings and their wider generalisation in the field of educational digital technologies. A recent second-order meta-analysis of study results from the past 40 years of research, examining learning gains arising from uses of digital technologies (Tamim, Bernard, Borokhovsi, Abrami, & Schmid, 2011), takes a methodological approach seeking to collate evidence from the widest possible range of sources. From this analysis, the authors concluded that both average effect sizes from their second-order meta-analysis and from their validation study, both accounting for fixed effects and random effects, were low (or moderate at best); they calculated effect sizes that ranged only from 0.30 to 0.35. As the authors said, this means a learner in an environment with digital technologies will on average perform 12 percentile points better than someone in a learning environment without them. Importantly, the authors went on to say that it can be argued that: "aspects of the goals of instruction, pedagogy, teacher effectiveness, subject matter, age level, fidelity of technology implementation, and possibly other factors . . . may represent more powerful influences on effect sizes than the nature of the technology intervention" (p. 17). The authors went further, recommending that future researchers focus on how these different factors contribute, so that uses of digital technologies might be most effectively applied to support learning.

Some researchers, however, believe that impacts on learning arising from specific uses of digital technologies are either very hard to measure, or, actually, impossible to measure. Reasons are based on the difficulty of associating selected impact measures with affordances and uses of the digital technologies. As a recent research group (Association for Learning Technology [ALT], 2012) stated, "The outcomes of education extend beyond examination results and timescales extend beyond the period at school. Learning was also context dependent and there was an issue of the currency of the results of any research" (p. 6). Other reasons for concern about impact measures are based, in cases where control groups are involved, on difficulties of ensuring matched sets of control and test groups are contextually the same in all other respects. As the same research group went on to say, holding variables constant in an educational environment is not necessarily the same as that within a medical environment. So, in an educational environment: "It was not clear what a control group would do in a large scale education experiment and whether this were indeed possible as teachers would find it hard to stand dispassionately back from that group and teacher attitudes affect results" (p. 6).

Such considerations about efficacy of research methodologies and study findings go beyond a concern associated with delineating a simplistic division of quantitative and qualitative approaches. For, although it is clear that quantitative approaches allow extents or levels of outcomes or gains to be identified, they do not necessarily enable an understanding of how or why those outcomes occur (see, for example, in the context of integrated learning systems, the limitations highlighted by Underwood, Cavendish, Dowling, & Lawson, 1997). Fundamentally, however, a perspective that suggests that quantitative methods enable extents and levels to be known can itself be potentially misleading—what needs to be asked here is extents or levels of what, exactly.

Choice of Method and Relationship to Findings about Contribution

To explore this issue further, an example will illustrate quandaries readily found in quantitative studies, even where associated qualitative elements are undertaken alongside them. In the United Kingdom (UK), a well-known quantitative study from the early 2000s explored impacts of uses of information and communication technologies (ICT) on learning—this was the ImpaCT2 study (Harrison et al., 2002). Their study involved 60 schools, divided into three groups, dependent on learner age. Learners were grouped into age categories, from 10 to 11 years, 13 to 14 years, and 15 to 16 years. The study analysed outcomes and impact according to levels of use of ICT, identified in each of the age group categories from answers learners gave to questions asking how often computers were used for school work during the previous year in separate subject areas. Respondents were then grouped into 'high' and 'low' use categories by subject.

The final analysis looked at mean relative scores across three Key Stages (age ranges), at 11, 14 and 16 years of age. For 11- and 14-year-old learners, scores came from national standard assessment tests (SATs) and at 16 years of age from national general certificate of school education (GCSE) examinations. A comparison of 'high' and 'low' ICT users then allowed relative gains to be identified. Results indicated where there were positive associations, and at a statistically significant level. For example, findings at the end of Key Stage 2 (11 years of age) in English indicated statistical significance between level of ICT and national tests, that high ICT use was estimated to raise performance in the national test by 3.12 marks (0.16 of a level), and that high ICT use was estimated to accelerate progress towards the national test by 16%; but in mathematics indicated non-statistical significance between level of ICT and national tests, that high ICT use was estimated to raise performance in the national test by 1.69 marks (0.061 of a level), and that high ICT use was estimated to accelerate progress towards the national test by 6.1%.

There are methodological questions to be raised about this study, and also about ways in which averages and estimates are considered by teachers in how they apply these to each learner in their class. Although an extensive study:

- Learning was viewed mainly through subject measures of knowledge and understanding. As such, the most commonly tested aspects of learning would have been recall and memorisation, with some levels of application also being tested. It was 'test learning' that was being measured; learning arising at the time of the use of digital technologies, and longer-term learning arising in terms of transfer to the next stage of education or training, was not tested. The test results did not tell us a great deal about preparedness for learning, or the ways that learners might have changed their thinking about their learning, for example.
- Learners tested were selected by teachers as being representative of their classes. However, this had clearly not necessarily included learners who would have been representative of all learners. Details about categories of learners and populations of learners will be discussed later, but it is not clear that learners in one age category from 20 schools would be representative of the 1,474,300 learners in the 10- to 11-year-old population from across the UK recorded in 2007 to 2008 (Department for Children, Schools and Families [DCSF], 2008), which is unlikely to vary hugely from the figures in the years 2000 to 2001.
- There was limited information in this report about different forms of ICT being used, or the ways the ICT were supported through teacher or tutor interventions. It cannot be assumed that these were the same.

Overall, this study took a quantitative approach, although qualitative evidence was gathered and used to provide additional and valuable insights. However, none of the tests were completed using ICT as a direct vehicle, or as a means to support activities required to complete the tests. These tests removed the ICT from the context used to support learning within classroom situations. The link between uses of ICT to support prior learning, and ways that tests identified those aspects of learning was not clarified or identified within the report.

This UK approach to studying learning and impacts of ICT is rather different from that proposed and undertaken in the United States (US). The advice given by the US Department of Education, Institute of Education Sciences, and the National Center for Education Evaluation and Regional Assistance (2003) is to consider impacts identified through controlled studies. This group advises that statistical significance effects are to be identified whenever possible to validate efficacy, meaning that a study should have a sample size large enough to demonstrate this. They suggest a study of about 300 learners, with 150 in a control group and 150 in a test or intervention group. If classrooms rather than learners are used, they suggest 50 to 60 schools or classrooms are used, with half as control and the other half as test groups. They caution, however, that initial starting attainment or achievement should be roughly the same across all these learners, or schools, or classrooms.

There are clearly differences between the UK and US approaches. Overall, in terms of research designs and ways to identify impacts:

- Controlled studies enable differences between use and non-use of a specific digital technology used by learners to be identified. So, studies using US approaches are often much more specific; they focus on an individual educational digital technology or product.
- A wide range of digital technologies used in or across a range of classrooms, levels of use and associations with impacts can be identified through non-controlled quantitative studies. In the UK, controlled studies have been used less, and digital technologies and products have been delineated less.
- In specific situations and with specific individuals, qualitative studies have allowed reasons for impacts to be identified rather than average extents of impact. Indeed, average extents of impacts can potentially hide a skewed result. They might also, importantly, hide the fact that there are learners where high or low levels of gain are arising, and these are not cases highlighted and explored further. If these were explored more, this might tell us more about the levels and the qualities of some more specific groups of learners.

A Four-stage Methodological and Analytical Approach to Measuring Contribution

Before selecting a research method for any study exploring benefits and gains arising from uses of educational digital technologies, however, it is important to distinguish between and consider the relative and related contributions of four key elements: affordances; uses; outcomes; and impacts.

Affordances describe the features that a digital technology provides (such as a real-life context offered within a video of an event, or the ways that text can be amended, removed or added to online). Gibson (1977) originally defined affordances in terms of features of an environment, that they offer a provision or function, allowing actions to be observed as a consequence (which might be beneficial or otherwise). Later, Kirschner (2002) considered the concept of educational affordances more specifically, and defined these as features of artefacts determining or allowing particular learning activities or behaviours within a learning environment, but additionally and importantly, that learner characteristics play an important part and may subsequently determine aspects of learning that are possible or not. Affordances are determined initially by features or properties of both hardware and software; for example, the 'comment box' in *MS Word* is an affordance that can be used by a teacher or a learner. Some studies focus specifically on identifying and investigating affordances of digital technologies. For example, Deng and Yuen (2011) identified important affordances of blogs that could lead to emotional and social aspects of learning, while Maher (2011) identified affordances from observing uses of e-books via interactive whiteboards in year 3 and 4 primary classes in Australia.

Uses, on the other hand, describe how a digital technology (whether hardware or software) is applied, either by teachers or by learners. For example, a teacher can use a video clip in which an author describes his approach to writing with a group of learners in a classroom, offering them ideas about creative writing approaches they might take. Here the teacher uses affordances of the video clip resource. Studies that have closely linked affordances with uses are those of Robertson (2011), who looked at uses of blogs recorded in design diaries completed by 113 computer science undergraduates, Jones and Cuthrell (2011), who considered uses of *YouTube* for learning, of Banister (2010), who explored uses of iPads, iPhones and iPods with learners in grades K to 12, Murphy, Rodríguez-Manzanares, and Barbour (2011), who examined uses of both synchronous and asynchronous online teaching, and Dalgarno and Lee (2010), who looked at uses of 3D virtual learning environments, developing spatial awareness and representation, experiential learning, collaborative learning, and learning in contexts related to real-life situations.

Outcomes describe what results from or after use. For example, learners can use an online test of mathematical tables, and their ability to remember certain times tables afterwards is an outcome. Many of the studies in subsequent chapters of this book examine and report outcomes of different forms of digital technologies. *Impacts* go further; they describe measurable outcomes arising (often through the use of test results, which might be teacher-devised or they might be national standard tests). For example, if a learner having used online tests to revise mathematical times tables has remembered them better afterwards, then a test to measure the difference before and after in terms of outcome allows an impact to be identified. Impact is, of course, dependent on individual learner characteristics and attributes (such as starting abilities or attainment in knowledge areas and interest levels), as well as being dependent on teaching and environmental contexts (such as the approach taken by the teacher, or the attitude of a group of learners within a class). So, contextual factors also need to be considered in an analysis of impacts. To identify impact as a legitimate measure, the relationship of these four components needs to be established and to be clear: the affordances from an educational digital technology need to be identified and these must clearly be linked to the next three elements; teachers and learners should use technological affordances and features of digital resources as well as accounting for individual characteristics and attributes of learners, teaching and environmental contexts; outcomes should arise from uses; and impacts need to be measured by instruments that identify outcomes arising from uses that are related to affordances. Some of the studies in later chapters of this book focus on identification of impact, and levels of impact are given where possible.

This four-stage approach will be returned to later, to consider how different research studies provide us with measures that indicate results in one or more of these stages.

Selection of Literature

It is worth noting here that this book relies as far as possible on more recent research findings. Although some less recent research is referred to throughout, the contemporary context in which learning occurs is important. This is demonstrated well when we consider forms of 'hypermedia' included in the meta-analysis of Liao (1998), who stated that: "interactive multimedia, multimedia simulators, and Level III or above . . . interactive videodiscs as delivery systems were considered" (p. 341). It is clear from this description of the digital technologies contemporary at that time, that the way in which 'delivery systems' can impact on learning would have been quite different from the way in which collaborative tools now do so. Highlighted further within the meta-analysis of Rosen and Salomon (2007), who looked at potential differences in learning outcomes of constructivist environments versus more traditional environments, as they said: "Different learning environments provide different learning experiences and ought to serve different achievement goals" (p. 1). They conjectured that constructivist learning environments would provide different forms of attainment and achievements, consistent with those environments, which would be different from the attainment arising from traditional environments. From a meta-analysis of 32 experimental studies exploring this form of comparison, they reported that results showed constructivist learning environments were more effective than traditional environments, with an effect size of 0.460, and that this effect size increases to 0.902 when tests identify more selected constructivist-focused measures. They found that when traditionally focused measures were selected, however, there was no significant difference between the two environments. They suggested this could be due to traditional settings incorporating more constructivist elements over time. It was certainly clear from their study that impacts arising could vary according to the selected measures used. The importance of contemporary factors was also highlighted by Jenks and Springer (2002), who concluded at the time they were reviewing research literature on computer assisted instruction (CAI) that: "In view of the age of the research, and in examining the potential shortfalls of much of that research, more research should be conducted on what makes CAI effective. Does CAI fair as well in contemporary settings with contemporary learners?". As they went on to say, contemporary factors need to be considered in terms of applicability of subjects to uses of digital technologies, and the ways in which interventions and instruction operate.

In terms of the selection of literature to inform a text such as this, a point made by Zhao (2003) is also worth noting. When reviewing existing analyses of effects of digital technologies on the outcomes of language learning, he stated that reports should be read with caution, as journals and reports might not report negative or neutral outcomes. This could of course be correct, but from my experience of conducting over 60 different studies in the past 12 years, I can say that there have been none of these (qualitative, quantitative and mixed method studies) where statistically significant negative levels of outcome have arisen; they have all identified positive or neutral level outcomes. From my experience in looking at studies that are reported, I would say that the balance is about the same. The selection of supporting literature in this text attempts to provide a balance, but at the same time to provide a picture that is detailed enough to understand when and why neutral, as well as positive or sometimes negative, outcomes arise.

Chapter 2

Educational Digital Technologies and Learning

Learning is Where We Start

A great deal has been written about digital technologies enhancing learning. An early meta-analysis of 120 studies completed between 1987 and 1992 by Fletcher-Flinn and Gravatt (1995) concluded that while there was evidence for benefit, further analysis suggested additional influential factors were also important. As they said, "studies which controlled for teacher and materials, and were of longer duration and studies using pencil and paper equivalents of CAI showed no learning advantage over traditional forms of instruction" (p. 219).

Although research studies since then have continued to identify learning benefits arising, sometimes using diagnostic and standardised tests or national and public examinations as measures of gains (see, for example, Wenglinsky, 1998; Wood, 1998; Schachter & Fagnano, 1999; Harrison et al., 2002; the Metiri Group, 2006; Somekh et al., 2007), these studies have not always delineated and detailed how the impacts identified and reported have arisen in terms of interventions and pedagogies used, or the learning focus involved. There have sometimes been uncertainties about even the age groups where learning benefits have arisen. While Roblyer, Castine, and King (1988) from their meta-analysis reported that impacts measured by effect size were more significant in the case of college and adult age learners than they were with elementary or secondary school age learners, Harrison et al. (2002) identified more significant impacts in primary than in secondary school, and in certain subjects. A more detailed view needs to be taken to start to unravel ambiguities and uncertainties.

Learning can be defined in a general sense (as a gaining of knowledge, ideas or concepts not already known or recognised), but while this is a single overarching definition, learning is not a single thing. It is made up of many constituent parts; for example, learning how to make a cake, learning how to find the time a bus leaves, or learning how to analyse data from a scientific experiment about the growth of yeasts all demand different forms of inquiry and lead to different forms of learning outcome. So, considering detail within individual studies identifying benefits, and relating these to specific elements of learning, is important.

Similarly, learners are not a single individual, but as a population (or populations) are made up of widely different individuals and groups, with different needs and taking different approaches to learning. Those supporting learners recognise these differences readily, and consequently, may support individuals or groups of individuals in quite different ways. When digital technologies are used, they may be applied in different ways, according to the support focus that is felt to be most appropriate at any particular time.

Digital technologies are not a single thing either; they need to be considered in terms of the more specific affordances that a group of technologies bring to particular learners and to their particular needs. The overall approach taken in this book is to delineate as carefully as possible using appropriate taxonomies—to consider benefits that can arise when specific digital technologies are used, impacting specific aspects of learning, for specific groups of learners, with specific mediators supporting learning. In all of these instances, in subsequent sections and chapters, research evidence will be used to identify and explain extents and scopes of benefits that can arise. Evidence presented will show that digital technologies can support learning and learners widely; indeed, digital technologies can offer inclusive opportunities, in that their application to different learners and their more specific needs is very wide. But this statement should not be taken to mean that they offer the same support to each learner. Inclusive technology enhanced learning should be considered more as a ubiquitous opportunity; understanding differences that apply to the individual, then, will enable those opportunities to be realised.

Learning is Not a Singularity

We will now return to learning, and focus on what constitutes learning and how we conceive learning. Learning is a wide conceptual term encompassing very many specific and distinctive elements and processes. When it is stated that a digital technology enhances or supports learning, such a statement is likely to be over-generalising in terms of describing influence or impact. It would be extremely unlikely that any specific digital technology or application would enhance or support all aspects or elements of learning. To find ways to explore this issue within the context of educational digital technologies, we will consider taxonomies to distinguish different elements constituting learning, and then look at ways these can be constructed to allow a more detailed and secure analysis of ways educational digital technologies impact learning.

Learning can be considered through a number of different perspectives or lenses:

- Neurobiological (the way that biological structure enables learning).
- Cognitive (processes that occur internally that constitute ways of learning).
- Emotional (approaches we individually take in understanding and being involved in our own learning, and short- and long-term interests we take in that learning).
- Social (ways that learning occurs in different social settings and circumstances).
- Societal (long-term interests and opportunities that drive our commitment to learning).

Different researchers have given us insights that build our understanding of learning through these different perspectives. So, while Piaget (1972) took a more cognitive and developmental perspective (how learning developed in children over time, and what processes were brought into play at different stages or ages), Vygotsky (1978) took a much more social perspective (concerned with how learning arose through social interaction, and within a sense of social development and integration). More recently, further constructs of learning have been defined and identified, and applied to learning associated with digital technologies (or ICT or e-learning). In summary, some key elements and constructs of particular pertinence are:

- Behaviourism or behaviourist approaches—were initially based on observations of animal behaviours, demonstrating responses to stimuli (see, for example, Skinner, 1935). Features of conditioned reflexes and operant conditioning were applied to learning situations more widely, and although these ideas are now considered as somewhat outdated, examples demonstrating these features are still reported in certain situations (learning engagement arising when rewards are promised and given, for example).
- Social constructivist approaches—are based on the work of, for example, Vygotsky (1978), and relate learning to active roles of the learner, building knowledge and understanding in ways relating to external social dimensions and interactions. The importance of background social culture and context are highlighted in this construct.
- Social constructionist approaches—are based on the work of Berger and Luckmann (1966), and take the nature of social interactions into account more, and highlight the importance of social agreement, institutional practices and collective social action on our knowledge and ideas. This construct asks us to consider differences between objective reality and human subjectivity (see, for example, Searle, 1995).
- Computer assisted learning or e-learning—is a term indicating that computers (digital technologies) can be used to support aspects of education and training. The nature of the interactions that might be involved is not specified, but it is argued that existing theories of learning are not adequate in explaining outcomes observed in e-learning contexts (see, for example, Andrews & Haythornthwaite, 2007).
- Computer supported collaborative learning—is more specific in terms of considering the nature of interactions involved. It focuses much more on the fact that interactions using computers allow sharing and collaboration, perhaps within specific situational contexts or in communities of practice (see Lave & Wenger, 1991).
- Networked learning—is perhaps more specific still, in focusing on the nature of interactions concerned with networking (see Jones, 2004), where technologies and social interactions are integrally linked, each playing their part in supporting actions in situations where learning can arise.

Rather than taking one or all (and there are others that could be added) of these constructs to consider ways digital technologies can support learning, a more fundamentalist (or perhaps reactionary) approach is taken here. For this approach, a construction will be used which will seek to integrate these different constructs. To say that any one of these is more important than the other, or that they are exclusive, seems a rather strange notion; indeed, the concepts have been identi-fied through different perspectives rather than through the same perspective, so it is arguable that their exclusivity is more questionable than their inclusivity. Sayer (1992, cited in Jones & Czerniewicz, 2011, p. 174) describes theory through three dimensions: as an ordering framework permitting observational data to be used for prediction and explanation of empirical events; as a conceptualisation, prescribing a particular way of conceptualising something; and as a hypothesis or explanation. Accepting these, and particularly accepting the second of these three dimensions, it seems more likely that they constitute a potential comple-mentarity, working together in certain respects. An integrative approach would seem especially relevant to situations where activities of learners are varied, using different forms of educational digital technologies at different times, rather than working separately. In taking this integrative approach, it will be possible to see whether these constructs are each supported by evidence rather than each being an ideological frame that is singularly important. The key point here is that different researchers have taken different perspectives, and that different constructs are viewed from different positions (see Figure 2.1).

The constructs themselves have often been researched with specific and small groups of individuals, and when studies continue to explore these constructs, if

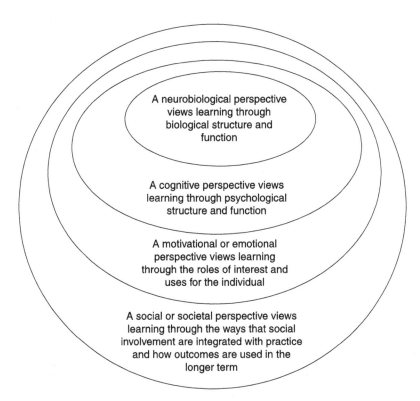

Figure 2.1 A way to view learning constructs and their varying perspectives

opportunities for alternative or other dimensions are not sufficiently considered, the result will then be a refining of the construct rather than a review of the construct. Certainly, in this respect, the research of Andrews and Haythornthwaite (2007) has been important, and has raised questions about applicability of existing constructs to the field of learning when educational digital technologies are employed. Accepting that an integrative approach to different constructs can provide a picture that can be wide-ranging, it also then seems possible that learning approaches by a wider population but at a more individual level could be accommodated. It is certainly feasible to think about certain constructs having a more prominent part to play when learners are considered as individuals, or where uses of specific educational digital technologies are considered. Then, the patterns of their learning interactions can be quite different, illustrated by the different patterns shown in Figures 2.2 and 2.3.

In Figure 2.2, the learner is concerned with cognitive endeavour, internal thinking and analysis, with a great deal of internal and intrapersonal activity, without a great deal of interaction with others through social environments; in Figure 2.3, the learner is concerned with social interaction and discussion, in developing ideas and thinking through dialogue with others, and in questioning ideas held with others. Both learners are highly motivated, and while they might well be addressing the same learning need, their approaches are clearly different.

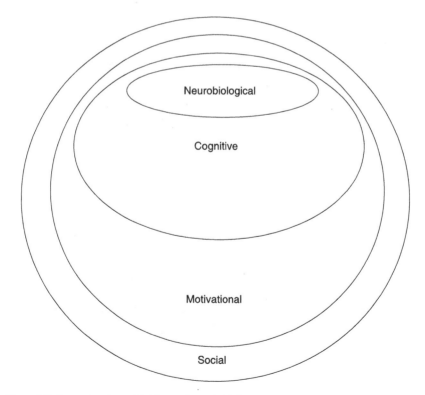

Figure 2.2 A way to view a highly motivated thinker

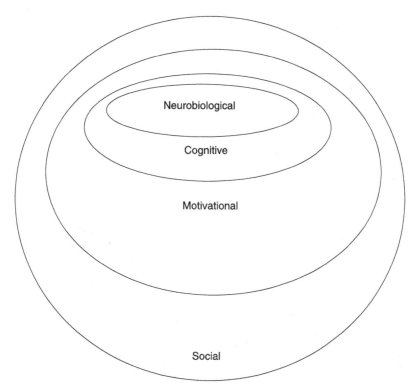

Figure 2.3 A way to view a highly motivated social learner

How would educational digital technologies be used in each of these circum-stances? Probably they would not be ideally used in the same way. Taking another, perhaps more extreme, look at this issue, Edelson (2012), talking about his experience with learners who are on the autistic spectrum, says that they may well rely on one style of learning more than another. He contrasts the learner who talks a great deal, who enjoys talking and being involved in discussion and who enjoys listening to audio broadcast and music (an auditory learner) with another learner who takes things apart, moves things around and handles items frequently (a kinaesthetic learner).

Descriptions of ways that other children learn offers other sharp contrasts. For example, Wishart (1993) stated that for a learner who has Down's syndrome, is shy and has low levels of literacy, such a learner might put a great deal of effort into avoiding learning, since the learner feels that being involved might put them in a position where they would feel at a distinct disadvantage cognitively. So, to say that learning is the same for each is clearly false. Indeed, looking at how learning is conceived for practice purposes, what is intended is that learning outcomes should be the same as far as possible. Making an association here between an intended universal or singular set of learning outcomes and a singularity in terms of learning approaches of all learners is clearly a false premise on which to start developing appropriate and useful practice. It is clear that learning for the two learners illustrated in Figures 2.2 and 2.3 is a quite different matter—in terms of the ways they are likely to engage with learning, the processes they will choose to bring to their learning endeavours, and the ways they will externalise their learning. Learning is concerned with choice on the part of the learner; imposing learning through a singular approach or concept or theory may not do this choice justice. When educational digital technologies are involved, choice of learning adopted by the learner becomes not only more important, but provides for more potential—so long as those supporting learning can recognise the potential range of alternatives and options, and these are also made available to the learner.

Considering the Neurobiological Level and Implications for Cognition

Learning is concerned at a more neuro-cognitive level with ways that knowledge, ideas and experiences are brought to and held in mind, allowing these to be integrated with other knowledge, ideas and experiences, as well as recall and association with other ideas. Psychologists have described roles of mental schemas in holding different forms of knowledge, ideas and concepts in mind. Fiske and Taylor (1991) described how schemas as 'background theories' help us make sense of new events or situations, which certainly highlights the importance of 'background theories' when encountering new knowledge, ideas or concepts. If this is true, it is likely that these schemas, or the ways that details are held in schemas, however, vary from individual to individual. Many people hold mental schemas of ideas or events in forms of moving, colour images so that details associated with these forms are those generated when they recall concepts or ideas. But it is worth considering how details that individuals describe when they are recalling ideas and events relate to forms of memorisation and back to engagement.

An additional factor at this level is also the distinction between working (short-) and long-term memory. While working memory enables individuals to handle knowledge and ideas in the short term, it is the creation of schemas with links to associated ideas that allows individuals to both retain and recall ideas, concepts and facts in the future. In terms of these forms of memory and ways teachers in schools support them, short-term or working memory is often the major focus for activities within classrooms, relying on and using text-based resources. These resources, as they can be scanned and skimmed readily, are ideal for supporting short-term memory interactions. Longer-term memory on the other hand is often constructed through mental schemas in the form of moving imagery and associated sensory, emotional and kinaesthetic links. These forms of memory may well be supported better, therefore, through use of sensory forms that are visual, moving, auditory, olfactory, emotional or kinaesthetic.

Research by the author illustrates this in context. Data were collected from teachers, using response (interactive voting) devices in four different conference sessions. The teachers held a range of roles; 13 head teachers, 54 senior leaders, and 27 practitioners. These teachers were asked to recall concepts, ideas and

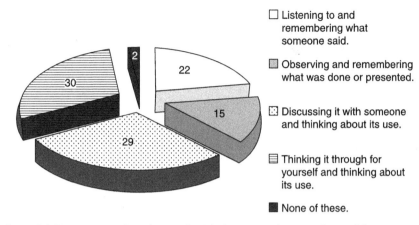

Figure 2.4 Proportions of teachers indicating how something was learned from a conference

events, choosing appropriate forms in which they brought them to mind through recall.

The first case asked teachers to think of something learned from the conference they were attending, or from a previous conference (proportions and numbers are shown in Figure 2.4). They were asked in what form it had been learned: listening to and remembering what someone said; observing and remembering what was done or presented; discussing it with someone and thinking about its use; thinking it through and thinking about its use; or none of these.

Different individuals reported learning specific things from the conference in different ways, but discussion played a major role for one-third of this audience. From a range of previous research studies (Pask, 1975; Vygotsky, 1978; Alexander, 2008) it is clear that dialogic learning and discussion do indeed play important roles in learning. In thinking about how the different reported forms of learning could be supported by digital technologies, roles of educational digital technologies applied could be quite different for each group of individuals identified in Figure 2.4: someone observing and remembering what was done or presented might well benefit from accessing video clips; while someone discussing with someone and thinking about its use might benefit more from online discussion or a video-conferencing session.

The second case asked teachers to think of a volcanic eruption. They were asked in what form they recalled this concept: as a black and white diagram; in a moving form; in a moving form in colour; in a moving form in colour with sound; as a piece of text; or none of these. Proportions and numbers are shown in Figure 2.5.

Although most recalled it in a moving form in colour, only about half of them recalled it with sound. Again, thinking about how digital technologies could support these different groups, it is clear that video films could provide a means to match this form of recall with the form of engagement, while for others a

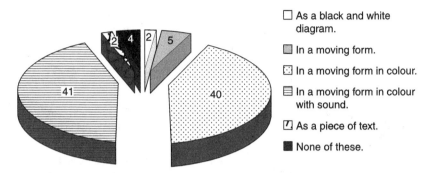

Figure 2.5 Proportions of teachers indicating the way a concept was recalled

black and white diagram might build a mental schematic more easily. Whether different optional forms of digital resource when matched to these different learners' reported recall would make a difference was not the focus of this research; but certainly the match could be made.

The third case asked teachers to bring the image of a square to mind. Teachers were asked in what form they recalled this image: in sketch form; an exact image with sides of equal length subtended by angles of 90 degrees; an exact image in outline in black; an exact image in outline in colour; or an exact image in outline where the centre is a different shade or colour. Proportions and numbers are shown in Figure 2.6.

Although very many teachers (92%) recalled it in exact form, more specifically about half (54%) recalled it in outline in black. Digital resources can now provide exact imagery through media such as interactive whiteboards, so that these can match the form of engagement with the form of reported recall from long-term memory.

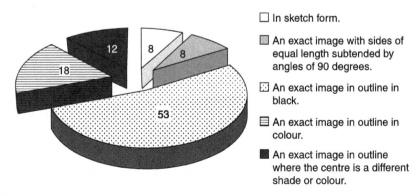

Figure 2.6 Proportions of teachers indicating the form in which a square was brought to mind

It should be noted that these responses are from a teacher audience. The audience is a sample, and although the results provide evidence about that sample, it should not be assumed that this evidence is necessarily representative of all teachers (for example, evidence from teachers of art might not be proportionately the same as evidence from teachers of music or history). Similarly, this evidence might not be representative of learners of different ages, or of those with different interests. This evidence should be considered, therefore, as illustrative; it points to the need to consider different needs.

Educational digital technologies can offer a means to provide forms of match between forms of presentation and ways that concepts are held in mind and forms in which they are reported as being recalled later. Showing the extent or level of this match could offer an important key to understanding both the way that digital technologies such as video films can bring about deeper and longer-lasting learning, and the way they might support initial and longer-term developments of conceptualisation, wider interest, and engagement with future activities, such as those that are science based. Kim and Olaciregui (2008) explored ways that an electronic portfolio system, organised through a concept map-based system, could offer access to learning needs of grade 5 learners. The authors provided images, graphics, videos and text about the Earth's atmosphere, organised either through a folder-based system or a concept map-based system. The learners were randomly assigned to a control or experimental group (25 in each group). Using a test to identify how easily learners could find answers to questions posed, and a test three days later to examine memory retention, learners using the concept map-based system performed significantly better than the control group. The results indicated also that visualisation was the most significant predictor of performance.

The aspect of media richness and its effects on learning was a focal concern of a meta-analysis undertaken by Timmerman and Kruepke (2006), who looked across 198 studies published between 1985 and 2004, comparing CAI with traditional instruction. They found learners using CAI performed better than those involved with traditional instruction. More specifically, they found gains were highest in social science subjects, then physical sciences, life sciences and finally humanities and languages. Gains with CAI were also found to be highest in the case of comparisons to instruction involving lectures and discussion, as well as in the case of undergraduate learners, and when the CAI was used more often rather than only once. In terms of the media supporting gains most, they found audio supported the highest gains, followed by text, text with graphics, video, and then physical resources. For these groups of learners, therefore, video was not the medium providing the highest levels of gains, but it was also clear that social science subjects and topics might well be associated more with 'listening', and potential memorisation for the long term might then be more auditory in nature. The researchers found that feedback did not have a significant effect, but course-specific resources led to higher gains than general material. This suggests these learners were often concerned with skimming and scanning in order to gain factual material in a readily-accessible form, and handling and development of concepts might not have been a strong focus of the studies they explored.

Indeed, Gupta and Sehgal (2012) studied the difference between video and text materials on instructing 10- to 12-year-old learners about physical therapy exercises. In their study, 115 learners were randomly assigned to two groups—those instructed through video, and those instructed through text materials, accounting for suitable readability and language. A statistical t-test indicated no significant difference between the two groups in terms of both acquisition and retention. The authors concluded that feedback and memory recall were affected equally by text or video. However, the study did not look at ways in which the children described their previous retention of concepts and similar facts. Looking at impact of visualisation on acquisition and memory in more detail, Spanjers, van Gog, and van Merriënboer (2010) reviewed a range of studies exploring aspects of dynamic visualisation, through video and animation media, and concluded that segmentation (the breaking down of video or animation into short elements that could be repeated) was an important facility aiding learning. They concluded from their review that for learners starting to learn about a subject or topic, segmentation could produce positive effects. They proposed that positive effects arose in two ways: by reducing cognitive load, as shorter pieces offered more time for details and information to be processed; and by breaking the video into pieces that each had more meaning, so specific details could be assimilated more readily according to times needed to understand them and integrate them into thinking and meaning making.

The important role of teachers and mediators in supporting understanding when learners are using video and visualisation forms also needs to be considered in this context. This factor was highlighted by Kolikant and Broza (2010); in their study, they explored whether a video clip would support understanding of fraction expansion for a group of learners who had low prior attainment in mathematics. From their study of three students, they concluded that although the learners felt the video had helped them to remember the story, there was no evidence they had used this to explain their understanding of the concept. As the authors said, "It was the tutor's careful interventions in the discourse, building on the students' recall of the story, which led to a synergy effect that facilitated the students' understanding and articulation of the meaning of fraction expansion" (p. 23). The authors concluded that successful strategies to support learning involved both use of visualisation and mediation of tutors in combination, as shown by subsequent discussion and performance in tests comparing understanding before and after the intervention.

A range of literature has explored aspects of this field and sheds light on its complexity, but also offers some insights and implications for practice. For example, Kollöffel (2012), in a study with 48 undergraduate students, showed clearly that cognitive style (defined as verbalisers or visualisers) and learning outcomes were not related, so those preferring visual materials did not necessarily gain more if they used visual materials for learning, but their outcomes did seem to be influenced more by cognitive processing abilities. Liu, Kinshuk, Lin, and Wang (2012) also looked at these cognitive styles, and how learners engaged with and gained from simulation-based online resources, concluding that both groups gained similarly, but visualisers tended to scan and skim and to integrate ideas from across resources, while verbalisers tended to read resources thoroughly and to work in more linear ways. The effects of media formats were studied by Kühl, Scheiter, Gerjets, and Gemballa (2011) in a controlled study involving 75 university students, showing that inferences were generated more from visual than from textual resources, but no differences were shown between static and moving visual resources, although students working with static resources tended to play them more often. Özmen (2011), in a controlled study, explored how animation and supportive texts would impact grade 6 learners' understanding of the change of matter, showing that animation with supportive texts challenging preconceptions and then offering alternative explanations had the most positive impacts on understanding, while Starbek, Erjavec, and Peklaj (2010) in a controlled study involving 468 grade 3 and 4 learners in high schools showed that learning about protein synthesis with short animations or text supplemented with illustrations led to improved knowledge and comprehension compared to those receiving lectures or reading text only. Similarly, Lin and Atkinson (2011), in a controlled study, showed that, across 119 undergraduate students, those using animations retained more concepts than those using static images, but those receiving visual cues learned the same as those without but in less time. For learners in elementary schools, however, Barak, Ashkar, and Dori (2011) in a controlled study involving 1,335 learners from 11 schools, showed that animated movies enhanced learner abilities to explain and understand scientific concepts, as well as motivation, connecting concepts to real-life situations, and considering the value of science for their future. In another subject area, learning a new foreign language, a study by Samur (2012) involving 22 undergraduates in the US, found that on-screen text as well as animation and narration supported vocabulary learning positively.

In terms of another additional element of multimedia, background music, a study by Fassbender, Richards, Bilgin, Thompson, and Heiden (2012) did not find conclusive evidence about its impact when learners used digital environments (whether immersive or non-immersive). However, some studies have pointed to other elements that influence learning outcomes when multimedia is used. For example, Slof, Erkens, Kirschner, and Helms-Lorenz (2013) found that, with 16- to 17-year-old learners in secondary schools in the Netherlands, creating a visualisation is more beneficial than inspecting a visualisation, and leads to higher gains. Wu and Pedersen (2011) examined how 142 grade 8 learners across eight classes in two public middle schools in Texas used different scaffolding techniques, and the study found that a combination of continuous computer-based and early teacher-based scaffolds was the most effective in terms of learners acquiring skills of inquiry, but had no impact on scientific knowledge gains.

While some external or additional features are highlighted as being important for maximising learning effectiveness, forms of visual evidence and representation appear to be less crucial. For example, Trundle and Bell (2010) showed that in 157 early childhood pre-service teachers, developing concepts about moon phases was equally well supported by a software program, direct observations as well as using the program, and direct observations alone. Concerning working memory, Garcia, Nussbaum, and Preiss (2011) in their study found no clear relationship between grade 7 learners' uses of ICT and performance on tasks involving working memory. Other studies point to the more crucial importance of sensory and cognitive processing in terms of learning outcomes. For example, Mason, Tornatora, and Pluchino (2013) looked at approaches that students took when integrating information from texts and images, and found those integrating information best took more time looking at the images on a first pass, more time to integrate verbal with visual information, and then the longest time integrating text and images when re-reading or re-inspecting images.

But digital technologies that offer resources in multimedia formats do not necessarily always impart benefit. Wecker (2012), in a study involving 209 university students, showed that slide (*MS PowerPoint*) presentations could suppress information being taken in from spoken sources, and argued that concise slides should be used wherever possible to avoid this overload. Other forms of overload are reported also. Charsky and Ressler (2011), studying learners from three grade 9 classrooms playing a history game (*Civilisation III*), one group using an expert generated concept map, one group constructing their own concept maps, and a control group using no map, showed that learners using the concept map had lower levels of motivation on the game play task due to overload. Distraction has also been reported in studies. Lin and Bigenho (2011) found, with 21 undergraduate students watching videos and subsequently needing to recall words, that with no distraction note-taking on paper was more effective as a recall technique, if distracted no note-taking was more effective, and that many participants used strategies to remember and recall words, but these were used less as the environments became more distractive. In terms of avoiding and addressing these forms of features, Spanjers, van Gog, Wouters, and van Merriënboer (2012) identified the importance of both cueing and pausing to alleviate cognitive load and leading to higher learning outcomes measured in their controlled study involving 161 secondary school learners.

Many factors come into play when digital technologies are used for learning purposes. While the mode of learning resource can clearly have effect, so too can the background of learners, ways resources can be accessed according to learner choice, and forms of involvement of mediators. The neurobiological cognitive dimension is one that can throw light on ways that digital technologies can affect certain aspects of learning, but there is a need to explore the other fundamental dimensions to gain further insights and understanding.

Defining a Learning Framework Accommodating Different Learning Constructs

A very wide range of terms are commonly used to describe learning. Taking some common elements—'cognitive processes', 'social aspects', 'memorisation', 'recall', 'creative approaches', 'conceptualisation', 'long-term educational goals', and 'reflection'—it is clear that some of these terms are used to identify a specific process or element of learning (such as conceptualisation), while others cover a wider group or category (such as cognitive processes). A taxonomy can be used to organise these elements more usefully, grouping elements and processes of learning through two main hierarchies: a higher-level category termed 'aspects' of learning (referring to perspectives, approaches or domains), and a lower-level category termed 'elements' of learning (referring to much more specific processes of learning within each aspect).

Considering first the groupings or aspects of learning, the literature (including that referred to in previous sub-sections), offers a number of these higher-level aspects that are distinct in terms of how they are used and the perspectives they take. These were initially defined and described in a paper looking at influences of specific digital technologies (Passey, 2006b), which defined five aspects of learning, all of which affect motivations for learning—megacognitive (elements leading to deeper and wider learning), metacognitive (knowing how to learn), cognitive (internal processing of knowledge, ideas and concepts), social (interactions with others for learning purposes) and societal (longer-term purposes and intentions that drive learners to learn). Each of these aspects will be considered in turn, and following a fuller definition of each, discrete elements of learning within each will be detailed. The elements of learning listed and defined have all been identified through a selective literature, taking a number of research and curriculum guidance texts that identify prominent elements rather than all elements necessarily. The purpose here is to exemplify an approach, to identify a useful range of elements of learning appropriate to later analyses, rather than providing a fully exhaustive range. The reasons for taking this approach will become more evident later, when this more detailed list of aspects and elements of learning is used to explore uses and impacts of digital technologies. The reader may wish, of course, to take this form of approach further, and to define and detail a more complete or exhaustive list, or one that meets the needs of a more specific analysis.

Megacognitive Concerns—Leading to Deeper and Wider Learning

This aspect of learning consists of elements becoming recognised as fundamental to developing 'expert learners', deeper learning, and wider learning, concerned with learning that goes beyond the ability to just memorise facts or understand a topic range. These elements encompass abilities that enable learners to transfer their learning both within and across subject or interest domains, with applications of involvement in real and authentic learning situations.

In their review of school-based practices and effective learning in the US, Bransford, Brown, and Cocking (2000) identified three key elements fundamental to effective learning:

- Knowing about the 'big picture'—having a sufficient overview of a field to understand how additional details fit within a wider canvas, being able to reposition understanding or ideas on the basis of comparison, contrast, match and integration with that wider picture and building it further.
- Transfer of learning—recognising that learning in one setting can have potential value in other settings, being able to draw on previous knowledge through a 'past' transfer, or thinking about how to use learning in possible 'future' transfer situations.
- Reflecting on previous learning—on knowledge and ideas, selecting and accessing appropriate mechanisms to do this, and considering the way new knowledge and ideas fit within an existing canvas, perhaps challenging, adding to or reinforcing previous details.

In his seminal work on learning, Vygotsky (1978) introduced the important element of the Zone of Proximal Development, which Luckin (2010) explored further. Luckin added more detail to this concept, introducing elements of a Zone of Proximal Adjustment, a Zone of Available Assistance, and a Zone of Collaboration. These four elements are key features concerned with effective learning:

- Working in a Zone of Proximal Development—recognising background knowledge and understanding brought to a learning situation, recognising the 'distance' of the next step or steps to learning, and considering whether and how the step is achievable and within reach.
- Working in a Zone of Collaboration—drawing on abilities to collaborate, to engage with others and with materials and resources the learner can identify in the immediate learning environment, as well as in other more distant locations and at times that might go beyond the immediate setting in which the learning activity is placed.
- Working in a Zone of Available Assistance—recognising the range and qualities of resources and assistance that can be drawn on, which might include teachers, tutors and peers, as well as physical and online resources.
- Working in a Zone of Proximal Adjustment—drawing on abilities to 'negotiate' the presence and nature of agents and resources to allow learning to be constructed from its present to a future position or stage.

Finally, for this aspect of learning, McFarlane (1997) argues the value of learners engaging in meaningful and authentic learning, a point also highlighted by van Merriënboer and Kirschner (2012). Here the element of meaningful and authentic learning is concerned not just with the fact that a learner looks at the potential for any learning in terms of its application to real and authentic situations, but can extract learning from real situations, and can undertake learning concerned with real and authentic audience and purpose (the production of a news item that will be broadcast widely on the web, for example).

These eight key elements fall within this megacognitive aspect of learning, shown within a simple framework structure in Table 2.1.

Table 2.1 Framework of individual elements in the megacognitive aspect of learning

MEGACOGNITIVE
Knowing about the big picture
Working in a Zone of Proximal Development
Working in a Zone of Proximal Adjustment
Working in a Zone of Available Assistance
Working in a Zone of Collaboration
The transfer of learning
Involving meaningful and authentic learning
Reflecting on previous learning

Cognitive Concerns—Content and Process

The cognitive aspect concerns elements affecting impact of information or external stimuli on the internal mind, forms of sensory stimuli engaging learners, ways in which information is handled within an existing internal information context, and ways a learner can demonstrate or use acquired learning. In his text on cognition, Child (1973) defined three distinct areas in this aspect:

- Internalisation—how knowledge and ideas are engaged, and how they are brought into mind.
- Internal cognitive processes—active processes in mind, manipulating knowledge and ideas, allowing them to be considered in the context of existing knowledge and ideas already held in mind, and integrating into a wider learning canvas.
- Externalisation—ways the learner makes their learning known to others.

Taking each of these three areas in turn, Child (1973) described three fundamental elements of internalisation:

- Attention—the focus on the activity, willingness to give attention to task, and level of focus on accessible knowledge or ideas.
- Sensory stimulus—the form of accessible knowledge or ideas, and how the learner engages through one or more senses, in turn stimulating interest and interaction. Gardner (1991), while he considers learning approaches in a wider sense, then goes well beyond sensory stimuli in his analysis of different learning approaches, but nevertheless offers ways to think about forms of external knowledge and ideas relating to forms of sensory stimuli. He identified nine different approaches to consider in terms of distinctive forms of sensory stimuli:

  o Visual—knowledge or ideas accessible or presented in visual forms, perhaps as still images, in black and white, or in colour, or as moving images, or through video-conferencing formats, or in living or real situations.
  o Auditory—knowledge or ideas perhaps accessible through 'teacher talk', or through cassettes or audio files, or via telephones or video-conferencing.
  o Kinaesthetic—the learner handles materials or resources, involving motor skills, perhaps developing skills allowing access to details, or practice through manipulation, through a keyboard, an abacus, or a mouse, for example.
  o Emotional—the learner recognises emotional link or quality to knowledge or ideas presented, perhaps relating these to previous experiences of an emotional nature, recognising joy, empathy, sympathy or sadness.
  o Social—describing knowledge or ideas accessible through forms of social interaction, where the learner is involved in a social encounter, discussing or questioning, perhaps, with peers or teachers or others.
  o Textual—material is in text form, the learner is involved in recognising symbolic forms presented (mathematical as well as literacy symbols), reading in ways allowing a representation of material to be accepted.

- o Musical—the form of material is musical or has musical elements, perhaps with music accompanying a message or through song, or where the music itself describes a scene or sets a part of the context of the learning activity or environment.
- o Interpersonal—interaction between the learner and one or more others, whether these are peers, a teacher, or another adult.
- o Intrapersonal—interaction within the mind of the learner, where discussion is internal, where the learner is stimulated to ask internal questions (discussed by Vygotsky (1978), in terms of 'inner talk', for example).

- Acquisition or reception—the learner recognises knowledge or ideas have impinged upon the consciousness, are accepted into the mind, in a form that can be taken further and handled through a range of internal cognitive processes.

In terms of internal cognitive processes described by Child (1973), elements can be defined through:

- Subject knowledge. The educational curriculum requirements across a range of different subject areas in primary and secondary education in England (Department for Education and Skills [DfES], 2005), refers to:
  - o Searching—seeking information or details, in one or more sources, or through large data sets.
  - o Summarising—selecting key, important or comparative detail to provide a précis, or add to current ideas and knowledge.
  - o Generating or developing ideas—taking existing knowledge or ideas, and recognising that these allow a generation or development of other ideas.
  - o Hypothesising—taking knowledge or ideas, and being able to generate questions needing to be tested or validated through additional knowledge or questions.
  - o Imagining—taking existing knowledge and ideas leading to questions such as 'what if?' or 'can you imagine that?'.
  - o Gaining skills—recognising certain skills have been gained as a result of access to certain knowledge or ideas.
  - o Gaining understanding—recognising there is an understanding of the content and context of additional knowledge or ideas gained.

- Ways knowledge can be handled or manipulated. Using the work of Bloom (1956), knowledge might be handled in six different ways:
  - o Acquisition—recognising knowledge gained, additional to existing knowledge.
  - o Comprehension—understanding knowledge, at a descriptive or definitional level.
  - o Application—using knowledge in another situation, in another setting or context; this setting might be strongly related to, or only weakly related to, the original setting.

- o Analysis—questioning knowledge, drawing other ideas from it, perhaps to categorise, or contrast, compare or argue points arising in other material.
- o Synthesis—bringing knowledge and ideas together from a range of sources, building a wider picture with deeper understanding or conceptual levels of understanding arising.
- o Evaluation—questioning knowledge in terms of its use, its value or how it might be used or judged or assessed in particular situations or circumstances.

- Approaches to thinking and thinking skills. Educational guidance material about thinking skills from the government education department in England (DfES, 2006) and the particularly useful review by Moseley et al. (2005), details:

  - o Creativity—taking existing knowledge or ideas, creating new ideas or knowledge that go beyond the originating items and have certain unique qualities associated with them.
  - o Enquiring—abilities to look at a situation or area of interest using techniques allowing more details or ideas to be collected.
  - o Questioning—abilities to question ideas or knowledge rather than accepting them uncritically.
  - o Conceptualising—abilities to develop or generate a concept, allowing ideas or knowledge to be shaped within a set of dimensions or criteria. Two discrete elements are the formation of concepts, and how ideas are reconstructed in order to create or amend or develop concepts already held.
  - o Comparing—abilities to use existing or other knowledge and ideas to compare and contrast, to look for similarities or differences.
  - o Reasoning—abilities to make comparisons and contrasts and reason with them, considering alternatives and possibilities, to draw conclusions or hypotheses that might be clear or might need further refinement.
  - o Interpreting—abilities to take knowledge and ideas and to work with these in ways allowing other conclusions or results to be drawn, allowing additional understandings to emerge not necessarily stated within originating material.

- Elements concerned with memorisation. Child (1973) details:

  - o Rehearsal—abilities to consider existing knowledge and ideas, to recognise differences or additions that might be of interest or value. According to circumstances and use, items then might be accessible from short-term or long-term memory.
  - o Retention—knowledge and ideas are retained in memory in appropriate forms, which might relate to sensory forms through which they were accessed, such as visual, auditory, textual, emotional or social forms.
  - o Recall—abilities to recall knowledge and ideas from memory, through associations or hooks from mental schemas.

In terms of externalisation, forms learners use to externalise their understandings include:

- Writing—relating knowledge or ideas in textual or symbolic forms.
- Reporting—relating knowledge or ideas through a report structure, defined in structural terms to a greater extent than is generally used for free-form writing.
- Speaking—perhaps through a one-to-one discussion or through responses to questions from a group.
- Presenting—to a wider audience, perhaps using images or presentation materials as a background, or using a more dramatic or musical form of presentation.
- Drawing—relating knowledge and ideas through forms of drawing that might be either more structured in terms of design, or more unstructured in terms of artistic presentation.
- Completing—having a structure with gaps that need to be completed, perhaps having to include appropriate words or texts or making choices from a series of options.
- Moving—using motor skills and manipulative skills to move items into order, or to move them into patterns of sequences that show knowledge and understanding.

There are 51 elements identified within this aspect of learning. They can be placed into a simple framework structure, listed in a form recognising relationships described in the underlying texts, and are shown in Table 2.2.

Metacognitive Concerns—Recognising How We Can Learn

This aspect includes elements concerned with ways learners learn to learn and know how to learn. It covers elements describing how learning strategies can be identified, adopted or chosen, or ways information or knowledge are transferred from one scenario or situation to another.

Presseisen (2001) identified two broad areas and six specific elements detailing this aspect further:

- Monitoring task performance—recognising how a task is proceeding:
  - Keeping place and sequence—identifying different stages, perhaps milestones reached, and a current position along a sequence of stages.
  - Detecting and correcting errors—reflecting on work as it proceeds, reviewing what has been done, identifying errors, and correcting them as far as is possible.
  - Pacing of work—using concepts of time and scope, recognising an end point, and at any one time the effort that might be needed to accomplish the task and levels of detail relating to possible scope and quantity of feasible output.

Table 2.2 Framework of individual elements in the cognitive aspect of learning

COGNITIVE

Internalisation		
Attention	*Sensory stimulus* Visual Auditory Kinaesthetic Emotional Social Textual Musical Interpersonal Intrapersonal	*Acquisition or reception*

Internal cognitive processing		
Subject knowledge	Searching Summarising Generating or developing ideas Hypothesising Imagining Gaining skills Gaining understanding	
ICT knowledge	Skills Understanding	
Knowledge handling Acquisition Comprehension Application Analysis Synthesis Evaluation	*Thinking* Creativity Enquiring Questioning Conceptualising Comparing Reasoning Interpreting	Concept formation Reconstruction of ideas
Retention	*Rehearsal* Short-term memory Long-term memory	*Recall*

Externalisation	
Motor stimulus	Writing Reporting Speaking Presenting Drawing Completing Moving

Table 2.3 Framework of individual elements in the metacognitive aspect of learning

METACOGNITIVE	
Monitoring task performance	Keeping place, sequence
	Detecting and correcting errors
	Pacing of work
Selecting and understanding	Focusing attention on what is needed
appropriate strategy	Relating what is known to material to be learned
	Testing the correctness of a strategy

• Selecting and understanding appropriate strategy—having a range of strategies to be drawn on, selected and tried out in the context of any learning task:

   ○ Focusing attention on what is needed—selecting appropriately from a range of strategies, and matching needs of the task with strategies that might be used.
   ○ Relating what is known to material to be learned—using previous experience, drawing on techniques used and applied in those previous situations.
   ○ Testing the correctness of a strategy—recognising if a strategy selected is appropriate, whether a result appears to be feasible, reasonable or correct, and perhaps selecting alternatives allowing feasibility of outcome to be checked.

These six elements are placed into a simple framework structure, shown in Table 2.3.

Social Concerns—the Roles of Others

This aspect includes elements concerned with ways learners interact with others. These interactions might be within classroom environments as well as in home or other external environments. Different forms of interaction allow different forms of engagement and output, allowing learners to access or use information, as well as share it, or work co-operatively with others.

The importance of social interactions in learning has been highlighted in a wide range of contexts. Pask (1975) identified key roles of social interactions in developing understanding through discussion (where, in a series of interactions, the focus of intention shifts as understanding builds), while Vygotsky (1978) highlighted the importance of social integration for ideas and knowledge to become learned. Lave and Wenger (1991) developed the idea of 'communities of practice', and the roles that engagement with specific communities have, as well as the roles of discussions and interactions that take textual forms as well as those happening through spoken forms. In terms of classroom settings, Twining and McCormick (1999) identified 12 different forms of social interaction in which learners might be involved (defined here by Passey, 2006b):

- Instruction—a teacher indicates what learners should do, how they should do it, and what is expected as outcomes.
- Explanation and illustration—a teacher explains ideas or concepts, verbally, and may illustrate these with gesture, images, or other resources.
- Direction—a teacher offers overall ideas of what needs to be done, and what is expected, without giving precise detail.
- Demonstration—a teacher provides a demonstration as an example of what happens, or what learners should do.
- Discussion—a teacher elicits ideas from learners, picks up on specific points, and encourages other learners to contribute ideas or comments.
- Scaffolding—a teacher provides a series of steps, or a number of interim stages or frameworks, to help learners approach an activity in a structured way.
- Questioning—a teacher asks questions, and elicits responses from learners, either to closed or to open questions.
- Speculation—a teacher offers a scenario, together with different ideas about outcomes or implications.
- Consolidation—a teacher reviews a previous topic or activity, exploring the extent to which learners appear to have remembered details or grasped concepts.
- Summarising—a teacher pulls out key points, messages, or ideas, providing an overview as a summary of a topic or activity.
- Initiating and guiding exploration—a teacher introduces a topic or activity, and indicates possible ways to explore, with ideas of how to begin or approaches that might be taken.
- Evaluating learners' responses—a teacher provides feedback to learner responses, and indicates features concerned with quality of those responses and how improvements might be brought about.

These 12 elements are listed in a simple framework structure, shown in Table 2.4.

Table 2.4 Framework of individual elements in the social aspect of learning

SOCIAL	
Learner interaction	Instruction
	Explanation and illustration
	Direction
	Demonstration
	Discussion
	Scaffolding
	Questioning
	Speculation
	Consolidation
	Summarising
	Initiating and guiding exploration
	Evaluating learners' responses

Societal Concerns—Long-term Drivers and Purpose

This aspect includes elements concerned with reasons why certain information is selected or recognised as being more fundamentally interesting or useful than other information; reasons concern how information is perceived in terms of its longer-term interests and potential usefulness within particular societal, cultural or wider environmental contexts.

McFarlane (1997) highlights the importance of meaningful and authentic learning, and the need for learners to consider how their learning relates to situations they regard as real, not only in the immediate but also in the longer term. In terms of societal concerns learners have for undertaking learning (defined here by Passey, 2006b):

- Lipman (1995) describes ways learning might relate to learners' concerns about caring, defined through five distinctive elements:
    - Appreciative—of caring or being cared for.
    - Active—involving positive action concerned with caring.
    - Normative—caring thinking considered as a norm or standard.
    - Effective—feelings or emotions aroused in relation to caring.
    - Empathetic—empathy (such as agreement, belief, or understanding) associated with caring.

- Moseley et al. (2005) described four overarching long-term concerns in which thinking might be contextualised by learners:
    - Education—relevance to other aspects of or longer-term concerns for further involvement in education, or concerned with education in the wider sense.
    - Citizenship—implications for ways in which people live, relate, or behave within a wider society.
    - Work—concerned with the realm of work, either in the present, or potentially for the future.
    - Recreation—related to outside interests, hobbies, or games, concerned more with recreation than with work.

These nine elements are placed into a simple framework structure, shown in Table 2.5.

Table 2.5 Framework of individual elements in the societal aspect of learning

SOCIETAL	
Caring thinking	Appreciative
	Active
	Normative
	Effective
	Empathetic
Contextual thinking	Education
	Citizenship
	Work
	Recreation

Using a Learning Framework to Identify Where Specific Elements of Learning are Located

By detailing the range of elements of learning within each of the broad aspects, and bringing these together into a single framework, the taxonomic representation produced can be used as a way to record elements of learning where evidence indicates uses, outcomes or impacts when certain digital technologies or resources are used, or when a learning activity takes place. An example of such a learning framework analysis is shown in Figure 2.7. This example is taken from a report of a study that examined uses and reported outcomes of learning when teachers used a specific set of online digital resources within classrooms in primary schools (Passey, 2011a). Evidence of outcomes and impacts gathered from teachers in this study were recorded in the learning framework to show where levels of outcome or impact arose most strongly. In this example: dark grey shows a very high level of response; mid-grey a high level; and light grey a lower level. Areas shaded with diagonal lines show evidence of outcomes but where the level cannot be easily quantified in broad terms through forms of responses provided; and white shows there is no evidence from responses in the study.

This learning framework analysis shows us that:

- Learning can be considered through a wide array of different and varied elements.
- If a single learning activity is considered, it is highly likely to involve one or more of these elements, but is not likely to cover all of them.
- For the set of online resources studied, where impacts were reported, some elements were reported more often than were others.
- There are some strengths of influence on learning for that particular digital technology resource. It should be noted, however, that different resources can produce somewhat different profiles, see Passey (2006a), for example.
- There are some weaker elements identified for that particular digital technology resource. It should be noted in this context, however, that 'weakness' can mean teachers or learners are not focusing strongly on that element of learning, rather than it necessarily meaning the resource itself is not able to support that element with impact.

The form of learning framework shown in Figure 2.7 will be used in the next chapter to consider in more detail evidence about uses, outcomes and impacts of specific types of digital technologies on elements of learning, in a range of different curriculum contexts and for different learners with different attributes. This form of learning framework will be used to identify, from across a range of research literature, those elements where digital technologies are recognised as having influence or impact. It will be seen in subsequent chapters that this level of detail is needed if we are to ensure that both our uses of digital technologies are focused adequately and their uses are supported effectively.

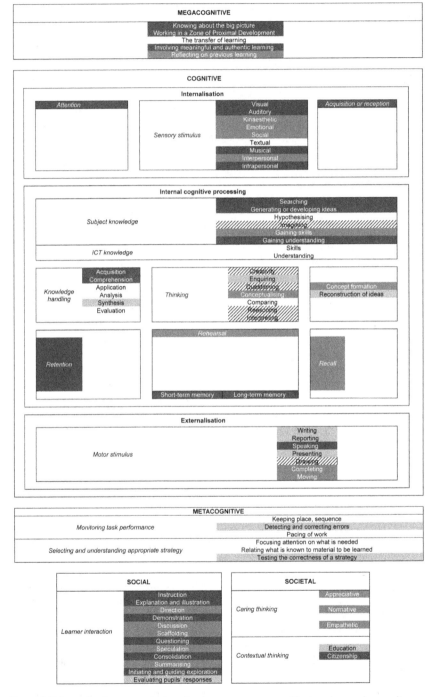

Figure 2.7 Learning framework showing hotspots reported by teachers when online resources supporting curriculum-wide needs are used to support learning and teaching (Source: Passey, 2011a)

Chapter 3

Types of Digital Technologies and Their Applications in Educational Settings

An Introduction

Reports of contributions to learning arising from uses of digital technologies have often focused on a specific hardware—such as laptops (see Roschelle, Penuel, Yarnall, Shechtman, & Tatar, 2005, reporting on US studies), interactive whiteboards (see Moss et al., 2007, reporting a UK study; or Hansson, n.d., reporting a study in Sweden), or mobile telephones (see Thomas and Orthober, 2011, reporting a study in the United States). Earlier studies in the UK (for example, Watson, 1993; British Educational Technology and Communications Agency [Becta], 2001, 2003; Harrison et al., 2002) looked at contributions according to levels of uses of digital technologies, categorising schools and access according to 'high' or 'low' levels of usage. At times when levels of digital technologies in schools were somewhat limited (and certainly that was the case when these latter studies were conducted), the value of this approach can certainly be recognised. However, many schools in many countries now have access to much higher levels of digital technologies, and indeed learners and supporters have high levels of access and use outside schools; consequently, this approach is clearly not only much more difficult to adopt in terms of attempting to differentiate between 'high' and 'low', or 'control' and 'test' groups, but indeed it is the qualities offered by the different forms of digital technologies, and the ways they are used in an integrated sense, that can bring about contribution for an individual. As Livingstone (2012) said, "It seems that a simple increase in ICT provision does not guarantee enhanced educational performance" (p. 11), while Lei (2010) stated that "to examine the relationship between technology use and student outcomes, the quality of technology use—how, and what, technology is used—is a more significant factor than the quantity of technology use—how much technology is used" (p. 455). Lei (2010) went on to say that in an empirical study where both methods were used, a quantitative approach identified no significant association, but a qualitative approach identified significant association between use and outcomes.

While access to digital technologies is clearly important, there are concerns that digital technology access should be at an individual level to achieve personalisation supporting most appropriate use. As Liu and Milrad (2010) said: "The argument that one-to-one computational environments may alter the way people learn is largely based on the ratio of students to computers and readiness for students to access the computers" (p. 1). But, there is still a need to consider whether all purposes for learning are best served by a one-to-one level of provision. It can be argued that fulfilling social or work or citizenship purposes might be best served through this level of provision. However, in a study looking at levels of shared interactions involving graduate students, Liu, Chung, Chen, and Liu (2009) found that: "In the environment with shared displays, each discussion thread attracted more students and demonstrated more shared visual focus than in the one-to-one setting by a significant margin" (p. 127). But the argument, from classroom (formal) contexts compared to outside school and home (informal) contexts, is far less clear. As Larkin (2011), in the introduction to an article detailing a study in Australia reported, orthodoxy at that time appeared to favour one-to-one computing as it could achieve most effectively outcomes such as "individualised learning, collaborative environments, or constructivist pedagogies" (p. 101), but his findings showed that one computer to two learners was preferable in primary schools, as it achieved "a balance between productivity, student engagement, social activity, and individualised learning". For the study, Larkin gathered data across a one-year period from four year 7 classrooms, with 11- to 13-year-old learners accessing netbook computers, and found that: "The sharing of ideas and collaborative learning identified in these comments from the classes with 1:2 access was conspicuously absent in the 1:1 computing scenarios, where student comments indicated a preoccupation with individual productivity tasks" (p. 114).

If collaborative learning is important (and authors such as Bay, Bagceci, & Cetin, 2012, and Zhu, 2012, argue that this is so), then levels of digital technology access can determine pedagogies that can affect contributions to learning. That there is a relationship between pedagogy, technology and learning outcomes is clear. This concept is explored in more detail by Mishra and Koehler (2006), through their technological pedagogical content knowledge framework. Relationships between levels of digital technologies, content and pedagogies is not an aspect that will be dealt with in specific detail in this book, but it is an aspect considered through the taxonomy of digital technologies in this chapter.

Digital Technologies Need to be Categorised According to the Support they Offer

Eight separate categories of educational digital technologies are proposed here. Each one will be discussed in turn, and the contributions (benefits, affordances, uses, outcomes or impacts) that each one makes to learning will be detailed using the learning framework described in the previous chapter (Figure 2.7). The discussion and learning framework analyses will show that each category of digital technology has its own 'learning fingerprint', contributing to learning in different ways. The learning framework will show aspects where there are strengths, as well as where there are gaps. Those gaps might be in our knowledge about contributions, or elements or aspects of learning that need to be focused on more, fulfilled through other pedagogic and learning approaches (perhaps by learners themselves, or by supporters involved).

Educational digital technologies vary widely. Some are more teacher-centred, for example interactive whiteboards are often used in teacher-centred ways and less often by learners directly, as described by Smith, Higgins, Wall, and Miller (2005). Others are more learner-centred (mobile devices used on school trips, for example, as described by Passey (2010)). As is shown in these and other research studies (such as Lave & Wenger, 1991; Laurillard, 2001), ways digital technologies are used make a difference to learning that is both supported and how it is supported.

Different ways have been used to categorise digital technologies in the past. For example, Hoyles and Noss (2003) categorised different technologies used to support mathematics education (summarised in Laborde, 2007, p. 69) as tools for mathematical activity (such as calculators or spreadsheets), resources for teachers or learners (such as the internet or learning environments), tutorial environments, and technical devices (like interactive whiteboards or mobile devices). By contrast, Conole (2007) categorised digital technologies through forms of learning activities—assimilative, adaptive, productive and experiential.

Digital technologies are categorised in this book, not by hardware device or platform (such as interactive whiteboards, desktop computers, mobile telephones, or internet-based online resources), or by learning activity (describing forms of learning that are engaged), but according to ways they are used by learners and supporters, and the functions they perform in terms of learning support. In other words, the taxonomy used here describes different learning landscapes. This taxonomy is used in part because a single digital technology can be used in a wide variety of ways—the technology does not itself usually determine the way in which it is used and applied to support learning, either by the learner or by those supporting the learning through mediation. Hence, the taxonomy used here is based on an earlier categorisation (Passey, 2012a) that considered the taxonomy from a learning support (rather than a technological or activity) perspective. Another category (online resources to support revision purposes) has been added since that research was completed. Each category is defined according to ways the digital technology is used within a learning environment or landscape, which can vary from formal (classroom settings), to informal (in homes or public areas), and to non-formal settings (in after-school clubs or community groups or societies). The eight categories are described in outline before a more detailed exploration of each one is offered.

Topic-specific resources and software focus on a specific topic or area of subject content, supporting individual users or small groups of learners, which might well be supported by oversight from a teacher or a peer. This category includes software in specific subjects, such as computer algebra systems (CAS) and dynamic geometry environments (DGEs), for example. It also includes resources such as robotic and electronic kits, which can be used to develop understanding and ideas in specific subject topics. This form of digital technology might involve the learner through one-to-one access, but some uses might involve one-to-two access or access in small groups.

Curriculum-wide learner-centred software provides a large range of resources and activities that cover (more or less) entire curriculum areas, but which are learner-focused and used more directly by learners than by teachers. This category includes software referred to often as integrated learning systems (ILSs), enabling individual learners to access wide-ranging content, often with oversight from a teacher, although oversight might well range from individual on-hand guidance to very limited or minimal interaction. This form of digital technology usually relies on one-to-one access.

Curriculum-wide teacher-centred software covers resources developed specifically for teacher use within classrooms but designed to cover an entire curriculum for one or more years. These resources are delivered through learning activities, accessed through a number of technological devices, including networked computers, graphical calculators or interactive whiteboards. Examples include the UK *RM MathsAlive* programs, covering the entire mathematics curriculum for 11- to 14-year-old learners. In all cases, involvement and oversight from a teacher is assumed, as activities are largely classroom-based. This form of digital technology may involve some levels of one-to-one access, but much of the access will be through group work or at a class level.

Software involving and supporting parents includes resources that cover specific subject topics, identified by the teacher, but where access is happening in homes. Learners will generally have some level of parental oversight or involvement, ranging from checking that the learner is undertaking the activity, through to taking interest in the child's achievement, to being involved alongside the learner with exploring the activity and its needs. This category includes mathematical software and resources such as those provided by *Mathletics* or science and literacy resources such as those from *Education City*. These resources are often provided in the form of online educational games, matching or complementing activities or topics undertaken in classroom lessons. This form of digital technology will rely to an extent on one-to-one access, but with parental involvement the access will move to a one-to-two or small group level.

Online resources supporting curriculum-wide needs are sets of resources developed to support an entire curriculum, but which more specifically cover a range of selected topics within that curriculum rather than every topic. These topic or subject resources are selected and used by teachers and integrated with other forms of resources and activities, over a number of years. The software supports activities in forms accessible online by teachers as well as sometimes by learners at home, and in classrooms resources used on interactive whiteboards, in the form of video clips, teaching screens, mental activities or revision questions, such as those provided by *Espresso Education*. This form of digital technology will largely be accessed at a class level, although some follow-on work may be at a one-to-one level.

Online resources supporting revision needs are sets of resources developed to support an entire curriculum, but which more specifically cover topics through revision exercises, enabling preparation for tests or examinations. Topic or subject resources can be selected and used largely by learners and may be integrated with other forms of resources and activities, over a number of years or within a more narrow time-window. The software supports activities in forms that can be accessed online, such as those provided by *SAM Learning*. This form of digital technology is largely accessed at a learner level, although some access through classwork may be undertaken in some schools.

Online learner support includes technology-supported interactions focusing on an individual learner's work and queries, provided through online contact with mentors or counsellors. The interface might provide links to websites that offer related content, highlighted by mentors during their online discussions. Activities and work might or might not be connected to teacher approaches within a classroom. This form of digital technology largely involves the learner at a one-to-one level, although some online interactions could be at a group or collaborative level.

Project and after-school club activities involving digital technologies are focused on learning arising through team work and team-based practices, perhaps with specific roles being designated to individuals, focusing on technical, artistic or editing skills. Examples of activities in this category are the annual *BBC News School Report*, or *Interactive Opportunities'* after-school clubs involving uses and creation of video games levels, or activities run through the regional, national and international levels of *First Lego League*. This form of digital technology may involve the learner at a one-to-one level for certain activities, but a main focus of the project will be to establish group work, team work, collaboration and communication.

Points to Consider

It is worth noting here that when considering how educational games and video games fit into this taxonomy, it is the affordances they provide that determine an appropriate category. As an overall pointer to main selection criteria for computer-based games, some are not able to be changed or created—they provide a player route for the learner, while others enable games or levels to be created by one or more learners. Crawford (1984) created an early taxonomy: skill and action games (including combat games, maze games, sports games, paddles games, race games and miscellaneous games); and strategy games (including adventures, dungeons and dragons games, war games, games of chance, educational and children's games and interpersonal games). For learning, strategy games are used far more than skill and action games (although sports games and race games are sometimes used in specific subjects, so would be regarded as topic-specific software). For strategy games, some adventures are included as topic-specific software, or parent-involved software, while some project or after-school club activities also use these games. Examples will be discussed in relevant digital technology categories.

It is also worth noting that the term informal learning is used in this book to describe those activities that happen outside classrooms and outside structured or organised group or team activities. Informal learning in this text is concerned with learning happening in unstructured ways—in the home, in the playground, in the street, during ad hoc visits to the beach, a museum or a gallery, or on the way home, for example.

Topic-specific Resources and Software

Topic-specific resources and software focus on a specific topic or area of subject content, supporting individual users, with oversight from a teacher or peer, and include uses of software in classroom settings, such as word completion exercises. Studies exploring uses and outcomes in this category include Apostol (1991), a study showing ways computer-animated videotapes could be used to support mathematical understanding (and highlighting particularly the affordances of

Regularity of use									
Selected by teachers									
Used by learners									
In classrooms									
In projects or after-school									
Involving parents at home									

Figure 3.1 How topic-specific resources and software offer support for learning

this software), and Wiest (2001), who reviewed a range of digital technologies supporting mathematics education, looking at benefits and weaknesses of alternative forms of specific software. In summary, these resources are used at irregular times; they are selected by teachers and used by learners in classrooms (see Figure 3.1).

There are many examples of studies that have explored uses and outcomes of topic-specific software. Huang, Lin, and Cheng (2010) reported uses of a plant identification and information system on PDAs used by learners in elementary schools in Taiwan for fieldwork, Silva, Pinho, Lopes, Nogueira, and Silveira (2011) also described uses and outcomes of a computer-based plant identification system but with high school and undergraduate learners, and Wrzesien and Raya (2010) explored the use of a virtual world to learn about environmental issues in the Mediterranean Sea with 48 learners in the grade 6 (showing higher levels of reported engagement and participation, but not in terms of learning impacts). In another subject context, González, Jover, Cobo, and Muñoz (2010) in a controlled study with 121 undergraduate students in an introductory course in statistics identified an improvement of 0.48 points on a 10–point scale in a final examination, with an effect size of 0.63 for the 94 students using the software, and Wang, Vaughn, and Liu (2011) in their controlled study explored forms of animation interactivity and how they related to an understanding of statistics in 123 college students, reporting that animation interactivity had a positive impact on understanding. Similarly, Owusu, Monney, Appiah, and Wilmot (2010) compared CAI with traditional teaching methods for senior high school students learning a science concept (the cell cycle) in two schools and showed that initial low achievers gained most when using CAI, while Zhang et al. (2010) described how mobile technologies were used to create three science lessons in a Singapore primary school that were more context-based and learner-centred. A number of studies have focused on learning mathematics with topic-specific software, such as Bai, Pan, Hirumi, and Kebritchi (2012) who reported a controlled study involving 437 grade 8 learners showing that use of a 3D mathematics game led to enhanced knowledge in algebra and engaged learners more, Tan (2012) who reported a study with 65 high school students in Malaysia showing that use of a graphing calculator could improve abilities in and understanding of probability, whether baseline mathematics scores were low, medium or high, and Pilli and Aksu (2013) reported a controlled study with grade 4 learners in North Cyprus, using *Frizbi Mathematics 4* software, showing that learning gains resulted in enhanced multiplication and division competencies but not in fractions. Other studies have reported on other subject areas, such as Coutinho and Mota (2011) who reported a study of grade 6 learners in Portugal creating a podcast in music education classes published online, and Papastergiou, Gerodimos, and Antoniou (2011) detailed how a multimedia blog was used by undergraduate physical education students to reflect on basketball skills and activities, but without significant gains being shown. Some studies have also looked at more kinaesthetic uses and outcomes, such as Benitti (2012) who reviewed the literature on use of robotics in schools and reported a general outcome of enhancement of learning, but with some exceptions where no learning gains were identified, and Schönborn, Bivall, and Tibell (2011) who reported a controlled study involving a haptic device giving the user a feedback of force, used with tertiary students who needed to find the best fit for two biomolecules, finding that those using the haptic device produced outcomes with a better match.

Learning Contributions are Widely Recognised by Teachers

Topic-specific resources and software have been used for many decades, and their use has not diminished. More features and affordances have become available over those decades, and technologies used to access these resources have shifted from desktop devices, through carry-around disc players such as those running compact discs (CDs), to internet access via mobile devices. These resources can be used with all age groups, in many subject domains, with ranges of learners with different cognitive abilities.

A recent article by Kaveh (2012) discussed how teachers in Tehran, Iran, accessed and used resources certainly including topic-specific software. The author argued that these forms of resources were necessary and fundamental, to match learner expectations, and to enhance creative and dynamic approaches. The author argued that impacts depended on knowledge and understanding of how to apply uses of these digital technologies, and investigated the forms of educational technology and media used by elementary school teachers in Tehran, gathering evidence using a questionnaire from a sample population of 400 teachers. Findings indicated use of "computers, video projectors, smart boards, and visualizers were below average. . . . Most frequently utilized media and tools by more than 50% of the teachers are: posters, maps, oral explanation, white/black boards, plays, alphabet cards, and educational CDs" (p. 30). Media knowledge of the teachers was found to be 'average', but, importantly, the author highlighted why teachers were using the resources. Teachers recognised contributions topic-specific resources offered to learning, focusing learners' attention on subject or topic concepts, enhancing their commitment to learn and to collaborate, and motivating them through audio and visual sensory routes.

The identification of such contributions by teachers occurs very widely. In a study completed in a district in Pakistan, Suleman (2011) also explored uses and outcomes in primary schools. In this study in a Karak district (Khyber Pukhtunkhwa), 366 primary school teachers and 2,002 learners were involved (constituting 25% and 5% of each of these total populations respectively). From results gathered using questionnaires, the author concluded that "educational technology is very useful for the effective teaching learning process at primary level" (p. 85). The author identified from teacher responses some main ways in which contributions to effective teaching and learning were recognised: encouraging participation; enhancing motivation; enhancing effective pedagogy; engaging learners through a variety of sensory routes; and enriching the classroom environment and attitudes of learners positively.

Learning Contributions from Television and Video

What are being identified in the previous studies are contributions in terms of sensory engagement, attention, motivation and interest, participation and an effect on learning environment or ethos. Contributions to sensory engagement through visual and audio routes were identified and summarised also by the Metiri Group (2006), in reviewing outcomes and impacts across a wide range of prior studies. They concluded that, "The *power of television and video for learning* lies in the use of multimedia to engage students visually, cognitively, emotionally, socially, and civically in facets of the academic content" (p. 6). They reported that the sensory visual element enhanced engagement, but, importantly, would allow complexity (wider ranges of contributory factors), depth (more detail) and breadth of experience (more examples) to be enhanced, and that these improved performance. However, they stressed that content needed to be of high quality, and teachers needed to adopt sound pedagogy.

Learning Contributions from Using Calculators

Other studies have indicated strong links between routes of sensory engagement and cognitive processes, within certain subject areas. Penglase and Arnold (1996) identified three contributions arising from the use of calculators: a greater understanding of graphical concepts; abilities to make meaningful connections between functions and graphs; and higher levels of spatial skills. Ellington (2003), in a meta-analysis of studies looking at learning outcomes arising from uses of calculators, also identified positive contributions to operational and problem-solving skills when calculators were used for testing and in learning activities. At the same time, however, the author highlighted the fact that longer-term retention of those skills and the transfer of the skills to other situations had not been identified through studies at that time. A large-scale study in the US by Bridgeman, Harvey, and Braswell (1995) found that college-bound juniors (18 years of age) who used calculators did significantly better on selected test items from the scholastic aptitude test (SAT) than students who were not using them. Of the four ethnic groups represented in the sample, Latinos gained most, while the other three ethnic groups (Whites, African-Americans and Asian-Americans) as well as both genders, gained equally. A later controlled study by Pennington (1998) reported by the Metiri Group (2006), again in the US, but this time using calculators with some learners (in middle schools) gaining instruction on how to use them and others not, looked also at gains. The results indicated that grade 7 and 8 students (12 to 14 years of age) using calculators outperformed those not using calculators when tested for basic mathematics skills, irrespective of whether they were given instruction on how to use the calculators.

From their review of studies investigating contributions to learning arising from uses of calculators, the Metiri Group (2006) concluded that "the *power* of this technology for learning mathematics is unleashed when the tools are used *long-term* (more than nine weeks), are *integral to the instruction, not just computational tools*, and are used in both *instruction and assessment* activities" (p. 7). They reported studies showing calculators had a positive effect on learners' scores for algebra, but results were more mixed in terms of other topics, and slightly negative for learners in grade 4.

Learning Contributions from Games-based Activities

Games-based resources have been the focus of a range of studies looking at contributions to learning. A large-scale controlled study by Rosas et al. (2003) in Chile, involving 1,274 first- and second-year (early elementary) students, compared a group using games-based resources to support reading comprehension, spelling and mathematical skills on handheld devices with control groups that were based both inside and outside the school. The results indicated that, after 30 hours of using the devices over a three-month period, those students using the games-based resources gained significantly more than those in the control group outside school. However, when compared to the control group inside school, no significant differences were identified.

In their review of games-based learning activities and their contributions to learning, the Metiri Group (2006) found that when used in educational settings, games positively impacted attainment in reading comprehension, algebra and decoding. Additionally, they found evidence of impacts on motivation, attitudes to learning engagement and on self-concept when uses were compared to traditional instruction. They identified reasons why these impacts were occurring; these included immediate feedback, enhancement of learner engagement and participation, and increases in knowledge. They also stated that educational games could support the "development of complex thinking skills and problem solving, planning, and self-regulated learning" (p. 13). One point they raised indicated that a major factor influencing impact on learning was the level of interaction between the learner and the game itself, and level of attention and degree of concentration "continuously *reinforces knowledge, scaffolds learning*, provides levelled, appropriate challenges, and provides *context to the learning of content*" (p. 13). As an important rider, however, they stated that, from studies of uses in schools over many years, impacts were not always positive, but that mixed results were reported. These differences they attributed to forms of software used, content covered in the game, context in which the game was used, pedagogy adopted and affective and cognitive factors of learners themselves. They concluded by saying positive significant gains were possible if appropriate pedagogy and relevant subject content were considered adequately.

Rosas et al. (2003), in a review of research studies looking at uses and outcomes of educational games, reported they could strengthen and support aspects of school achievement, cognitive abilities, motivation towards learning, and attention and concentration. But at an individual research study level, not all studies show all of these outcomes, and there are important key determining characteristics to consider at an individual project or games-use level. For example, Kebritchi, Hirumi, and Bai (2010) studied a total of 193 students and 10 teachers using a mathematical game and identified significant gains in mathematical attainment of the experimental versus control group, but no gains were identified in terms of motivation of the experimental group. In addition, the authors found that what teachers prior to and following uses of the game did was crucially important, and Hirumi argued it was potentially more important in terms of learning outcome than the effect of the game, indicating the critical role that design and pedagogy play.

By comparison, Panoutsopoulos and Sampson (2012) studied learning outcomes arising from uses of "a general-purpose commercial digital game (namely, the *"Sims 2-Open for Business"*)" (p. 15). Their rationale for the study was based on the premise that such a game provides experiences allowing the learner to draw links between concepts covered in the game and real-life events or practices. The study involved students aged 13 to 14 years, "from families with an average or high socio-economic background" and "our research subjects were familiar with the use of computers" (p. 17). They looked at achievement in terms of both "standard curriculum mathematics educational objectives" and "general educational objectives as defined by standard taxonomies" (p. 17). They gathered student views about their participation in the digital game and any potential "changes in their attitudes towards mathematics teaching and learning" (p. 17). Their results showed the 'general-purpose commercial game' did indeed contribute to general educational objectives, but not to mathematical objectives, shown by comparisons of the control and experimental groups using both Levene's test (p=0.006, showing no equal variances) and the two-tailed t-test (t=0.418, df=48.041, p=0.678). They concluded from their findings that the game supported educational objectives in general, but there was no statistical proof it impacted attitudes towards mathematics teaching or learning.

Importantly, perhaps, these studies focus on areas of subject or topic learning that each specific game can support, but across short time periods only; future impacts and transfers of learning outcomes are not explored. Curriculum match, teacher approaches, and forms of measurement are all shown here to be important, but another finding emerging is that engagement with games-based learning is not necessarily gender biased. Carbonaro, Szafron, Cutumisu, and Shaeffer (2010) studied game construction in grade 10 English classes and found girls enjoyed the activity as much as boys and were equally successful. These researchers concluded overall that computer game construction was an activity supporting teaching of higher-order thinking skills (in this case focused on science), computer game construction involving scripting enabled teaching of abstract skills in computing science, the activity enabled teachers to introduce computing science in a way learners enjoyed, and outcomes showed girls and boys gained equally in terms of higher-order thinking, abstract skills in computing science, and enjoyment of the activity itself.

Some studies have looked at learning contributions arising when games-based activities are run on handheld devices. Savill-Smith and Kent (2003) reviewed research at that time identifying contributions of palmtop devices to learning, and concluded there were positive correlations between the use of educational games on PDAs and enhancements to reading comprehension and improvements in mathematics performance. Their explanations of these gains centred around forms of engagement that were encouraged—deep levels of concentration, high levels of positive motivation, high levels of attention and enhanced self-regulation.

From a recent literature review, Connolly, Boyle, MacArthur, Hainey, and Boyle (2012) reported wide gains arising from using computer games for learning with learners 14 years of age and above, in terms of knowledge acquisition, understanding and motivation. Recent studies aligned with this trend are those of Berns, Gonzalez-Pardo, and Camacho (2013) who looked at uses of games in a three-dimensional (3D) virtual environment, providing multi-player facility and texting, and reported learner gains in German language in writing, vocabulary, pronunciation and listening, and Wouters and van Oostendorp (2013), who looked at how computer games and instructional support might be related, and reported instructional support enhanced learning outcomes when computer games were played, but was most effective when targeted at providing new information. Reports from studies of uses of computer games to enhance the learning of mathematics continue to be divided, with, for example, Ke (2013) reporting a study in two middle schools and not finding statistically significant effects on mathematics results when computer mathematics games were used, while Miller and Robertson (2011) in their study, involving 634 learners 10 to 11 years of age in 32 schools across Scotland in using a commercial computer game to support the development of mental computation skills, found, after nine weeks of use, both accuracy (50% more) and speed (100% more) of computations were gained by those using the game, with no gender differences, but those with lower starting scores gained more, and those with middle starting scores gained most in terms of speed. In terms of collaborative uses of computer games for learning, Meluso, Zheng, Spires, and Lester (2012) in their study showed collaborative or individual video-games led to no marked differences in terms of science knowledge, but use of games overall did lead to enhanced results.

Simulations and Modelling

Another group of resources included in this category, and studied in different subject contexts, is simulations and modelling. Cox et al. (2003) reviewed research literature at that time on contributions to learning arising from uses of simulations and modelling in science, and concluded findings showed enhanced retention of knowledge, and sequencing and scaffolding were important factors contributing to that outcome.

In a more specific context, Akpan and Andre (2000) conducted a range of experimental and controlled studies in the US with grade 7 students (aged 12 to 13 years), with a frog dissection simulation. They looked at performance when dissection only was involved, when the simulation only was used, when the simulation preceded an actual dissection, and when a simulation followed a dissection. Their results indicated significant gains arose when the dissection simulation was used on its own or when it preceded an actual dissection, compared to lower gains when the dissection was undertaken on its own or when the simulation followed the dissection. This result suggests that order of activities can be important, and placement of simulations and modelling in a series of activities is an important factor to be considered by teachers when they plan curriculum events.

In another context, Huppert, Lomask, and Lazarowitz (2002) looked at learning outcomes when students used a microbiology simulation program.

Students needed to explore 'what if' scenarios, and could manipulate three different independent variables. The results showed learners using the software gained significantly more than a control group. Again, no gender bias was found in terms of gains. As the groups involved were identified as those with lower cognitive ability levels, the authors concluded that students in this group could be supported in terms of gaining problem-solving skills.

Overall, the Metiri Group (2006) concluded from their review of simulations and modelling programs and their contributions to learning that: "The *power* behind the use of simulations in the life sciences is in the opportunity for students to explore 'what-ifs' in ways that enable the student to *build schemas of understanding*" (p. 10). They also reported in summary that simulations and modelling enable a visualisation of concepts or structures, that this reduces cognitive load, so younger or less experienced learners are able to understand more complex ideas and concepts at an earlier stage. From a recent review of the literature, Rutten, van Joolingen, and van der Veen (2012) found that impacts of simulations on science learning were positive overall, with effect sizes up to 1.5 for learning gains, but with larger gains arising where simulations replaced laboratory activities or where they were used in a preparative way.

Word Processors

Word processors are a set of resources used by many young people to support certain subject or topic needs, and ways they might contribute or not contribute to learning have been hotly debated for decades. Most research, however, indicates advantages arising for learners when word processors are used. Bangert-Drowns (1993) looked at impacts of using a word processor with students in experimental and quasi-experimental groups. The students received the same forms of writing instruction, but one group used a word processor for writing. The study identified a small, positive effect (ES=0.27) when the word processor was used. The only statistically significant relationship with regard to effect size, however, was with writing ability, with 'weak' writers benefitting more than 'average' or 'strong' writers when using a word processor (ES=0.49). 'Weak' writers also displayed less variance in terms of writing ability after instruction when using a word processor. The author concluded that using a word processor for writing had a positive motivational impact on 'weak' writers.

Concerns with a detrimental effect on handwriting skills, spelling, and abilities to think creatively have been raised over the years, but few research reports have highlighted negative effects, even at relatively early stages of using word processors (see Hunter, Jardine, Rilstone, & Weisgerber, n.d., for example). The only negative report (rather than neutral or positive) they reported was Kurth (1987), who reported that while there were no qualitative or quantitative improvements in the writing, junior high school learners made fewer spelling mistakes when a spellcheck facility was used with the word processor. Kurth (1987) also reported that text on screen seemed to enhance more discussion about the writing, and concluded that quality of writing was impacted more by teachers and quality of instruction than it was by the word processor (or any writing tool in general). On a more cautionary note, however, Hunter et al. (n.d.) concluded that while there seemed to be evidence of enjoyment arising and little evidence for supporting writing quality, the studies themselves often involved students at university level, not assigned to random experimental and control groups, not taught about affordances of word processors in advance, previous expertise in using word processors was not accounted for, and the study practice itself was not integrated with other writing or revision practices. A recent concern about uses of digital technologies has been that of texting affecting spelling and literacy. However, Wood, Jackson, Hart, Plester, and Wilde (2011) from a controlled study looking at impacts of text messaging on literacy skills of 9- and 10-year-old learners, found no differences at statistically significant levels for those texting and those not texting, but interestingly found levels of text abbreviations were related to literacy skills positively; the authors concluded texting not only does not adversely affect literacy skills but is related positively to improvements in spelling. Similarly, Powell and Dixon (2011) in their controlled study showed exposure to misspellings could have negative effects on adults' spelling, but exposure to text forms had positive effects on their spelling.

Studies have continued to show that learners can benefit from uses of word processors. Goldberg, Russell, and Cook (2003) conducted a meta-analysis of studies looking at writing with word processors, and found students using them wrote more, were more engaged and motivated, received early ideas and support from teachers offering more scaffolding for their subsequent work, and the quality of their writing was higher when compared to students not using word processors. In a summary of their literature review, the Metiri Group (2006) concluded impacts arising from uses of word processors were due to abilities to undertake writing as and when required, ease of access and use of the facilities and affordances, the prompts generated within the program to alert learners to issues, and ease of revising or redrafting. Certainly in terms of importance of prompts, it is interesting to note similar points highlighted by Bartolini Bussi and Mariotti (2008), who, in the context of mathematics learning, found uses of 'artifact signs' were crucially important, concluding that prompts allow a construction of 'semiotic chains' supporting the goals of teachers working across a series of interventions with learners. As they said, "reaching a mathematical definition does not only mean the production of a mathematically correct statement, but also the construction of a web of semiotic relationships supporting the construction of the corresponding mathematical concept" (p. 778). They found that teachers constructed semiotic webs using computer-based tools and artefact signs, enhancing mathematical symbolism and signs, but maintaining links students could follow and associate with a discourse, to return to whenever they felt it would be of value or use to them.

Learning Contributions and Other forms of Software and Resources

Apart from resources considered above, there are other resources used by teachers and learners to support topic learning. Uses of concept maps (such as mind-mapping tools) have been used by some learners in both formal and informal settings. Providing ways to identify key elements, to show how these relate, how ideas link and progress, and how concepts are depicted in terms of the general to the more detailed, was argued by the National Reading Panel of the National Institute of Child Health and Human Development in the US as contributing to learning. The Metiri Group (2006) summarised their findings as follows: "the generation of such concept maps offers an excellent opportunity for students to 'visually think' about and visually represent stories, concepts, theories, and passages they have read" (p. 11). They stated further that use of concept or mind-maps offered ways for learners to represent learning elements such as comparison, similarity, difference, causal relationship and direction, structures and hierar-chies, process and time sequences. They reported studies showing that concept maps can enhance reading comprehension.

Another element of learning in another topic field, visualisation in mathe-matics, has also been shown to be supported through software resources such as DGEs. The Metiri Group (2006) cite an unpublished doctoral dissertation by Lester (1996), which looked at the use of one DGE, *Geometer's Sketchpad*. This study showed skill of geometric conjecture was significantly increased by students using this software, when compared to a control group. Isiksal and Askar (2005) conducted a controlled study with grade 7 students in Turkey, with students randomly assigned to one of three groups: those using a DGE (*Autograph*), those using *MS Excel*, and those taught through more traditional methods. Results indicated the group using *Autograph* gained significantly more than those using either *MS Excel* or those in the group receiving more traditional teaching.

In the area of science, Linn and His (2000) described use of a web-based envi-ronment to support learning of the scientific concept of thermodynamics. In this study, students were involved in a range of activities on the web-based medium, including simulations and online discussion. Results of the study indicated those students using the online tools gained significantly more than those in a control group. In summarising their view of contributions to learning arising from what the Metiri Group (2006) call 'visualisation tools', they stated that: "Emergent research indicates that visuals can serve as a scaffold to deeper, more complex thinking, without causing cognitive overload. In other cases dynamic visualiza-tion tools enable students to explore cases and concepts" (p. 10).

Digital technologies can not only support aspects of 'visualisation' but also aspects of 'auditory access and development'. Crawford (2010), in a study in Australia, gathered evidence for a school case study, where music technology was used by teachers with year 7 to 10 classes. The evidence was gathered using surveys, semi-structured interviews with a teacher, and student journals. The author concluded that the evidence was strong, and music technology could be used to support effective music teaching and learning if resources were used in "a holistic way that encompasses valued knowledge and nonlinear/multi-dimensional platforms to create authentic learning" (p. 34).

Other topic-specific programmes have been used to support the development of social skills, and social responsibility. Blood, Johnson, Ridenour, Simmons, and Crouch (2011) reported findings from a study using an iPod, where: "A ten year-old boy exhibiting frequent off-task and disruptive behaviour during small group math instruction was taught to use an iPod Touch for video modeling and self-monitoring purposes" (p. 229). The study involved two phases of intervention; in the first, the student viewed a video just three minutes long demonstrating peers modelling appropriate behaviour in a mathematics group; and in the second, the student was taught how to self-monitor his behaviour during the mathematics group sessions. The authors found, following the first intervention, a significant increase in positive on-task behaviours and a decrease in disruptive behaviours, but these behaviours were not found to be consistent. Following the second intervention, the authors reported a consistent effect as well as increases in the two forms of positive behaviours, with on-task behaviours reaching nearly 100%. The digital technology used was a short video specifically designed to provide positive behaviour modelling: "In the video, peers demonstrated appropriate math group behavior including on-task behavior, following directions, and completing work" (p. 305). The video had an audio track describing expectations for positive behaviours during a mathematics group session. The authors concluded from the quantitative and qualitative results that the video modelling resource run on the iPod "had a positive impact on a student's on-task and disruptive behaviour during small group math instruction. The effectiveness of video modeling appears to have been enhanced with the addition of self-monitoring procedures" (p. 311).

Some studies have looked at uses of emerging digital technologies in specific topic contexts. In terms of uses of audience response systems, Blasco-Arcas, Buil, Hernández-Ortega, and Sese (2013) reported a study involving 198 university students in Spain, showing high levels of interactivity leading to more active collaboration and engagement, improving learning outcomes. In terms of augmented reality facilities, Wu, Lee, Chang, and Liang (2013), from their review, identified three categories of augmented reality facilities—focusing either on specific roles, or on specific tasks, or on specific locations—and while they identified potential benefits, they also cautioned that the complex environments could easily lead to cognitive overload, especially for some learners.

In terms of software shown to impact longer-term interests of learners, Miller, Chang, Wang, Beier, and Klisch (2011) in a study involving more than 700 secondary age learners in using a web-based forensic science game, indicated gains in knowledge but also motivation towards a science career.

Elements of Contribution

From evidence of contributions (uses, outcomes and impacts) described and detailed above and elsewhere throughout the text, a learning framework analysis highlights elements of learning where contributions arise. This picture is shown in Figure 3.2. No attempt has been made to indicate strength of reported contribution; where contributions are reported, these are shown using shading.

It is clear that topic-specific resources and software covers a wide range of resources and tools, and learners may experience very different patterns of access and use with regard to these resources. In this sub-section, the contribution to learning from across the range of resources will be considered, rather than at a more specific level.

Many topic-specific resources and software are either designed for or are selected by teachers and supporters to be used by learners starting with certain background abilities or skills. The evidence from across the range of resources considered here indicates that learners use topic-specific resources and software in order to support their working in a Zone of Proximal Development. Through their own interactions and the interventions of their teachers, they subsequently work in a Zone of Proximal Adjustment, and often, with peers or with their

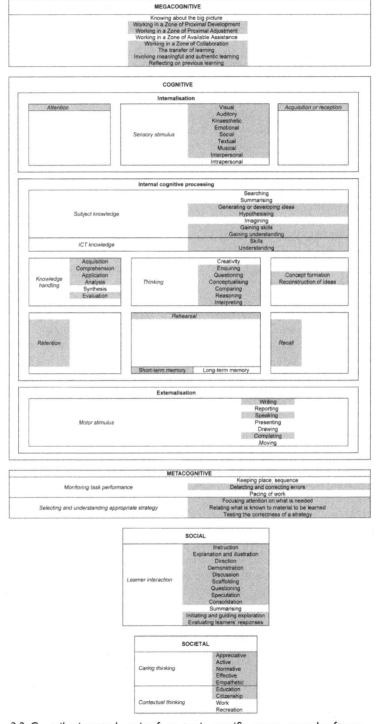

Figure 3.2 Contributions to learning from topic-specific resources and software

teachers, in a Zone of Collaboration. With some topic-specific resources and software such as some computer games or simulations or modelling, a transfer of learning has been shown, and in some cases experiences offer either direct or associated examples linking to authentic learning experiences. In many cases, learners or teachers are concerned with a reflection on their previous learning.

Heightened attention is often evidenced through use of topic-specific software. That heightened attention is related to the software being visual in nature, offering auditory output, and involving kinaesthetic input (such as inputting text or characters, or moving items on-screen). At the same time, the resources often offer access to learning through textual material, and either a musical background, or indeed focus on music skills and experiences themselves (take, for example, the opportunity to play a gamelan). Some topic-specific resources and software engage at a social and emotional level, and enhance engagement at an interpersonal level. Acquisition and reception of knowledge and ideas is encouraged through this range of sensory engagement routes.

A range of topic-specific resources and software encourages generating and developing ideas (video models, for example) and hypothesising (even word processors, encouraging ideas to be offered that can be viewed by others and reviewed by them). Gaining subject skills and subject understanding is widely identified (in science, in mathematics, and in areas of social responsibility, for example). Additionally, gaining ICT skills and understanding is also evidenced, for example, in gaining skills in using comment boxes or tracking in a word processor. Across the range, acquisition of facts and knowledge are evidenced, as is comprehension, application of facts and knowledge gained in one area being used within another, analysis of data provided, and in some cases evaluation (deciding how and when to use models exemplified through video, for example). The resources also lead to enquiring and questioning (through the use of simulations, for example), and conceptualising and the reconstruction of ideas (through the use of video and video clips, for example). Topic-specific resources and software also support processes such as comparing (in simulations), reasoning and interpreting (with CASs).

There is evidence of retention of facts and knowledge, and evidence of rehearsal (association of ideas and knowledge through cues, for example), and of recall (through tests and examinations). The use of resource ideas within short-term memory is evidenced also. Topic-specific resources and software are shown to contribute to writing, speaking and completing activities.

In metacognitive terms, topic-specific resources and software offer opportunities for learners to detect and correct errors (particularly where these are identified and discussed by teachers and supporters), and for focusing attention on what is needed to complete or take activities or tasks forward (through cues provided by teachers or supporters). Relating what is known to material to be learned is identified in a range of topic-specific software, as is the testing of the correctness of a strategy (particularly in terms of simulations or modelling, for example).

In terms of the social aspect of learning, topic-specific resources and software provide opportunities for instruction (in specific subject and topic areas), explanation and illustration (through video clips, for example), direction (indicating positive behaviours, for example) and demonstration (again, through exemplification in video clips). The software is seen to provide opportunities for discussion (in some cases with other learners and in other cases with teachers), scaffolding (even with generic programs such as word processors), questioning and speculation (in simulations and modelling), and consolidation (when students use mathematical games to re-try skills used before). The software supports the initiating and guiding of exploration (offering ideas learners might try), and evaluating learners' responses (by giving feedback at the end of an activity, perhaps in the form of a score such as '7 out of 10' or in the form of a comment such as 'that was very well done').

In terms of the societal aspect of learning, topic-specific resources and software can support caring thinking, some resources offering material that looks at ways to be socially responsible or to be safe, supporting an appreciative perspective, offering active ways to engage responsibly, as well as a normative perspective. Some software that considers elements of social responsibility also offers ideas of effective as well as empathetic perspectives. Overall, topic-specific resources and software support learners particularly in terms of longer-term educational and citizenship needs.

Gaps in the Picture

In terms of megacognitive aspects, topic-specific resources and software do not generally provide a wide overview or a big picture; they focus on a specific topic, and offering the big picture is not usually the intention at that point in time. Learners are generally focused on the use of the software, rather than working in a wider Zone of Available Assistance that considers other potential resources.

In terms of cognitive elements, the focus is not generally through an intrapersonal route (except through discussion with the teacher or supporter). As the software is concerned with completion of one or more activities, searching and summarising are not involved generally, and imagining is not a major focus. Creativity, synthesis and evaluation are similarly not focused on to any great extent generally. The focus on memorisation in terms of contribution is not always clear, and while some topic-specific resources and software support working memory, long-term memorisation is not necessarily built into the structure of the individual resources. As completion is a main focus, reporting to others, presenting, drawing or moving of items are not generally involved in terms of externalisation through affordances.

In terms of metacognitive elements, there is not generally an involvement of keeping place and sequence, as the completion determines this pattern in itself. Pacing of work is usually determined by the teacher, and is not an element the learner is concerned with generally.

In terms of social elements, summarising may be involved, but completion rather than summarising is often the key focus. In terms of societal elements, the key purposes of this software are usually on education and citizenship, rather than work or recreation (in terms of software provided for use by young people rather than adults in work).

Curriculum-wide Learner-centred Software

Curriculum-wide learner-centred software offers a large range of resources and activities covering entire curriculum areas. The pattern of use (shown in

Regularity of use													
Selected by teachers													
Used by learners													
In classrooms													
In projects or after-school													
Involving parents at home													

Figure 3.3 How curriculum-wide learner-centred software offers support for learning

Figure 3.3) can be described as regular, selected by teachers, used by learners, in classrooms and often with minimal teacher intervention.

Contributions (uses, outcomes and impacts) of software referred to often as ILSs, enabling individual learners to access wide-ranging content, have been explored; probably the largest national study into ILSs undertaken was reported initially by the National Council for Educational Technology in the UK (NCET, 1994), and later by Underwood and Brown (1997), followed by Wood (1998). Prior to these studies, a range of smaller studies had been conducted, reported by McFarlane (1997a) in her review of that literature. She reported the results of Becker (1992), when students used two different ILSs—*SuccessMaker* and *Jostens*. In both cases, significantly higher learning gains were identified when students used the systems, although effect sizes involved were lower with randomised control groups. Underwood et al. (1997) identified significantly higher learning gains in mathematics for students using the system compared to those not (with an effect size of 0.4), and this gain was retained when the study was repeated over a two-year period. The gain for those using the system for one year only was maintained for a second year when compared to those not using the system at all (with an effect size of 0.35).

ILSs and Different Learner Groups

In terms of more specific groups of learners using ILSs, Gardner (1997) looked at under-achievers, and the contribution that ILSs offered them in terms of their learning. In the under-achievement group, both very able and very weak students were included. Looking at students using and not using ILSs, and using vendor and independent test measures, positive impacts on attainment in mathematics and on behaviour patterns were identified for this group, with increased attention span and focus on task for all ability groups. However, it was noted that most impact arose for the very able and the very weak.

Of note also from the ILS studies was the fact that some students reported they did not like using the systems. Features or affordances of the system clearly determine whether some learners engage with it or not, and hence potentially affect ways activities accessible through the system can contribute to their learning. The ILS is an environment in itself; so, for some, this separate form of learning environment may be regarded as valuable, while for others it is not. This point is picked up further in Chapter 4, but other points to consider here with regard to this form of software, where completion and repetition can be seen as salient features, were raised by Cavendish, Underwood, Lawson, and Dowling (1997) in reporting a study by Hativa (1989) when they said "pupils have a love-hate relationship with ILS—they like it when the computer tells them they have got something right, but not when they have got it wrong, so the ILS is both motivating and demotivating" (p. 43).

How such programs respond to learners and their needs is clearly fundamentally important. If the available system works to support the learner, by working within their Zone of Proximal Development and can accommodate to a Zone of Proximal Adjustment, then what the Metiri Group (2006) state in their summary of contributions of such a system is likely to be valid: "The power of cognitive tutor programs is in their anticipation of common misconceptions students bring to the learning of specific concepts, and the intelligent feedback provided to students by the tutor that leads to correction of such misconceptions" (p. 11).

Learner-centred Mathematics and Literacy Software

Other forms of software in this category have focused on more specific subject areas rather than covering a range of subjects. One of these, called *Cognitive Tutor Algebra*, was studied by Morgan and Ritter (2004), and outcomes were reported by the Metiri Group (2006). The study outcomes reinforce some of the findings from the ILS studies. As the Metiri Group (2006) reported, this was "a large-scale experiment conducted in the Moore, Oklahoma, Independent School District during the 2000–2001 school year in which students were randomly assigned to either the Cognitive Tutor Algebra 1 program or a traditional Algebra 1 course" (p. 11). When results for both groups were viewed, those learners using the *Cognitive Tutor Algebra 1* system outperformed those not using it, as measured by an Educational Testing Service (ETS) algebra end-of-year assessment. The greatest gains were found in learners who performed least well in traditional settings, and a survey indicated these learners felt more confident in their abilities having used the system, although not at the same level as grade 8 honours students who were also involved in the study.

A study exploring outcomes of software that 'listened' to children's reading and responded to it (Poulsen, 2004 cited in the Metiri Group, 2004) produced some mixed results. As the Metiri Group (2006) reported, the *Project LISTEN Reading Tutor (RT)* was a programme designed to support English language learning for learners in grades 2 to 4. The study involved 34 students who were randomly assigned to experimental and control groups, and then switched at the midway point (one month into the study). The results showed the *RT* group made significant gains when compared to the other group (sustained silent reading). These gains were in fluency of reading and timed sight recognition of words. With untimed sight recognition of words and comprehension, however, there were no significant differences identified.

Another study in the US (Pearson, Ferdig, Blomeyer, & Moran 2005), looking at reading supported by intervention software, identified significant improvements when the software was deployed according to needs identified by the teacher. Similar results were found also with intervention software used to support science learning. A meta-analysis conducted by Bayraktar (2001), looking at studies between 1970 and 1999, identified most gains for software supporting physics through use of simulations and tutorials (not involving online tutors, but involving CAI). This meta-analysis also indicated that access to computer systems had an effect, with an effect size of 0.37 for one-to-one access, while the effect size was only 0.1 for three-to-one access. Significantly, the study reported CAI was more effective when used as a 'supplement' rather than as a 'substitute'.

Computer Assisted Instruction

The integration of CAI, or drill and practice programs, with other forms of more traditional classroom practice is an approach that has been explored in a number of studies. Blok, Oostdam, Otter, and Overmaat (2002) studied the teaching of English and Dutch in schools in the Netherlands when CAI programs were used and not used. Their results, from a study of students aged 5 to 12 years, showed those using CAI gained more in terms of learning to read when compared to those not using CAI. Cox et al. (2003) reported similarly, that a study in England comparing academic achievement of primary age students where CAI was used as a supplement to traditional classroom learning gained more than those not using CAI.

In terms of contributions to learning from such systems, the Metiri Group (2006) stated that "The *power of CAI* was in the provision of *supplementary activities* to strengthen learning and skill levels through provision *of immediate feedback*" (p. 12). They noted also from their review of CAI that it offered only small levels of advantage, even though these were significant, but it was believed new software based on concepts of neuroscience would offer potential advantages in the future. They provided an example of this form of software, with some indications of early findings of learning contributions from *Fast ForWord*, software supporting the development of reading through oral comprehension. As they said, the particular feature identified as being important was "its ability to adapt to each student's skill level and rate of progress. As a student moves through an exercise, the level of difficulty gradually increases and modified speech sounds gradually change to natural speech sounds" (p. 12). They reported study findings showing the software used visual and auditory processing routes to support reading through an oral training approach.

A more recent form of curriculum-wide learner-centred software has been the development of online virtual laboratories. Chen (2010), in a survey of 233 online virtual laboratories to support science learning particularly, found hypothetico-deductive logic was used most commonly in designing these environments, and cautioned this could reduce engagement with holistic approaches to science learning, potentially reducing appropriate scientific inquiry and application to everyday problems.

Elements of Contribution

From evidence of contributions (uses, outcomes and impacts) described and detailed above and elsewhere throughout the text, a learning framework analysis highlights elements of learning where contributions arise. This picture is shown in Figure 3.4. No attempt has been made to indicate strength of reported contribution; where contributions are reported, these are shown using shading.

This category supports learners by providing opportunities to work in a Zone of Proximal Development, either identified within the system through a series of

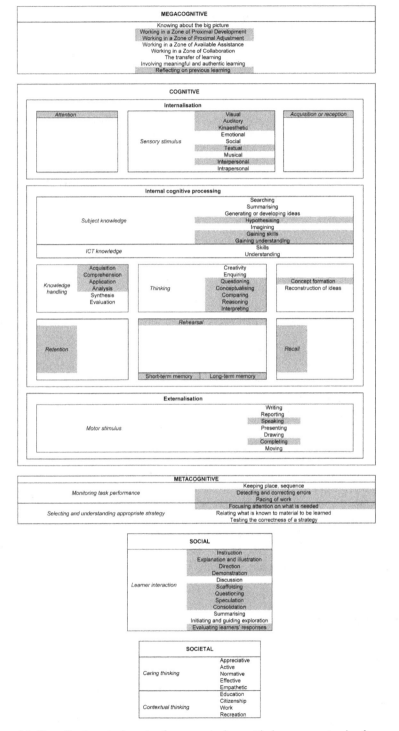

Figure 3.4 Contributions to learning from curriculum-wide learner-centred software

baseline tests, or identified by a teacher who selects an appropriate starting point. Feedback within the systems enables students to work in a Zone of Proximal Adjustment. Activities and exercises often bring up previous or prerequisite learning, and hence support a focus for reflecting on previous learning.

Many learners are seen to engage with the systems, and some gain from heightened attention. Visual and auditory formats of the systems support these sensory routes of engagement, as does the need for learners to complete tasks or activities through kinaesthetic engagement with a keyboard or other input device. Tasks within the systems are often provided in textual form, and frequent brevity of text is reported to support engagement. Systems provide quite rapid and regular feedback and these features support engagement at an interpersonal level, although it should be noted this can have negative affect if feedback regularly indicates learners are 'wrong'. Overall, features and affordances support engagement for a range of learners, leading to acquisition or reception of ideas or knowledge.

Within activities themselves, learners are asked to hypothesise, although some observations indicate 'guesswork' happens in some cases to a greater extent than hypothesis and reflection. There is evidence from studies that a range of learners gain subject or topic skills and understanding. The level of acquisition of knowledge and understanding supports at a level of comprehension, while follow-on activities provide opportunities for learners to apply this knowledge in other task contexts. Some activities, such as those in science, encourage knowledge handling at the level of analysis. Questioning and conceptualising is encouraged in some activities and programs, while comparing is a key feature of some activities. Reasoning and interpreting are encouraged in some programs supporting mathematics learning, for example.

Evidence from studies indicates retention of knowledge and ideas does result, at least in the medium term. Many programs encourage rehearsal of prior knowledge and ideas, and test outcomes indicate both short-term (working) and long-term memory can be affected by programs and activities. Recall is encouraged when learners regularly use these forms of programs, especially if they are integrated across a period of time through a series of interventions determined by the teacher.

In terms of forms of externalisation, speaking is encouraged in a range of programs, but for many programs, completing tasks and activities is the main route for externalisation of knowledge and ideas. Some programs now focus increasingly on identification, detecting and correcting of errors, but the programs often appear to be more responsible for this set of actions than the learner. Pacing of work can be determined by the learner, and although this can have advantages, some research indicates pacing of work determined by a teacher might be an important feature in terms of longer-term success. Certainly the programs focus attention on what is needed, but how much of this is taken up by the learner to use in other situations and contexts is not clear.

In terms of forms of social interaction, the programs are focused heavily on instruction, although they also offer explanation and illustration, especially in some subject areas and topics, such as science. The programs offer direction, as well as demonstration. Scaffolding is seen as an increasingly important development feature across this group of programs. Questioning is encouraged in a variety of tasks and activities, but the form of answering devices (such as multiple choice) can lead to guesswork from learners rather than answers arising from more reasoned trial and reflection approaches. Similarly, speculation is encouraged but not ensured. Consolidation is a key feature of many programs, as is evaluating learners' responses through immediate or rapid feedback, involving in some programs quite extensive reward and praise systems.

Gaps in the Picture

In terms of megacognitive elements, learners do not generally have a big picture of a subject area or topic provided through the software; they focus on a series of specific topics and tasks. As they use this software intensively, they are not working in a Zone of Available Assistance or in a Zone of Collaboration as their uses are frequently very individual. Transfer of learning is not a key focus, whereas completion of tasks or activities is. The software does not provide an environment where learning can often be described as real or authentic, especially as the tasks and activities also provide the environment for learning outcomes.

In terms of cognitive elements, learners are not generally engaged through emotional routes (although competitive features such as rewards do have some emotional impact on some learners). Social engagement is not a widely developed or used feature of these systems, and musical engagement is not generally featured. Intrapersonal engagement is not generally involved, as the focus is on individual interaction and completion. The system normally provides series of tasks that are fairly stand-alone, so there is no specific focus on processes or resources leading to searching, summarising, generating ideas or imagining. While subject skills and understanding are a focus in terms of desirable outcomes, ICT skills and knowledge are not generally widened for learners using these systems. Learning elements of creativity, enquiry, reconstruction, synthesis and evaluation are not generally included as a focus of tasks or activities. Forms of externalisation within and beyond the system tend to be limited, so writing, reporting, speaking, presenting, drawing and moving items or objects tend to be overshadowed very largely by completion of tasks and activities (except perhaps for some auditory records requested within some modern language learning software, or on-screen movement of items using drag and drop features).

In terms of metacognitive elements, keeping place and sequence is normally managed by the system rather than by the learner. In terms of identifying and selecting strategies, reports of guesswork rather than involvement of strategic processes indicates that relating previous material and testing correctness are not evidenced very largely.

In terms of social elements, discussion is not inherently built in as an integral part of the system. Summarising and initiating and guiding exploration are social features not included or expected. In terms of societal elements, the focus of tasks and activities is generally topic and subject based. Concerns of how tasks and activities, results and outcomes can be considered in wider societal terms are not a general function or feature of these programs.

Curriculum-wide Teacher-centred Software

Curriculum-wide teacher-centred software provides resources developed specifically for teachers to use within classroom settings. This software is designed to cover an entire curriculum, perhaps for one or more years, which might be delivered using networked computers, graphical calculators, or via interactive whiteboards. Examples of studies exploring uses and outcomes in this category include Lee and McDougall (2010), who investigated uses of graphing calculators by teachers in secondary schools, and Passey (2011c), who reported findings from a national UK evaluation study exploring uses and outcomes of digital resources to support an entire mathematics curriculum for 11- to 14-year-old learners. Overall, as shown in Figure 3.5, this form of digital technology is used regularly, selected by teachers, but accessed more than used directly by learners in classrooms.

A range of software development in the 1990s focused on production of curriculum-wide learner-centred software, discussed in the previous section. From evidence arising from studies exploring uses and outcomes of that software, teacher interventions were found to be critically important in a range of ways. Some subsequent software developments, starting around the year 2000, focused more on products placing the teacher at the centre of the management of activities, but offering learner-centred tasks and activities within that wider framework. It is those products, and evidence of their uses, outcomes and impacts, which are the focus of this section.

Science Curriculum Software

A primary school product in this category, covering a science curriculum, was studied by Looi et al. (2011). They reported how formats of the product, designed for learners in grade 3 (about nine years of age), enabled access through mobile technologies. The curriculum delivery and a parallel study were run across an entire year, in a single school, with a single class in Singapore. Affordances were clearly considered within the design of the curriculum and how they were integrated into individual activities and tasks. As the authors said: "The students had a total of 21 weeks of the mobilized lessons in science, which were co-designed by teachers and researchers by tapping into the affordances of mobile technologies for supporting inquiry learning in and outside of class" (p. 269). They sought to "exploit the affordances" of the mobile technologies, use activities to undertake formative assessment of learner progress, "facilitate collaborative interactions", "make use of community support and resources" and "support

Regularity of use									
Selected by teachers									
Used by learners									
In classrooms									
In projects or after-school									
Involving parents at home									

Figure 3.5 How curriculum-wide teacher-centred software offers support for learning

teacher development to be good curriculum developers and facilitators" (pp. 272–3). This curriculum was used with a randomly chosen class of 39 pupils. Other classes were "taught in the traditional way" (p. 275), and all learners in all classes completed a general science examination with multiple-choice and open-ended questions, before and at the end of the 21-week curriculum. Overall, the authors found positive contributions arising, across a range of aspects of learning; the experimental class gained higher results in assessment tests than the other five similar mixed-ability classes. Learners gained from mobile access in terms of greater personalisation of learning, deeper learning, higher levels of engagement and more positive attitudes. The authors reported learners were "able to conduct research by formulating questions, conducting online search, collecting data, and producing quality animations and concept maps, as well as other digital artefacts to reflect their understanding and negotiate meanings collectively" (p. 276). The authors related these contributions to changes in behaviours of learners, which in turn affected dynamics of the learning environment in positive ways: "We consider the behaviour of students asking their own questions and their changed mindset about not being afraid of asking questions (that might be deemed as 'stupid' by their peers and their teacher) as very significant cultural changes" (p. 277). The authors felt these changes were so significant that this heralded a pedagogical shift towards a different culture, concerned with construction of collective knowledge rather than copying items the teacher had written or given them. Test result differences, comparing before and after results with the control classes, identified statistically significant differences in terms of science knowledge and understanding, with an ANCOVA test $(F(5345)=31.619, p<0.01)$ showing class difference accounted for 4.1.% of the total variance between end-of-year examination scores, with the experimental class gaining highest scores. The authors indicated the learners believed affordances were supporting their learning and matching their learning needs, with 80% of learners believing the mobile device helped them to learn, both in and outside the classroom, and 62% believing they understood science concepts better and understood how these concepts were related to real-life situations. The importance of gaining understanding, developing an understanding of scientific concepts, and relating understanding to other contexts and real-life situations was clearly highlighted in findings from the study. The authors indicated how specific features and affordances were used to support aspects of learning. For example, "they drew and animated on the *Sketchy* to demonstrate their understanding; they listed ideas and connected them on PicoMap; they constructed comparison of concepts on Word; they searched for terms and ideas on the Internet" (p. 282). Additionally, learners watched videos on *YouTube*, researched individually and brought together ideas and knowledge they found in different places, looked at real-life situations and photographed these as a record, and captured learning of specific interest.

Mathematics Curriculum Software

These findings were echoed in an earlier study, reported by Passey (2011c). This study investigated uses of a three-year-long mathematics curriculum for lower secondary school learners (11 to 14 years of age). Uses and outcomes of the product, called *MathsAlive*, were studied across a three-year period, involving teachers in 20 schools using digital activities, of mental mathematics tasks, video clips, screen-based activities, homework sheets and creative screens teachers could choose from a bank or develop themselves. Teachers accessed these resources via interactive whiteboards largely, but access also involved using clusters of desktop computers, graphical calculators and learners' home computers. Findings from the study highlighted ways affordances engaged learners more fully in mathematical activities and learning. Particular outcomes identified by learners indicated that affordances:

- Enhanced visual clarity—providing them with 'exact and clear' images, so they could remember 'a real image'.
- Clarified a process—offering a point of reference everyone could see, supporting greater discussion about topics, with teachers explaining more how to solve problems.
- Developed conceptual understanding—helping understanding of certain topics, particularly shape and trigonometry.
- Encouraged participative learning—finding the games interesting, helping everyone to take part.
- Increased pace and variety—remembering things when they actively used the resources and did not need to copy and write.

Mathematics and English Language Software

A similar product supporting mathematics and English language learning was the focus of a study by Rosen and Beck-Hill (2012). They reported on product uses and outcomes in four elementary schools in Dallas, Texas, involving 20 teachers and 476 grade 4 and 5 learners (aged 9 to 11 years), who accessed the programs through one-to-one laptop devices. As the authors stated, findings overall were positive "in terms of student math and reading achievement, differentiation in teaching and learning, higher student attendance, and decreased disciplinary actions" (p. 225). Features of the program and its application within the curriculum echoed those identified within the studies reported above. In terms of program design, the report stated activities included "open-ended applets and discovery environments, multimedia presentations, practice exercises, and games" (p. 228). The sequence of activities was determined by teachers. An example given by the authors started with an animation to stimulate interest in a specific topic, followed by a class discussion to enhance curiosity or questioning, guided experiments undertaken by learners using an appropriate applet, learners uploading their work to a class gallery, the teacher selecting and projecting their work for the class to see, and involving the class in discussion. Five important components of the implementation were highlighted:

- Infrastructure—one-to-one laptop provision for learners and a workstation for the teacher.
- Interactive curriculum—recommended sequences for learning activities, matching policy and assessment needs, but allowing teachers to develop and integrate their own resources.

- Digital learning environment—a learning platform through which the teacher could construct sequences for lessons, and build in formative and summative assessments to give feedback both during and after lessons.
- Pedagogical support—each teacher taking a curriculum course and gaining regular support from a tutor.
- Technical support—available whenever the program was used in classrooms.

The researchers gathered a range of evidence across the first year-long study period, including "standardized assessment scores" at the beginning and end of the study period, "school records on attendance and discipline, student questionnaires, and [55] observations in experimental and control classes" (p. 230). After the first year, two experimental schools and two control schools were chosen, to match learner and teacher features, demographics and localities. The schools supported a diverse student population, "63.1% Hispanic students, 17.6% black students, 15.1% white students, 3.7% Asian students, and 0.5% American Indian students" (p. 231). All schools, experimental and control, devoted the same amount of time to a mathematics and English language curriculum (90 minutes each day). When standardised scores in mathematics and reading at the beginning and the end of the year-long trial period were compared between experimental and control schools, the results were statistically significant. The study used the "TAKS [Texas Assessment of Knowledge and Skills] tests" (p. 232). Results showed higher mean scores for grade 4 learners in experimental schools in reading (M=665.9 at the end compared to M=621.9 at the outset), and in mathematics (M=673.9 at the end compared to M=597.6 at the outset), while shifts for control schools were much lower in reading (M=650.3 at the end compared to M=643.0 at the outset), and in mathematics (M=660.1 at the end compared to M=611.6 at the outset). Results were similar for grade 5 learners; in experimental schools in reading (M=713.7 at the end compared to M=652.5 at the outset), and in mathematics (M=700.6 at the end compared to M=654.7 at the outset), while shifts for control schools were much lower in reading (M=696.1 at the end compared to M=656.0 at the outset), and in mathematics (M=674.1 at the end compared to M=646.4 at the outset). The program also affected behaviours, measured by both attendance rates and levels of disciplinary action being taken, with learner absences reduced by 29.2% in experimental schools and increased by 56.6% in control schools, and with learner discipline issues reduced by 62.5% in experimental schools and reduced by 15.4% in control schools. Importantly, the authors highlighted increases in levels of participation, measured by numbers of interactions between teachers and students; in experimental schools the level during two months was 40.3, while in control schools it was 17.0. After a further six months, the level in experimental schools had increased to 51.0, while the level in control schools was 30.0. The authors identified from their observations levels of forms of interaction occurring in both experimental and control schools. These outcomes are shown in Table 3.1.

The authors provided examples of each of the different forms of interaction observed:

- Independent learning—opportunities to increase independence, responsibility for learning and self-management of learning.
- Intellectual challenge—opportunities to reflect on their engagement and the challenge to move beyond the level of recognised abilities.
- Modelling—guiding practice, and providing scaffolding.
- Adjusting instruction—responding to progress achieved during the lesson.
- Descriptive feedback—about learning processes that had taken place.

Elements of Contribution

From evidence of contributions (uses, outcomes and impacts) described and detailed above, a learning framework picture shown in Figure 3.6 highlights elements of learning where contributions arose. Reported contributions are shown using shading.

In terms of megacognitive elements of learning, evidence indicates learners do gain knowledge of the big picture (being given ideas of the entire path of activities and how they relate to end points). Teachers tailor activities to enable learners to work in a Zone of Proximal Development, and they clearly also 'adjust instruction', for example, so that they also work in a Zone of Proximal Adjustment. The range of facilities provided for learners, and their access to teachers, peers and online materials, means they can work in a Zone of Available Assistance, and their interactions clearly indicate they also work in a Zone of Collaboration. The nature of the programs indicates learners generate outcomes and whenever possible transfer these using particular digital technologies or to other learners and teachers; so they are involved in a transfer of learning. Evidence indicates that learners recognise they are involved in meaningful and authentic learning, and are clearly encouraged to reflect on previous learning.

Table 3.1 Instances of key interactions between teachers and students (based on data presented in Rosen & Beck-Hill, 2012)

Interaction observed	Level (percentage) in the 3rd and 4th months in experimental schools	Level (percentage) in the 3rd and 4th months in control schools	Level (percentage) in the 8th and 9th months in experimental schools	Level (percentage) in the 8th and 9th months in control schools
Independent learning	100	50	84	14
Intellectual challenge	67	40	63	29
Modelling	75	100	84	63
Adjusting instruction	83	30	42	21
Providing descriptive feedback	58	50	84	85

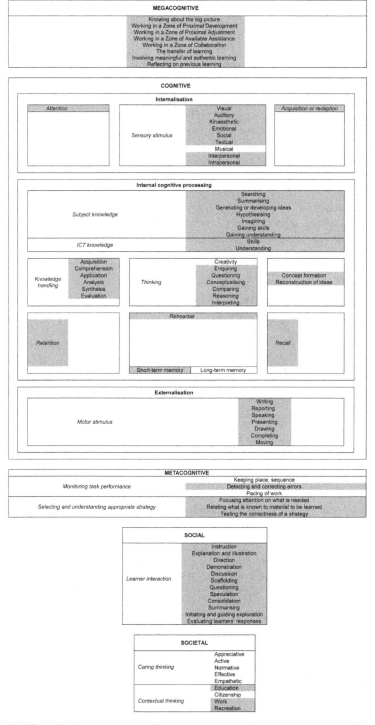

Figure 3.6 Contributions to learning from curriculum-wide teacher-centred software

These programs clearly engage learners' attention. Learners refer to affordances and the importance of visual and auditory elements, as well as kinaesthetic elements when they are involved in direct activity with the digital and other physical environments. Learners indicate emotional as well as social engagement, and their engagement with material that is textual. Both interpersonal and intrapersonal interactions are indicated as being important. The forms of sensory engagement involved, as recognised by teachers, lead to acquisition or reception of ideas and knowledge acquisition by learners.

In terms of forms of cognitive elements involved, learners are encouraged to search for knowledge and ideas, and summarise key facts. Evidence indicates learners generate or develop ideas, hypothesise both with their peers and with their teachers, and are encouraged to imagine outcomes such as 'what will happen then'. Results indicate there are not only subject gains in skills and understanding, but also in ICT skills and understanding.

Outcomes indicate learners are involved in acquisition of facts and knowledge, as well as comprehension, and application of knowledge and ideas beyond points when they are initially gained. Higher-order skills are involved, in terms of activities asking learners to analyse (what will happen if, or what do these results tell us), synthesise (bringing ideas and facts together), and evaluation (identifying the value or worth of outcomes or results). Overall, learners are involved in enquiring, questioning, conceptualising (including a reconstruction of ideas when teachers challenge them), comparing, reasoning and interpreting. As would be expected, the range of cognitive elements across an entire year of curriculum would be expected to be high. However, the balance of these cognitive elements is clearly important, and teachers and observers recognise higher-order elements arising more frequently than in 'traditional classroom environments'. Overall, retention of knowledge and ideas is demonstrated by the difference in results between experimental and control groups. The programs used, with appropriate interventions from teachers, ask learners to rehearse their knowledge and understanding, and recall facts and knowledge as these are needed. The programs are supporting working memory, and although tests suggest that long-term memory is affected, the extent is not clear. These programs do not determine a single form of externalisation of learning; but learners are involved in a wide range—writing, reporting to their peers and their teachers, speaking and discussing regularly, presenting to others, drawing in ways summarising and identifying key features and facts, completing tasks and activities, and moving items around on-screen as well as off-screen.

A number of important metacognitive elements are evidenced. Learners are encouraged through activities and teacher interactions to detect and correct errors, focus attention on what is needed (supported by affordances of the digital technologies), relating what is known to material to be learned (encouraged through teacher interactions as well as peer discussions), and testing the correctness of a strategy against comment and discussion from peers and teachers.

Forms of social interaction described and detailed are wide. Instruction is supported for the teacher, but also supported by materials provided through the program. Explanation and illustration is offered by teachers and the program, as well as direction and demonstration. A major outcome from these programs is enhancing discussion, between teacher and learner, and between learner and learner. Teachers can use the materials to scaffold learning experiences; they can support these through adequate and focused questioning, challenging learners to speculate, but also offering activities enabling them to consolidate and summarise, using the features and medium of the accessible digital technologies. The program and teachers can initiate and guide exploration, and teachers are evaluating learners' responses regularly, exploring ways learners gain as well as what they gain.

These programs focus largely on educational needs, but can provide learners with an understanding of how education might be delivered in the future to support their on-going engagement and educational needs. Some evidence indicates learners are considering their experiences in terms of work, as well as recreation.

Gaps in the Picture

In terms of megacognitive elements, this software provides the potential to focus on all of these elements, integrated through teacher interactions mediated in classrooms. In terms of cognitive elements, musical engagement is not widely used, although some specific instances are introduced by teachers. Creativity is not generally seen as a focus of activities, and there is no clear evidence of how these resources contribute to long-term memory.

In terms of metacognitive elements, keeping place and sequence and pacing of work often results from teacher interactions and decisions rather than learner actions. In terms of social elements, teachers can use these resources widely to support the full range of social interactions, while in terms of societal elements, the programs do not generally focus on caring thinking, or on citizenship.

Software Involving and Supporting Parents

Software involving and supporting parents often includes software focusing on specific subject topics, identified by a teacher, but accessible in homes by learners with parental oversight. This category includes software in the form of online educational games, which can be linked pedagogically to content covered in lessons; using these software resources, activities can be undertaken at home with varying levels of parental oversight, depending on age and form of activity. As shown in Figure 3.7, this software is used on occasions to match teacher needs, can be selected or encouraged by teachers, but used by learners, involving parents at home.

Networking infrastructure now enables connectivity and communications between homes and schools; these facilities can support learner, teacher and parent involvement through a range of activities. Early implementation activities

| Regularity of use |
| Selected by teachers |
| Used by learners |
| In classrooms |
| In projects or after-school |
| Involving parents at home |

Figure 3.7 How software involving and supporting parents offers support for learning

using networking infrastructures have been explored since the 1990s; some were reported in a joint UK government department initiative by Scrimshaw (1997). It was not until about a decade later, however, that wider networking infrastructure supported broadband access at sufficiently high bandwidth to enable affordances (colour imagery, video transfer, and high level data transfer) to support educational activities for a full range of learners.

Exploiting Home–School Internet-wide Infrastructure

In 2007, Somekh et al. reported a favourable picture in the UK about levels and qualities of technological access in homes and schools, supporting the notion that digital technologies across the home–school landscape could support learning where parents would be involved from lesser to greater extents. In 2008, Plowman, McPake, and Stephen reported on a two-year empirical investigation of three- and four-year-old children's uses of digital technologies at home. Evidence was based on a survey of 346 families and 24 case studies, and identified a range of affordances supporting children's interactions and engagement with the outside world. They found "children had learnt to switch items off and on, rewind, fast-forward and navigate websites" (p. 308). They also found that parents potentially could support key elements of important learning environments: "operational, by acquiring technical skills; extending knowledge of the world, by finding and developing information; dispositions to learn, by finding pleasure in these activities and, sometimes, learning the need for persistence" (p. 315). As the authors said, this meant parents were supporting a learning environment in a range of ways, not just concerned with operational but with more cultural aspects.

Just prior to that article being published, the government department in England set up an ICT Test Bed project, providing learners of primary and secondary school age with computer access in homes as well as in schools. A selected number of schools took advantage of this opportunity, looking to encourage development of computer-based activities reaching across from schools into homes, and involving parents where possible. Different schools developed these practices to different extents, but outcomes of the project, involving 28 schools in total, were evaluated to explore whether such practices might affect impacts on learning. Somekh et al. (2007) evaluated differences in national test results for the 28 schools with high levels of ICT over a four-year period by comparing them to a comparison group without those levels of ICT access (as well as to national test averages). At the start of the project they reported test schools were attaining at levels below control schools, measured by Key Stage 2 national tests (at 11 years of age) in English, mathematics and science and according to an average points score across all subjects. Test schools were attaining at lower levels than national averages, particularly with regard to English and mathematics. By the end of the project, the authors reported a shift; they reported high levels of digital technologies enabled learning activities to be undertaken in schools and in homes, leading to statistically significant results at the end of Key Stage 2. These higher results were in mathematics, with a shift from 64% of levels attaining level 4 (the expected norm for that age) and above in the national test in 2002, to 75% in 2006, compared to 74% at level 4 and above in control schools in the same national tests in 2002, rising to 73% in 2006. Statistically significant shifts were not identified at Key Stage 1 (for learners aged seven years) or at Key Stage 3 (for those aged 14 years). At Key Stage 4 (for those aged 16 years) the only indicator with a comparative shift was in percentage of five A*–C grades (highest grades in the national examinations) at GCSE (39% for test and 36% for control schools). It was not clear from the report why such results were only found in the one age group, but it could be argued parental involvement for 7- to 11-year-old learners might have had a more profound effect, or be more common, than at other ages. An alternative explanation could be those teachers set tasks for the 7- to 11-year-old age group, followed up at home with parent-supported or online activities more. Certainly involvement with parents changes with age. In terms of relationship between parents and children of different ages, Davies (2011) highlighted from his study that parents experience a 'loss of control' with uses of digital technologies as children move into later years of adolescence, but he also reported some children find their learning uses are limited as they become older due to parental views of appropriateness.

Home–School Access and Commercial Online Resources

A range of later studies explored this category of digital technology further. For example, Sandberg, Maris, and de Geus (2011) reported a controlled study involving three groups of primary school learners, using mobile applications to support English language learning. They found those who took the devices home gained most, using their home time for learning purposes. Another example was reported by Holmes (2011), of a case study looking at uses of digital games to support young learners at home, enabling a linking of parental support to help those finding it difficult to read. At a more general level, Selwyn, Banaji, Hadjithoma-Garstka, and Clark (2011) studied ways parents used school-provided VLEs in six primary and six secondary schools in England and how these were considered in developing school–home relationships.

Outcomes and impacts arising when learners aged seven to nine years in eight primary schools were supported by their teachers in developing and implementing home-based activities, following up and linking with their in-school practices, was evaluated by Passey (2011d). In this seven-year project, initial implementation activities supported a community-wide ICT development, with funding to support interactive whiteboards in all classrooms, PDAs in two schools, computers into homes initially trialled and deployed through one school, and shared training and support facilitated across the schools. Additionally, local community centres were set up with computer facilities, a mobile learning facility was used at various community locations, and, importantly, a pilot wireless network was put in place across parts of the local area. By 2009, all eight primary schools were actively engaging parents in the project, asking them to consider investing in home-based computer facilities and internet access, providing training opportunities for family members, and encouraging teachers to use facilities to match home-based online learning activities with school-based practices. By 2011, some 2,680 computers, with wireless-based internet access, had been installed in homes across the area, meaning some 60% of homes could use the facilities (and with families sharing the facilities with friends and neighbours, there was leverage to a wider number). The project trained young learners to support their parents at home, trained parents and family members to be aware of what they could expect and do with the new facilities, and engaged teachers in matching home and school activities to support learning needs identified through internal and external assessment.

Teacher reports at the end of the project indicated levels of parental awareness and engagement with education and their children's learning had increased, "something in the region of a 72% shift in level of awareness, and in the region of a 34% shift in forms of engagement" (p. 5). Teachers reported a 61% shift in parental levels of engagement with their children's learning. The study looked towards the end of the project at more specific learning gains by comparing shifts in age-standardised tests over a nine-month period. Results indicated learners gained in terms of attainment in both mathematics and reading. A population of learners (738 in total) across years 3 and 4 (aged seven to nine years) in seven different schools completed a mathematics test *Progress in Maths 9* (GL Assessment, 2004) and a reading test *Suffolk Reading Scale 2* (GL Assessment, 2002a, 2002b) on two different occasions. The tests were age standardised; so, if a learner did not progress, their scores would remain the same, irrespective of age. Results showed gains at highly statistically significant levels in both mathematical scores for all learners (but particularly high for girls), and reading results for all learners (but particularly high for boys).

The development of parental engagement and online homework activities was part of a wider set of interventions by the schools to support enhancements in literacy and mathematics generally. Taking all of these interventions together, the impacts were nevertheless clear, and gains in learning arose over quite short periods of time. As the report stated with regard to mathematics, "For all matched pupil results, a paired sample t-test shows that the difference between the March and December 2010 scores is highly statistically significant (t=-8.58, p=.000)" (p. 54). Differences between results for boys and girls were also identified, "an ANOVA test shows that there is no difference in test scores between these groups in March 2010 (F=.397, p=.529), but there is a statistically significant difference between these groups in December 2010 (F=4.577, p=.033)" (p. 55). The difference in results widened across the period between the tests. High levels of shifts were identified in terms of reading scores, "the difference between the March and December 2010 scores is highly statistically significant (t=-3.778, p=.000)" (p. 58). Again, differences between results for boys and girls were identified, but this time, higher gains for boys were found, "a paired sample t-test shows that the difference between the March and December 2010 scores is highly statistically significant (t=-3.141, p=.002)" (p. 58). This result was particularly encouraging, as boys generally score lower in literacy tests than girls (although it should be noted that writing is the element of literacy that is often particularly weak, and reading was the element that was the focus of the test in this case).

A specific focus of the project was on offering homework activities involving reading and completing mathematics activities, using resources such as *Mathletics* and *Education City*. Teachers reported key shifts not only in terms of their own practices, but also in terms of their expectations and outcomes they recognised arising from their pupils. The project enabled different types of homework to be selected by teachers, and "it was clear that some teachers were then asking pupils to undertake tasks such as research, which were not demanded of them previously" (p. 67). This affected the ways some parents perceived school-based work and how they questioned homework as "work was more visible, the school intentions were more visible, and means of discussion were more visible. Some teachers noted shifts in terms of questions about homework being raised by parents, and questions about amounts of homework being set" (p. 68). Other evidence pointed to longer-term impacts arising from this community-based and family-involved project. National test performance in 2010 at the end of the educational intervention period indicated improvements: "the level of attainment in mathematics had reached 74%, and in English it had reached 73%" (p. 62). At the same time, the variation between the area schools and those across the entire local authority had halved, and no schools had been placed in a category of serious weakness following national Ofsted school inspections.

Elements of Contribution

From evidence of contributions (uses, outcomes and impacts) described above and referred to across other sections and chapters, a learning framework picture has been created, highlighting elements of learning where contributions arose, shown in Figure 3.8. Reported contributions are shown using shading.

Using digital technologies and resources in this category, learners are able to work in a Zone of Proximal Development (identified by their teachers in terms of appropriate online resources and activities), and in a Zone of Proximal Adjustment (with outcomes monitored by teachers, and activities adjusted to meet their starting points and shifting capabilities). Learners can work in a Zone of Available Assistance (which includes their parents in some instances as well as their teachers and the online resources), and in a Zone of Collaboration (with their teachers and parents particularly, but also with other family members). Transfer of learning is a key element in these cases, with learning experiences gained in school practices taken to and used in home environments, and vice versa. Reflecting on previous learning is a key element, with parents as well as teachers encouraging learners to talk about what is happening in the others' environments.

Teachers and parents both reported positively about ways affordances engaged their children in terms of attention. Visual and auditory qualities of online resources, and the need to engage with them kinaesthetically through moving items on-screen or by using input devices, was clear. Emotional engagement was reported by parents particularly, as was social engagement with parents, family members and teachers. Online resources demanded learners to often engage through textual routes, and their engagement was not only interpersonal (competing with themselves to get better scores, for example) but also intrapersonal (competing with other peers). Teachers and parents reported varying routes of engagement leading to reception of ideas and knowledge, followed by acquisition of subject elements of knowledge. Teachers reported that they required learners to engage in cognitive elements involving searching, summarising their findings, and generating or developing ideas as a part of their research activities. Teachers asked pupils to hypothesise about 'what might happen if', and overall, teachers and parents reported learners gained subject skills and

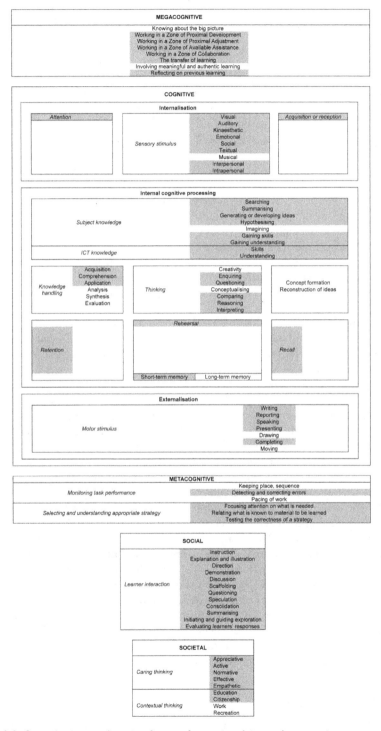

Figure 3.8 Contributions to learning from software involving and supporting parents

understanding (supported by findings from test results and analyses), as well as gaining ICT skills and understanding widely. Overall, learners were involved in acquisition of knowledge and ideas, as well as comprehension and application of knowledge in other contexts (in homes and in schools). Learners were involved in enquiring (researching and summarising), questioning (how to find details and to address problems), comparing (within some exercises and activities), reasoning and interpreting (within other activities, and in how teachers challenged them in classrooms). Findings indicated knowledge and ideas had been retained. Learners were asked by parents and teachers to rehearse their knowledge, and while it was clear this had affected short-term memory, teachers, parents and online activities themselves were demanding learners to recall their knowledge and ideas regularly. This category provided opportunities for learners to use a range of approaches to externalise their learning, through writing, reporting, speaking to parents and teachers, presenting and completing (online activities, for example).

In terms of metacognitive elements, these digital technologies and resources provided opportunities for learners to detect and correct errors (in some of the activities involved), focusing attention on what was needed to undertake activities and tasks, and allowing them to relate what was known to material to be learned. Online activities enabled them to test the correctness of a strategy, but to what extent these abilities were transferred to other situations was not clear.

Learners were involved through this category in a range of social interactions, sometimes directly resulting from affordances of the digital technologies themselves and sometimes from approaches taken by teachers. Learners were involved in instruction (in lessons and in some activities), in explanation and illustration, direction and demonstration. Discussion was encouraged with both teachers and parents and family members, while teachers provided ways to scaffold their learning through links between school-based and home-based practices. Learners were subject to questioning from both parents and teachers, speculation through that questioning, and consolidation through their completion of activities. Learners were asked to summarise results of their online searches, while other tasks set by teachers initiated and guided exploration of subject or topic areas. Overall, both parents and teachers were involved in evaluating learners' responses, and recognising their achievements.

In terms of societal elements of learning, the involvement of parents and online resources meant that learners were involved in caring thinking. Learners were involved at an appreciative level (how their parents showed interest and concern), an active level (being involved), a normative level (identifying expectations of how responses arose or were given), an effective level (recognising impacts of involvement), and an empathetic level (recognising the value of the involvement). Overall, experiences offered models of ways to engage with education in the current and the future, and with citizenship (how these approaches potentially modelled future experiences).

Gaps in the Picture

In terms of megacognitive elements, learners at home, working with or supported by parents, are not generally concerned with a big picture; they are more concerned with undertaking specific tasks or activities. Those activities tend, if online, to be offered through game-style or completion tasks, but it is possible for teachers to ask learners to engage in and gain information about the experience of family members or friends, which could be considered to involve a form of meaningful or authentic learning in the sense of context.

In terms of cognitive elements, musical engagement is not generally observed or reported, but some background music can be used in some activities. Cognitive elements such as imagining and conceptualisation are less prominent. Creativity, analysis, synthesis and evaluation tend not to be the main focus of home tasks or activities, and how short- or long-term memory is involved is not always clear (even though tests indicate subject learning is arising). Tasks do not generally involve drawing or moving items (although some on-screen activities do use drag and drop formats).

In terms of metacognitive elements, keeping place and sequence are not focal tasks asked of learners in these forms of activities. Pacing of work can be a focus, but generally in the sense of undertaking a series of tasks or activities within a period of time, rather than reflecting on achievements in terms of using these experiences for use beyond the programs themselves.

In terms of social elements, tasks and activities, and working with parents, provide for the full range of social interactions. In terms of societal elements, caring thinking is integrated into these activities, but work and recreation are not specific elements of focus. Indeed, it can be argued that some activities attempt to blur the recreation focus, by linking it to the education focus.

Online Resources Supporting Curriculum-wide Needs

Online resources supporting curriculum-wide needs can support an entire curriculum, but in this category individual resources are designed to cover a range of specific topics, and from the range available, these are then selected and used by teachers and integrated with other forms of delivery, over a number of years. These resources can be accessed online by teachers and sometimes by learners at home, often through interactive whiteboards in classrooms, giving access to content in the form of video clips, teaching screens, mental (perhaps mathematics) activities or revision questions. Studies exploring uses and outcomes in this category include Bos (2009), who explored impacts of different formats of web-based resources, and Passey (2011a), who explored impacts of online resources selected by teachers in classrooms, specifically looking at longer-term uses across schools. Overall, the pattern of uses of these resources (see Figure 3.9) can be described as regular, selected by teachers, accessed by learners sometimes directly and at other times indirectly, and used in classrooms.

Online resources to support curriculum-wide needs are becoming increasingly accessible. For example, Zhuzhu and Xin (2010) reported that in 2008, 260,000 rural schools across China had received online resources to cover all subjects and disciplines for all elementary and secondary schools. In the UK and many other countries, these resources are often accessed via interactive whiteboards, and the role of the teacher in supporting access and subsequent learning is clearly vital. In this context, Hennessy (2011) reviewed roles of interactive whiteboards and different roles of digital artefacts in generating learner dialogue,

Regularity of use								
Selected by teachers								
Used by learners								
In classrooms								
In projects or after-school								
Involving parents at home								

Figure 3.9 How online resources supporting curriculum-wide needs offer support for learning

at points in time, over time and across locations. VLEs are now also providing learners with access to resources for curriculum-wide needs. For example, Meyer, Abrami, Wadea, Aslan, and Deault (2010) looked at impacts of an electronic portfolio offering a text editor and audio recorder for creation of work items in the form of readings, music or oral presentations. In three Canadian provinces involving 14 teachers and 296 students, this study showed those using the system gained significantly ($p<0.05$) in both writing skills and some metacognitive skills. Positive gains arising from uses of online resources when teachers intervene and interact are recognised not only in individual research studies but also in meta-analyses (for example, Tamim et al., 2011). Passey (2011a) explored uses of this form of software (*Espresso Education*) through a mixed methods approach, involving qualitative and quantitative elements of enquiry. These resources are used by many schools in the UK, and increasingly in other countries too. In September 2010, a total of 8,978 primary schools (mostly in England) subscribed to the service. As Passey (2011a) reported, most teachers reporting in the study "identified strongly with positive qualities they associate with Espresso resources—allowing children to understand things more easily, engaging pupils through a range of sensory routes, positively motivating pupils to learn, and getting wider ideas about topics or subject areas" (p. 2). However, some researchers caution uses of certain resources in certain ways. For example, Yang, Chang, Chien, Chien, and Tseng (2013) showed with university students watching visual slides in *MS PowerPoint* that they required more decoding time than with text.

Affordances, Uses and Outcomes

Taking a specific example, *Espresso Education* resources have particular qualities and affordances. They are clearly laid out, colourful and uncluttered. They are rich in visual terms, but also in terms of auditory material, combined together through many short video clips. The material shows real-life events and situations, is up-to-date, with regular news items being produced, in different formats to suit different groups of learners with different levels of literacy abilities. The resources are designed to be largely used by teachers, rather than by learners directly. By contrast, *Education City* resources are designed to be used more by learners directly. Teachers in a study (Passey, 2011a) commonly reported wide use and regular use of the *Espresso Education* resources, for topic work, and to support learning in humanities subjects as well as in core subjects (literacy, mathematics and science). Lower levels of use were associated with curriculum areas such as religious education and personal, social and health education, but often fewer of these lessons ran during the week, but "the value of the resources in these areas is nevertheless commonly reported" (p. 2). Teachers recognised specific learning outcomes associated with particular resource qualities and affordances, in terms of: "megacognition (gaining a big picture, involving meaningful learning), cognition (acquisition of ideas and knowledge, generating ideas, gaining understanding, memorisation and retention of ideas and knowledge, encouraging speaking), and social interactions (explanation, illustration, consolidation, initiating exploration)" (p. 2).

In this study, the pattern of use by teachers across a number of schools was explored in some detail. In 72 primary schools, using national test results at 11 years of age, schools with higher levels of attainment were separated for analysis from those with lower levels of attainment in English. Levels of use of resources (identified by page access) were examined at each Key Stage: Early Years (up to five years of age); Key Stage 1 (between five and seven years of age); and Key Stage 2 (between 7 and 11 years of age). A comparison of the ratios of 'top 10' pages accessed was compared for the two different school groups—high levels of English attainment, and lower levels of English attainment. The results indicated that those schools with higher attainments at the end of Key Stage 2 accessed Early Years and Key Stage 1 resources by comparison more, and Key Stage 2 resources by comparison less. They also used mathematics resources less by comparison but other topic resources more by comparison. The differences between levels of access at the different Key Stages was statistically significant, (χ^2=6.446 and p=0.04). Schools attaining at higher levels at the end of Key Stage 2 were using more *Espresso Education* resources earlier, preparing learners using these resources in the longer term across the width of the curriculum, rather than focusing later on a more specific set of subject resources.

Elements of Contribution

From evidence of contributions (uses, outcomes and impacts) described above and elsewhere in the text, a learning framework picture has been created highlighting elements of learning where contributions arose, shown in Figure 3.10 using shading.

In terms of megacognitive elements, teachers and learners indicate they can select resources to allow working in a Zone of Proximal Development, but also in a Zone of Proximal Adjustment (recognising and adjusting to the needs of different learners and their starting points), working in a Zone of Available Assistance (with appropriate questioning, discussion and direction providing cues and ideas of how to tackle or widen or deepen understanding), and working in a Zone of Collaboration (with teachers and other learners). Similarly, a transfer of learning is evidenced by teachers and learners using ideas and understanding and applying them in different contexts, while meaningful and authentic learning is clearly evidenced from use of news and real-world resources. Reflecting on previous learning is encouraged commonly by teachers through discussion and questioning.

In terms of cognitive elements, attention is recognised as a key outcome; resources are highly visual (with video and still imagery), auditory (through news sections and video clips), kinaesthetic (linked to practical in-class

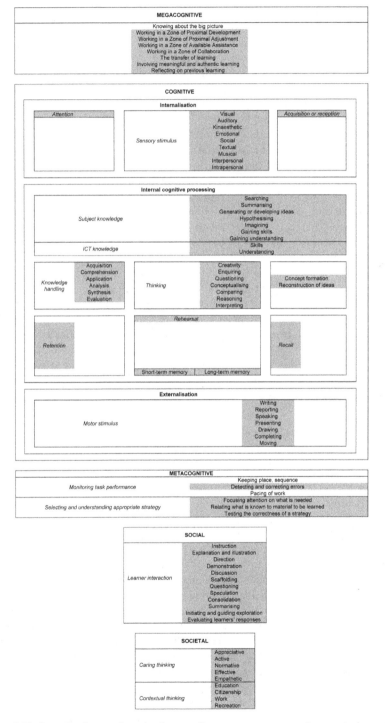

Figure 3.10 Contributions to learning from online resources supporting curriculum-wide needs

activities), emotional (generating empathy and feelings of joy or amusement or concern), social (showing interactions and leading to discussions), textual (in different forms to meet literacy levels of different learners), musical (they include songs and jingles), interpersonal (generating thinking and ideas), and intrapersonal (generating questions and stimulating discussions). The acquisition or reception of facts, ideas and understanding is commonly reported by teachers. They refer to learners searching for details, summarising key points and ideas, generating or developing ideas from those presented, hypothesising when seeing material that stimulates questions (without answers presented to them directly), and imagining what certain contexts might be like. Gaining skills and understanding are both recognised by teachers and are identified in some studies, while ICT skills and understanding arise, but less in some cases than in others (especially when resources are largely accessible to learners through an interactive whiteboard medium). Acquisition of facts is reported commonly, comprehension of facts and knowledge is aided by resources offering different perspectives, application of facts is supported when teachers question and ask learners to complete activities, analysis can happen when teachers ask searching questions, synthesis can arise when learners draw ideas together from different sources, and evaluation is required of learners when teachers ask them to review and reflect on what they have seen, heard or learned. Creativity is stimulated and supported by examples offered, as is enquiring, questioning, conceptualising, comparing, reasoning and interpreting. Retention of ideas, facts and understanding is reported by teachers and evidenced in studies. Rehearsal is a frequent practice demanded by teachers when resources are used to support in-class discussion, so that both short-term and long-term memory might be impacted, and recall is aided by the format of resources themselves and ways learners remember and associate key details. Writing (such as creative writing arising from resource stimulation), reporting (to others through discussion), speaking (arising from questioning), presenting (of summaries and key ideas), drawing (stimulated by resources), completing (activities both on and off-screen), and moving (again on and off-screen) are all forms of externalisation of learning that can be encouraged by teachers using these digital technologies.

In terms of metacognitive elements, detecting and correcting errors is aided by teacher intervention and learner practice, focusing attention on what is needed is supported by formats of activities, and relating what is known to material to be learned is supported by teacher intervention. Testing the correctness of a strategy can be undertaken through practice and teacher intervention.

In terms of social elements, instruction is an intervention aided by the resources, explanation and illustration is supported by many resources through examples and detail they offer, as is direction and demonstration. Discussion is encouraged by the wide range of stimulating features, but teachers also see opportunities when using these resources for scaffolding, questioning and speculation (when asking learners to consider more details, for example). Consolidation is supported when teachers and learners can revisit resources, and teachers often ask for a summarising of key points. Teachers use resources for initiating and guiding exploration, and for evaluating learners' responses.

In terms of societal elements, the forms of resources enable learners to gain an appreciative view of caring thinking (about others and the context of others' cultures, for example), active in terms of how to respond and to care in specific contexts, normative in terms of how appropriate concern and behaviour can be considered, effective in terms of what impacts on others certain behaviours (such as interactions with older learners when moving to a more senior school) can have, and empathetic in terms of thinking about the feelings of others. The resources cover aspects of education (in both short- and long-term contexts), citizenship (in terms of how to develop elements of social responsibility), work (with examples of how individuals work in their adult environments) and recreation (in terms of widening interest through a range of different experiences or activities).

Gaps in the Picture

In terms of megacognitive elements, while these resources support a wide range of megacognitive elements of learning, knowing about the big picture is not always evident from reports studying these forms of resources, and is highly dependent on the teacher introducing this element or not. In terms of cognitive elements, however, teachers use these resources widely so they can cover all elements.

In terms of metacognitive elements, keeping place and sequence tend to be managed more by the teacher, rather than being asked of learners. Similarly, pace is determined by teachers rather than by learners.

In terms of social elements, the resources provide for the full range of interactions. Similarly, in terms of societal aspects, the full range can be accommodated by teachers using these resources.

Online Resources Supporting Revision Needs

Online resources supporting revision needs can support an entire curriculum, but products and resource banks available are usually designed and grouped to cover a range of specific topics selected and used by learners when revising subject areas. This software provides activities in forms accessible online by learners at home, offering revision questions and aids through a range of formats. Overall, the pattern of use of these digital resources can be described as irregular but frequent at certain critical times, selected and used by learners largely outside classrooms (see Figure 3.11).

Online access to resources for revision purposes is widening. As Jewitt and Parashar (2011) reported, an initiative in England to provide computer and

Regularity of use											
Selected by teachers											
Used by learners											
In classrooms											
In projects or after-school											
Involving parents at home											

Figure 3.11 How online resources supporting revision needs offer support for learning

internet access for low-income households for learners 5 to 19 years of age across two LAs enabled enhanced time at home for learners to work on homework and independent learning.

A number of different digital devices or forms of hardware have enabled learners to access activities inside and outside classrooms. Perhaps the most widely used hardware technologies to date used in classrooms have been inter-active whiteboards, but some projects and studies have looked also at how access for revision purposes can be supported through online quizzes and quick response or voting devices. The Metiri Group (2006) noted that although at that time there was no rigorous research conducted on forms of response or voting devices, qualitative studies had looked at impacts of online quizzes with undergraduate students. Through forms of feedback, reflection and self-checking of answers, and comparing scores with their peers, these forms of digital technologies had focused on and supported metacognitive elements of learning.

Forms of online resources for revision purposes may well influence both access and outcomes. Bolliger and Supanakorn (2011) in a study involving 54 under-graduate students, explored relationships between learning styles, modalities and uses of online tutorials, and found that while students as a whole found tutorials useful, females tended to work in more bimodal or multimodal ways than males, but females tended to prefer unimodal learning while males preferred multi-modal learning, and males preferring multimodal learning were the only group to gain in terms of performance.

Some studies have reported on developments of affordances and features to more effectively support online resources for revision. Tong (2012) reported a study exploring uses of online surveys with undergraduate students, and found their use led to students reviewing previous material taught in class, as well as providing links to follow-up sessions, leading the author to conclude online surveys could be used to support coherence and linking of sessions across modules and courses. Hwang, Chen, Shadiev, and Li (2011), in a study involving 32 learners in the first year of junior high school using an online annotation tool and with access to homework solutions for four months, showed achievement was related to text annotations learners made, but not to annotations peers made on their work, and final achievements were predicted by levels of annotations made. Chen, Chen, and Sun (2010), in a study involving 56 high school learners in Taiwan using social tagging when reading texts online in English (as a foreign language) to encourage collaborative activity, showed significant improvements in reading scores after three months, and teachers felt more empowered to iden-tify literacy issues.

Online Revision Banks

McLoughlin and Reid (2002), reporting on the design of online quiz questions, indicated online forms supported a shift from what might be regarded as more memory-based assessment to "fostering learning and transfer of knowledge", since, they argued, more complex quiz questions helped to stimulate or foster deep learning. Certainly in terms of learners accessing online revision questions for tests (including online quizzes), the Fischer Family Trust undertook a range of studies over a number of years to explore potential relationships between levels of use (measured by hours of access) and levels of results (in national subject examinations). The Fischer Family Trust (2004) compared results from students using online revision practice exercises according to levels of amounts of revision exercises accessed. Using national examination result measures at age 16 years, across 105,617 students, the study found those with more than 10 hours' use of the revision exercises achieved 4.7% higher examination grades (one quarter of a grade per subject), with greatest increases for students in middle and lower prior attainment groups (nearly half a grade per subject for those in lower prior attainment groups). This result compares to levels of gains from uses of ILSs reported by Gardner (1997) with groups starting at similar attainment levels.

Elements of Contribution

From evidence of contributions (uses, outcomes and impacts) described above and in other sections of this text, a learning framework picture has been created highlighting elements of learning where contributions arose, shown in Figure 3.12 using shading.

In terms of megacognitive elements, learners indicate they can select resources allowing them to work in a Zone of Proximal Development, but also in a Zone of Proximal Adjustment (recognising and adjusting to their needs and their starting points), working in a Zone of Available Assistance (using prompts or feedback or ideas from the system itself), but they are largely not working in a Zone of Collaboration (with teachers or other learners). Transfer of learning is evidenced by test or examination results but this is not in different situational contexts, while the provision of meaningful and authentic learning is not clear. Reflecting on previous learning is certainly encouraged by questions posed through the systems or banks of resources.

In terms of cognitive elements, attention is recognised as a key outcome arising when these resources are used, but this largely results from the learner's attitudes towards their needs; resources are not generally highly visual (usually without video but with some still imagery), they can be auditory (especially for language revision exercises), kinaesthetic (in terms of using the mouse and keyboard to complete exercises), they are largely textual (in different forms to meet starting points of different learners), but not often musical (even with background music), although they are interpersonal (generating thinking and responses). Acquisition or reception of facts, ideas and understanding are commonly reported by learners, and learners refer also to the need to search for details and summarise key points and ideas. Gaining skills and understanding are both recognised by learners. Acquisition of facts is reported commonly, comprehension of facts and knowledge is aided by exercises in different formats, application of facts arises when questions ask learners to complete activities in another context or activity setting, and analysis can arise when exercises demand this of learners and learners respond appropriately. Enquiring is encouraged in some subject areas, as is comparing, reasoning and interpreting. Retention of ideas, facts and understanding is reported and evidenced in studies. Rehearsal is a frequent practice demanded by the revision systems or resource banks, so both short-term and long-term memory might be impacted, and recall can be aided by the format of the exercises themselves. Writing (such as creative writing arising from exercises),

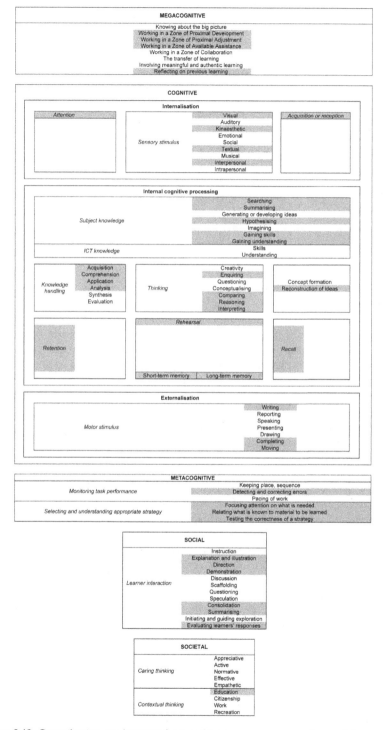

Figure 3.12 Contributions to learning from online resources supporting revision needs

completing (exercises on-screen), and moving (again on-screen) are all forms of externalisation of learning encouraged by these digital technologies.

In terms of metacognitive elements, detecting and correcting errors is aided by feedback provided, focusing attention on what is needed is supported by formats of the activities, and relating what is known to material to be learned is supported by content of questions posed. Testing the correctness of a strategy can be undertaken through practice and attending to feedback provided.

In terms of social elements, instruction can be provided in some subject exercises, explanation and illustration is provided in some exercises, as is direction and demonstration. Consolidation is a key element encouraged through revisiting topics and undertaking exercises posed, while summarising of key points can be requested in some exercises. The resources focus strongly on providing feedback and evaluating learners' responses. In terms of societal elements, the forms of resources do support aspects of education (in both short- and long-term contexts), while other elements of the societal aspect of learning are less often or well supported.

Gaps in the Picture

In terms of megacognitive elements, while revision resources support a range of megacognitive elements of learning, knowing about the big picture is not always evident; learners tend to select topics rather than considering the wider dimensions of the subject. Similarly, working in a Zone of Collaboration is less likely as learners access these resources individually, the transfer of learning is often not a specific focus other than for test or examination purposes, and exercises are not deliberately developed to involve authentic learning.

In terms of cognitive elements of learning, sensory engagement through auditory, emotional, social, musical and intrapersonal routes tends to be limited. The resources are not generally designed to generate ideas or to stimulate imagining. ICT skills and understanding are not generally enhanced, as exercises are designed to be easily accessed by as many learners as possible. Elements such as synthesis, evaluation, creativity, questioning and conceptualising are not included in major ways in the design of exercises. Similarly, reporting, speaking, presenting and drawing are not elements of externalisation focus arising often.

In terms of metacognitive elements, keeping place and sequence tend to be managed more by the system than by the learner. It could be argued that pace is determined by learners rather than by the system, but it can also be argued that pace is determined by success in answering rather than it being determined by learners taking a longer-term view of pace, or what could be accomplished over a length of time.

In terms of social elements, the exercises do not tend to provide instruction often, and do not lead usually to discussion, or provide scaffolding (except for cues or clues in some cases), or lead to questioning with others, or speculating (they tend to require a correct answer), or initiating or guiding exploration (they tend to be concerned with a more rapid end-point).

In terms of societal elements, only education in terms of test or examination success is a key focal element. Other contextual thinking (citizenship, work and recreation) and elements of caring thinking are not focal elements designed and built into these exercises.

Online Learner Support

Online learner support concerns interactions between learners and mentors (who might be teachers), supported or managed through digital technologies such as online learning environments, focused on an individual learner's work and queries. Direct support is offered by mentors or counsellors, while some interactions might provide links to websites offering related content. Overall, the pattern of use can be described as commonly irregular except by some learners or at certain times, selected by learners or parents and guardians more than by teachers, and not often undertaken in classrooms (see Figure 3.13).

A study exploring uses and outcomes in this category, Skouras (2006), looked at the creation of a learning environment and the ways computer screens supported a formulation of conjectures and a "gradual transformation of non-formal knowledge into knowledge that requires analytic description". A great deal has been studied in this category in a higher education context, but less in terms of school-based contexts. Although findings from studies having examined online learner support are often positive, a number of important factors need to be considered when these practices are deployed. As the Metiri Group (2006) stated, "Emergent research on visualization and learning through multimedia and a summary report from England suggest that results will be determined somewhat by learner control, dialogue, learner support, and opportunities for direct learner involvement" (p. 9).

Even though most reports are based in higher education settings, forms of online learning are being explored in some schools. Anastasiades et al. (2010) studied how 46 learners and four teachers in two elementary schools in Athens and Crete collaborated via interactive video-conferencing, and reported this led to enhancement of social relations among learners and teachers. Tsuei (2012), in a controlled study, investigated 88 learners 10 to 11 years of age who peer-tutored synchronously online in mathematics, and found this practice led to higher gains for those who peer tutored, as well as higher levels of self-concept and positive attitudes towards the subject, with vulnerable learners gaining particularly when they continued to engage.

In terms of preferences for learning medium and its impacts, Abdous and Yoshimura (2010) in their study found, when the same instructors delivered live video-streamed, satellite broadcast, and face-to-face instruction with 496 university students, no significant difference arose in terms of grade levels achieved or student satisfaction responses. In terms of synchronous and asynchronous online learning, AbuSeileek and Qatawneh (2013), in a study of

Regularity of use								
Selected by teachers								
Used by learners								
In classrooms								
In projects or after-school								
Involving parents at home								

Figure 3.13 How online learner support offers support for learning

oral discussions of English language learners aged 19 to 21 years, showed asynchronous discussions led to more discourse about questions and strategies, seeking more detail, explanation and clarification. Additionally, Oztok, Zingaro, Brett, and Hewitt (2013) found across 222 undergraduate students in a university in Canada, synchronous private messaging was being used to support asynchronous discussions. In this context also, Verpoorten, Westera, and Specht (2012), in a controlled study involving 54 learners, showed reflective triggers were valued and used by learners, but did not lead to outcomes statistically significantly different from the control group working online without triggers. Other forms of outcomes are reported also; for example, Lin, Hong, and Lawrenz (2012) showed in their study that college students developed argumentation skills after only one hour of scaffolding, and online asynchronous practice was slightly more effective subsequently. However, in terms of reflective opportunity, Kiliçkaya and Krajka (2012) in a study involving 25 learners aged 14 to 18 years in Turkey, completing an online comic strip following a weekly English language session, found learners using the comic strip produced longer and more varied texts.

In terms of collaborative or individual online tutoring, Jones, Antonenko, and Greenwood (2012) explored online responses of undergraduate students learning science, and found that while motivation initially dropped for users of both systems, females tended to improve in cognitive regulation in collaborative responses while males improved in individualised response systems.

Meta-analyses of Online Learning and its Impact

Studies looking at online learning compared to traditional instruction have not always found evidence to be conclusive in terms of identifying impacts at statistically significant levels. Coomey and Stephenson (2001), from meta-analyses of results from studies of online learning, reported learners generally perform as well as or better in formal online learning situations as those taught through more traditional instructional practices. They also indicated learners achieved slightly better when they were involved in courses using email or web-based virtual learning rather than more traditional approaches, but learner achievement was about the same or even lower for courses involving video-based virtual learning rather than more traditional approaches. They emphasised the importance of four critical factors: "dialogue, involvement, support and control". Cavanaugh, Gillan, Kromrey, Hess, and Blomeyer (2004), who conducted a meta-analysis of studies on distance learning, found a small positive effect when they compared web-based virtual learning courses with traditional approaches. They also found a small negative impact when video-conferencing was used as the main delivery approach. The analysis included primary and secondary schools as well as institutions of higher education. No significant differences between traditional teaching and online approaches were found, or between traditional teaching and video-conferencing approaches, but, learners using online environments outperformed learners using traditional approaches, but there were also lower retention rates for those using online environments. While learners using traditional approaches outperformed those using video-conferencing, differences were not found to be statistically significant. Slykhuis and Park (2006), in their study of subject attainment in physics by high school students, comparing those taking an online, hands-on unit on motion with those involved in a more traditional approach, found gains were statistically similar. In the study, gains in comprehension were identified using a pre- and post-test, and the results suggested online course delivery could be a viable alternative to a traditional route in this context.

In summary, the Metiri Group (2006) reported: "Educators are finding that reflective dialog augments learning. Social networking accelerates learning and is facilitated by technology. Students are highly motivated to communicate via technology be it text messaging, email, instant messaging, talking, or video-conferencing" (p. 12).They also emphasised that social networking resources do allow learners to be connected to resources that can deepen and extend their thinking, or enhance their curiosity. Certainly an early and now classical study conducted in Canada (Scardamalia & Bereiter, 1994), showed increases in higher-order social interactions, collaborative knowledge building, and deep understanding of concepts when knowledge construction was undertaken by learners using a computer-supported collaborative learning environment. More recently, Tan, Lin, Chu, and Liu (2012) studied "a ubiquitous learning environment termed the Environment of Ubiquitous Learning with Educational Resources (EULER) and conducted a natural science course for eight weeks. The participants included elementary school teachers and students" (p. 206). This study involved 36 grade 5 learners and four science teachers (all experienced in CAI), and the students had previously been involved in learning science (from the grade 1) and computer science (from the grade 3). These authors summarised the outcomes of their study in a table, linking affordances (both actual and perceived) to outcomes. The affordances are summarised here:

- Actual affordances:
  - Unconstrained knowledge accession—leads to construction of knowledge, and enhancement of comprehension.
  - Real-time evaluation—leads to an evaluation of learning outcomes, and an improvement in handling knowledge.
  - Individuality—leads to development of a personal portfolio, engages at an individual level, enhances individual experience and commitment, fosters abilities to manage their own learning, and improves outcomes.
  - Diverse interaction—leads to enhanced peer interactions, enhanced motivation, improves outcomes, improves relationships between mentors and learners, improves aspects of teaching, and develops thinking skills.
  - Arbitrary data collection—leads to data handling abilities, develops investigative approaches, and enhances cognitive abilities.
  - Ubiquitous game play—leads to increased interest in topics, enhanced motivation, enhanced levels of interactivity, and improves outcomes.
  - Authentic context awareness—leads to heightened engagement, and develops knowledge in authentic contexts.
  - Vivid immersion—leads to improved understanding.

- Perceived affordances:
  - Skilful application—leads to the application of ICT and associated skills to learning needs and problem-solving, exploring ways to learn, and encourages independent thinking.
  - Methodological analysis—leads to heightened data analysis skills, and willingness to explore other knowledge avenues.
  - Creative synthesis—leads to the combination of elements into creative products, and enhances self-satisfaction.
  - Ubiquitous revision—leads to an increased familiarity with content of lessons, and improved outcomes.
  - Seamless collaboration—leads to an increase in peer interactions, enhances motivation, improves outcomes, enhances relationships between mentors and learners, and enhances social identity.

Using Online Learning Environments

A study looking specifically at the use of an online learning environment in secondary schools (Passey, 2007), explored outcomes arising across two LAs in the UK. The learning environment offered a range of features to support learners and teachers, "a mentoring service, a bank of learning materials, a range of communication channels (including messaging, discussion forums and chat rooms), online assignment management, online communities, an incentive scheme for learners, and a continuing professional development programme" (p. 5). Reports about uses of the online environment were gathered from learners through questionnaires, completed by 1,486 learners (some 6.8% of the total learner population registered to use the system), with more girls represented in the sample (953 in number) than boys (533 in number). Reports from boys and from girls did vary to some extent: boys' responses were higher (by at least 5%) in reporting whether they had been given sufficient training and encouragement to use the system, whether *Virtual Workspace* helped with school work, whether they had used the Communities area most, whether facilities helped with discussion of work outside the classroom, whether facilities had helped to understand the teacher more, and whether online mentors had been contacted; while girls' responses were higher (by at least 5%) in reporting whether they used other online systems such as a school intranet, and whether they regarded themselves as being a 'quiet' person in terms of discussing ideas in class. But when responses from self-reported 'shy' or 'quiet' learners were compared to other learners, the study showed that these 'quiet' learners were more commonly gaining in certain ways. Comparing responses of 'quiet' boys with all boys, the percentage of responses from 'quiet' boys was higher (by at least 8%) in their being more involved in learning than might have been the case otherwise (16% difference), discussion of work outside the classroom (14% difference), allowing ideas to be expressed when this might not happen in class (13% difference), helping to understand teachers more (9% difference), helping with coursework or assignments (9% difference), mentors helping personally (9% difference), and wanting to see more use of *Virtual Workspace* (8% difference). Comparing responses of 'quiet' girls with all girls, the percentage of responses from 'quiet' girls was higher (by at least 8%) in allowing ideas to be expressed when this might not happen in class (9% difference), and being more involved in learning than might have been the case otherwise (8% difference). As the author noted, "The system, according to learner feedback (and supported by qualitative evidence from a number of teachers), is having an impact particularly on 'quiet' learners" (p. 7). The author also noted 'quiet' in this context was likely to encompass at least three different groups of learners: those naturally reticent in offering their ideas in classrooms; those with emotional or social reasons for not engaging in a classroom discussion; and those not wanting to be seen by others as being engaged or interested. This point will be further discussed in sections in Chapter 4.

Elements of Contribution

From evidence of contributions (uses, outcomes and impacts) described above and in other sections of this text, a learning framework picture has been created highlighting elements of learning where contributions arose, shown in Figure 3.14 using shading.

In terms of megacognitive elements, online learner support allows working in a Zone of Proximal Development, identified by the mentor or teacher, as well as working in a Zone of Proximal Adjustment, selected by the mentor or teacher, working in a Zone of Available Assistance, when mentors provide support or offer pointers to available material, and working in a Zone of Collaboration, with the mentor and maybe with other peers. Transfer of learning is encouraged, across members of the online space, as is a reflection on previous learning, drawn out through the efforts of the mentor.

In terms of cognitive elements, attention is identified by mentors and learners generally as a positive outcome, but effective techniques of moderation clearly can help this feature and outcome positively. Kinaesthetic engagement (through active interaction), emotional engagement (empathising with the interests and concerns of others), social engagement (with peers and a mentor), textual engagement (through iterative responses), interpersonal engagement (through individual contribution and response), as well as intrapersonal engagement (between members of the community), are all recognised as ways of engaging learners through this support environment. Acquisition or reception of ideas, facts and understanding are recognised. Searching is an element encouraged by moderation and appropriate questioning, as is summarising of key points or facts, generating or developing ideas in response to questions and comments from others, and hypothesising about possible ideas highlighted by mentors. Mentors and learners often recognise gains in both skills and understanding. Comprehension of topics and content, application of facts and knowledge through answering questions or discussion of ideas, analysis of content presented by mentors, synthesis of ideas to summarise outcomes, and evaluation of topics presented, are all identified by learners and mentors as outcomes arising. Enquiring is encouraged by appropriate moderation, as is questioning, conceptualising and the reconstruction of ideas when issues or weaknesses are identified and then addressed. Comparing different perspectives and approaches, reasoning when presented with new material, and interpreting material offered in

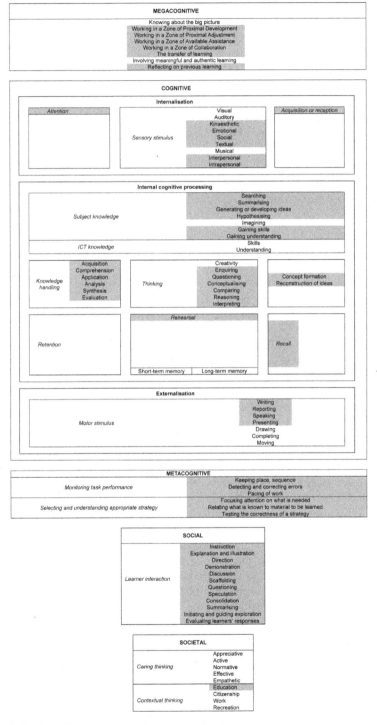

Figure 3.14 Contributions to learning from online learner support

challenging ways are all outcomes reported by learners and mentors. Rehearsal of facts or ideas is a key concern often of mentors and learners, particularly at early stages, as is recall, but often at a later stage. Writing is encouraged as a part of the medium, as is reporting when mentors ask learners to summarise or offer ideas or comments, speaking when facilities offer audio interaction, and presenting perhaps in a formal response.

In terms of metacognitive elements, keeping place and sequence is encouraged by the medium and by moderation by mentors, as is detecting and correcting errors and pacing of work, focusing attention on what is needed, relating what is known to material to be learned, and testing the correctness of a strategy. All these metacognitive elements are encouraged by skilled moderation techniques (see, for example, Salmon, 2000).

In terms of social elements, instruction can be led by the mentor, as can explanation and illustration, direction, or demonstration. Discussion is a key focal concern, either through a textual or audio (video) medium. Effective moderation enables scaffolding to be put in place, questioning to be used at key times, speculation to be brought up at other times, consolidation used as and when appropriate, and summarising points and overviews at key points. Initiating and guiding exploration is a vital moderation function and action, as is evaluating learners' responses. In terms of societal elements, education is a key focus of this form of activity.

Gaps in the Picture

In terms of megacognitive aspects, online support is generally specific to a topic or subject, and does not tend to focus on a big picture. Similarly, the context of the learning is between learner and mentor, and is not happening necessarily within a wider meaningful or authentic learning context (although authority of the mentor can provide an authenticity for learners).

In terms of cognitive aspects, visual, auditory and musical forms of engagement have not generally been involved when mentors support online, but increasingly mentor support via video-conferencing and Skype is developing rapidly in some instances. Although there is often a clear focus on subject knowledge, ICT skills and knowledge are not generally a focus or contribution of the interactions (indeed, it can be argued the learner needs an existing range of ICT skills in order to interact with a mentor). In terms of knowledge areas, imagining and creativity are not generally evidenced. Retention of facts or ideas is not a clear outcome in all cases (although it can be a clear focus for some levels of interaction), and contribution to short- or long-term memory is not clear (although studies suggest both are impacted at least to the extent of levels arising in traditional learning environments). Online environments now involve the learner in speaking to greater extents, especially as uses of Skype and video-conferencing become more widespread, but drawing, completion and moving of items are not generally used in terms of forms of externalisation of understanding or outcomes.

In terms of metacognitive elements, online support generally enables a focus on all these elements. Similarly, in terms of social elements, all are reported. In terms of societal elements, caring thinking is not generally a focus (except in specific cases with specific learners, and these will be explored more in Chapter 4), and the context of online interactions is usually on education engagement in the short-term rather than having wider concerns about citizenship, work or recreation (although the online medium and activity could model future forms of work or recreation interactions).

Project and After-school Club Activities Involving Digital Technologies

Some project and after-school club activities now integrate important uses of digital technologies, focusing on learning arising through team working and team-based activities. In some activities specific roles are designated to or taken up by individuals, perhaps asking them to focus on certain technical, artistic or editing needs, and all involving a range of 'soft' as well as technical skills. Examples of these forms of activities are the annual *BBC News School Report*, or *Interactive Opportunities* after-school clubs creating video games levels, or activities run through the *First Lego League* initiative. Overall, the pattern for this category can be described as regular use over specific project periods, often selected and facilitated by teachers, used by learners, but usually in after-school or out-of-class sessions, shown in Figure 3.15.

A variety of different project and after-school club activities involving digital technologies are reported in the literature. For example, Wishart and Triggs (2010) reported on an initiative involving 10- to 19-year-old learners in a number of museums across Europe, where learners gathered information during a visit and then created short multimedia presentations using authoring tools in teams to teach and question other teams. Ardaiz-Villanueva, Nicuesa-Chacón, Brene-Artazcoz, de Acedo Lizarraga, and de Acedo Baquedano (2011) reported a study involving 34 undergraduate students, requiring them to use online tools to collaboratively create an engineering-based outcome, showing the tools helped generation, evaluation and selection of ideas, and how to consider the forming of teams. Robertson (2012) reported outcomes from a six-week project in which 11- to 12-year-old learners created computer games leading to a variety of media storytelling skills, while Doyle (2010) described how a 3D virtual world was created by undergraduate students as a medium to host and display international art work.

Schools taking on board team-working projects integrating uses of digital technologies find they can work in different ways from those demanded by

Regularity of use										
Selected by teachers										
Used by learners										
In classrooms										
In projects or after-school										
Involving parents at home										

Figure 3.15 How project and after-school club activities involving digital technologies offer support for learning

activities they run within classrooms; they work more in ways described in extended school and extended curricula contexts (Barker et al., 2003). These forms of projects and after-school clubs focus on important aspects of educational practice—they demand a different form of organisation from that found in classrooms generally, and this puts the teacher more strongly in the role of facilitator (including technological facilitation). But schools find there are benefits arising, just as Kane (2004) concluded from four after-school programme evaluation studies in the US, saying these programmes "may be unaccustomed to holding center stage in the national education policy debate, but that is unlikely to change anytime soon. Some of the evidence so far is forcing a reconsideration of the magnitude of impacts we might reasonably expect" (p. 3). Indeed, Shurnow (2001) suggested schools should re-examine the role and centrality of after-school activities and clubs.

The important contributions of project-based and after-school club activities are becoming recognised in a number of countries. For example, in Turkey, Çubukçu (2012) states sufficient opportunities should be available for learners to work independently but not necessarily individually and: "teachers should allocate time for activities that increase student-centered learning, individual and social activities like extra-curricular activities, student club activities" (p. 49).

Projects Linking Schools and Learners Internationally

An important distinction is being raised here that can influence the conception and construction of the wider curriculum and variety of activities accessible to learners; learners need opportunities to learn on their own, as well as in groups and teams. The role of digital technologies within these activities, and outcomes arising, is currently beginning to be studied and identified. Leppisaari and Lee (2012), for example, reported findings from a cross-national study, saying that while learners may well be equipped with the technical skills to use social media in learning, "few international virtual learning projects have been implemented and researched. This article examines a trial which aimed to combine viable technology with future pedagogic solutions for primary students from Korea and Finland and create an international collaboration model" (p. 244). They went on to outline many challenges in implementing this type of project—concerned with organisation, language, technical issues and gaining collaboration. At the same time, the authors highlighted the potential benefits that could arise—developing virtual learning pedagogies, using visualisation to support learning, using online environments to support collaboration, and the potential of enhanced motivation and engagement that the environment would bring. They highlighted the need for a great deal of discussion between teachers at planning stages, and to consider how to integrate authentic learning opportunities that in turn encourage discussion and dialogue between learners in different countries.

The project involved Korean and Finnish teachers, and focused on the subject of environmental education, specifically on waste recycling. As English language lessons are introduced into both countries in the grade 3 (when learners are aged 9 to 10 years), this language was used as the medium for communication. The project involved some 120 learners in Finland (five classes aged 10 to 12 years in grades 4 to 6 in the same elementary school), and some 100 learners in Korea (three classes aged 11 to 12 years in grades 5 to 6 in three different elementary schools). The instructional materials used were developed by a Korean research group, and the learning platform used was '*Edu2.0*' (a free e-learning platform— see http://www.edu20.org/), selected for affordances it provided that would match project needs, being easy to use, having a background management system that would support all users, providing interactive facilities (and importantly a discussion forum), and features enabling knowledge sharing through documents or files in the form of images, videos, or commentary on items produced online. The project was staged through a number of sequenced activities or tasks: an ice-breaker; research on waste recycling in the local environment; and putting together and presenting ideas about novel ways to consider recycling of waste. While a Korean research team offered outlines for the activities and tasks, these were adapted by teachers locally to match their specific needs and those of their learners. The reasons for the choice of topic and activities were common to those of other projects and after-school club activities: the topic had real-world relevance and real-life application; the project focused on the need for learners to explore and solve real-life complex problems in depth; the activities would require a regular and sustained commitment of time from learners, to enable them to become immersed in the needs of the project, and to explore these in the context of other subject areas and knowledge.

Learners worked in groups on the tasks; they were involved in defining tasks as well as in problem-solving. Teachers offered guidance rather than initiating and directing, and learners were encouraged to work collaboratively through the design of the tasks. The project introduced aspects of culture as an element learners needed to engage with in a number of ways, and took learners beyond and outside 'normal practices' they encountered in schools.

The authors highlighted a number of key outcomes: "Technology can help us see things in a new way. Digital cameras and mobile phones make visualizing knowledge easy. Students can create documentaries which contain real-world phenomena in more visual form, giving them a better understanding of their own society" (p. 251). They found certain affordances of the digital technologies used were important in terms of supporting aspects of learning, "elements students found interesting (gifts, profile images)" (p. 252). They noted the digital technologies and the development of ICT skills were important, but these were integrated as vital support for the project rather than leading it, as "Students could acquire IT skills through authentic class activities, rather than formal instruction of IT skills" (p. 252). The authors noted the project as a whole impacted on elements of literacy—helping the development of writing skills for specific and real audiences; and enhancing the attention of boys to details to ensure correctness of grammar.

Similar and parallel findings and outcomes have been identified in other studies examining project-based and after-school club activities using digital technologies. Two examples are offered here.

Projects Focusing on Broadcasting

An evaluation of a project involving the creation of news by school teams, supported by the well-known UK broadcasting corporation, the BBC, identified similar and additional outcomes (Passey & Gillen, 2009). The project aims to support school teams, in creating and broadcasting their own video-, audio- or text-based news reports. The project began as a pilot in 2006, and has been run annually since then. School-based teams need to create their reports and put them on their school website by a specific time on a particular day (the News Day), which is a hard deadline teams need to meet. These website news reports are then linked to the *BBC News School Report* website, accessible to regional and national radio and television broadcasting teams, as well as to a wider worldwide audience.

The study (Passey & Gillen, 2009) gathered evidence from across the entire range of 514 schools involved in 2008 and 2009. The project began in October, and project team sessions then ran regularly, usually at least weekly, leading up to the News Day in March the following year. A range of methods were used to gather evidence, "pre- and post-News Day online questionnaires for students and teachers, observations of two News Day events, and follow-up visits to 25 schools to interview students and teachers" (p. 6). The schools involved were selected on the basis of their being representative of the wider UK picture. Student reports about their perceptions of benefits arising were very largely mirrored by those reported by teachers, "concerned not only with specific subject skills, but also with team working, creativity, attitude towards work, and social interactions" (p. 6). There were a range of areas of skills where differences before and after the project were at statistically significant levels: writing an article for an audience; taking pictures using different media; creating ideas for news stories; negotiating points with others during team work activities; working hard to contribute to the entire group effort; and meeting deadlines. Interestingly, the authors found "students indicated no significant change in their abilities to produce a video and an audio story, whereas teachers felt they had improved. These differences suggest strongly that the students' capabilities exceeded their teachers' expectations" (p. 7). Learners also reported their viewing and listening habits had changed to some extent: more said they were watching news on the television; more said they were listening to the news on the radio; but no more said they were reading news online. But importantly, students reported gains in terms of wider understanding, longer-term goals and interests, "they had learned more about news production and jobs. There was a big improvement in their understanding of how news is produced and about jobs in news" (p. 7). Learners indicated their interest in news reporting jobs had increased. The authors concluded the project had supported a range of learning aspects, "authentic learning; understanding through discussion; internal cognitive aspects; and the transfer of learning" (p. 8).

Projects Developing Video-Game Elements

By contrast, a project run across 15 secondary schools in one LA in the UK involved after-school teams (largely). Learners involved needed to create a video-game level so other players could access these across an international network. An evaluation of this project (Passey, 2012b) identified outcomes arising, again across all aspects of learning.

The project was set up "to encourage teachers in schools to bring together teams of young people to use a well-known video game, *Little Big Planet 2*, to create new levels that would be published and used by other players" (p. 1). Over 100 learners were involved at the outset, across the 15 schools. Teams of learners were selected by teachers, or needed to apply to take part in the project. Teachers recognised some of these learners did not participate in other school-based activities, so this project was encouraging learners with different interests to take part. The teachers supported the teams, facilitated work, provided a working space, and offered advice and guidance (sometimes about where to find solutions to technical or other problems); teachers did not create ideas or undertake programming for the project. The project was found to encourage elements of creativity; as the author said, "That creative endeavour has covered a range of different elements—artistic and planning, as well as technical" (p. 2). In some teams the members shared roles, while in others, members took on more specific roles and tasks, such as artistic roles (creating different images and scenarios), design roles (creating ideas for routes and challenges for players of the game), or programming roles (building the programming language to drive the game). A range of soft skills were developed by learners: communication skills; team working, planning and discussing details; social networking skills, using social networks they chose to meet project purposes; technical skills, finding details to overcome technical obstacles to create features in the scenarios; working with others, sometimes with people they had not worked with before; sharing skills; professional skills, concern with the finished product; and commitment, to work together and to achieve a professional outcome.

Elements of Contribution

From evidence of contributions (uses, outcomes and impacts) described above and in other sections of this text, a learning framework picture has been created that highlights elements of learning where contributions arose, shown in Figure 3.16 using shading.

Learners involved in this category gain widely in terms of megacognition. Their involvement leads to them knowing about the big (or a bigger) picture, engaging with wider societal and community groups offering wider experience and understanding. They are working in a Zone of Proximal Development (identified through peer as well as teacher mediation), but also working in a Zone of Proximal Adjustment (according to strengths and weaknesses they recognise in individual members of their teams), in a Zone of Available Assistance (facilitated by teachers or experts), and in a Zone of Collaboration (with teachers or experts, and definitely with each other). The context provides for transfer of learning (from their collaborative endeavours to selected and wide audiences), involving meaningful and authentic learning (focusing on real-world issues and audiences), and reflecting on previous learning (using learning from subject lessons and informal practice).

In terms of cognitive elements, learner attention to tasks and activities is commonly and widely reported. The effects reported involve visual engagement (working in visually stimulating ways), auditory (discussion is needed often and audio files and streams are also created and used), kinaesthetic (working with a range of digital and other tools and artefacts), emotional (requiring empathy and concerns for the tasks, their completion and quality of completion), social

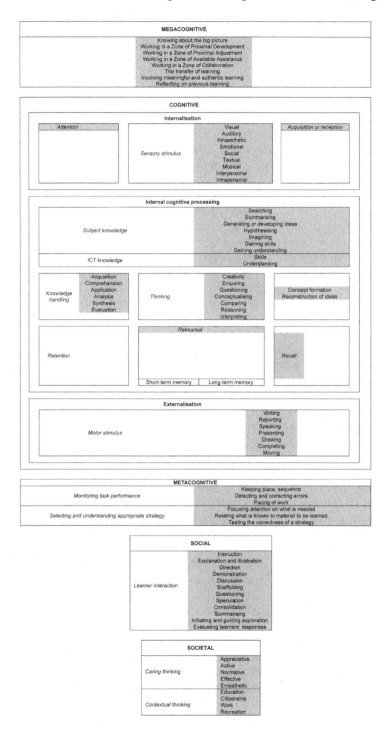

Figure 3.16 Contributions to learning from project and after-school club activities involving digital technologies

(working with others at the same level), textual (researching but also creating textual forms), musical (creating and handling musical backgrounds), interpersonal (encouraging personal problem-solving), and intrapersonal (encouraging discussion and collaboration focused on thinking and problem-solving needs). Consequently, acquisition or reception of ideas or knowledge is commonly reported. Learners are involved in searching (for ideas, information and details), summarising (key points or aspects of interest to others), generating or developing ideas (from a range of sources, guided by teachers and experts), hypothesising (thinking about 'what if' situations, perhaps applied to audience needs), and imagining (what end results or products might look like or how they would be perceived). Gaining skills and understanding in topics or subject areas are also reported commonly (in literacy or science, for example), as is gaining of ICT skills and understanding, often applied to specific digital technologies learners might not have encountered before in learning settings. Acquisition of facts and knowledge applied to topics and ICT are widely reported, as is comprehension of those facts and knowledge, its application to other contexts and for different audiences, analysis of how facts and knowledge might be applied to certain audiences, synthesis of ideas, facts and skills across teams and through the development of outcomes, and evaluation of outcomes in terms of impact on audience. Creativity in developing ideas and applying details to outcomes is widely reported, as is enquiring (perhaps across a learner team, or with teachers, or external experts), questioning (about processes involved and implications), conceptualising and reconstructing ideas to apply them in specific contexts, comparing situations and alternative ideas and outcomes, reasoning about what to do and how to do it, and interpreting the effect details might have on audience perceptions. Rehearsal of ideas, knowledge and skills is commonly reported. So too is recall, when learners need to use existing and new knowledge and skills in developing and emerging contexts. Learners are involved in writing (notes, scripts and reports), reporting (through articles or statements), speaking (about their ideas, knowledge and skills), presenting (to others, perhaps in audio or video form), drawing (ideas, or images), completing (tasks and activities, to deadlines), and moving (tools, materials and products as needed).

In terms of metacognitive elements, keeping place and sequence are required for planning purposes, detecting and correcting errors are elements applied throughout, pacing of work is a part of the planning required, focusing attention on what is needed is maintained by group and team efforts, relating what is known to material to be learned occurs often across the activity period, and testing the correctness of a strategy is a need of projects involving peer review and discussion, as well as teacher and external expert review.

In terms of social elements, instruction occurs across team members with teacher and external expert support, explanation and illustration occurs throughout the project, direction is an element of planning and team work, demonstration happens as needed and requested by teams, discussion holds the activities together, scaffolding is identified as needs arise and challenges emerge, questioning occurs frequently, speculation is encouraged by team thinking and review, consolidation is facilitated often by teachers or external experts, summarising occurs frequently and highlights key points arising, initiating and guiding exploration is an on-going need across the activity period, and evaluating learners' responses happens in an on-going way through team member, teacher and external expert responses.

Societal elements identified include appreciative concerns with caring thinking, raised often by team members, they are active often in considering the needs of others, and these concerns can lead to normative outcomes based on the needs across the team, involving effective thinking for others, and empathetic in terms of individual and team needs. Future concerns for education is a main focus for these forms of activity, but they also clearly offer opportunities for learners to think about and engage with concerns for citizenship (and values and contributions possible for a wider community and society), to work (looking at possible future work processes and ideas) and recreation (ways to use their knowledge and skills for their own leisure purposes and with others).

Gaps in the Picture

In terms of megacognitive elements, all are evidenced in terms of the activities in this category. In terms of cognitive elements, it is not always clear that retention or contributions to short- or long-term memory are intended or identified, although it is clear tests to measure these effects have not been widely deployed in research studies yet.

In terms of metacognitive elements, all elements can be supported through these forms of activities. Similarly, in terms of both social and societal elements, all are evidenced in terms of contribution.

A Comparison of Contributions from the Analysis of Different Categories of Digital Technology

Comparing contributions of the different categories of digital technologies to the different elements of learning is not in itself an easy task, although it can be considered initially quite simplistically. One way to view comparison is to say number of elements of learning covered could offer an indication of an overall contribution to learning. The total number of elements of learning in the learning framework used in previous sections is 82. Looking at frequency across the eight categories (shown in Table 3.2), it is possible to see width of contribution defined through simple numbers of elements covered.

The results in Table 3.2 suggest certain forms of digital technologies offer more opportunities in terms of learning coverage, but it should be stated immediately, of course, that this depends upon a number of factors. The importance of teacher and supporter involvement will be picked up in Chapter 5, where a more detailed analysis of these results will be considered. But, to emphasise the importance of the supporter in the context of using different digital technologies, as Cox et al. (2003: 3) stated, "the crucial component in the appropriate selection and use of ICT within education is the teacher and his or her pedagogical approaches" (p. 3). The authors went on to conclude that positive effects on learning arose where there was a close relationship between use and learning objectives.

The role different digital technologies play in supporting specific aspects of learning is, however, worth considering further here. In Table 3.3, those aspects

Table 3.2 Numbers of elements of learning contributed to by each digital technology category (ordered from highest to lowest number of elements)

Digital technology category	Numbers of elements of learning contributed to
Project and after-school club activities involving digital technologies	79
Online resources supporting curriculum-wide needs	79
Curriculum-wide teacher-centred software	71
Software involving and supporting parents	64
Topic-specific resources and software	64
Online learner support	59
Online resources supporting revision needs	43
Curriculum-wide learner-centred software	42

Table 3.3 Aspects of learning fully contributed to by each form of digital technology (ordered according to number of aspects from high to low)

Digital technology category	Megacognitive	Cognitive	Metacognitive	Social	Societal
Project and after-school club activities involving digital technologies	√		√	√	√
Online resources supporting curriculum-wide needs		√		√	√
Curriculum-wide teacher-centred software	√			√	
Online learner support			√	√	
Software involving and supporting parents				√	
Topic-specific resources and software					
Online resources supporting revision needs					
Curriculum-wide learner-centred software					

where all elements within that aspect can be supported by the digital technology are highlighted (as a tick).

The picture now tells a rather different story, but, dependency factors still need to be considered carefully:

- The purpose and aim of any activity needs to appropriately match the form of digital technology selected. For example, a specific topic can be supported effectively through topic-specific software, but, it is not likely that its use will contribute to every element of the cognitive aspect of learning. So, topic-specific resources and software supporting young learners in recognition of letters within words will not be likely in itself to lead to wide reasoning skills. It is how these experiences are used by teachers, developed further, and integrated and planned into wider and longer-term patterns of learning that is as important as the immediate uses and benefits arising.

- Teacher and supporter involvement can make a big difference, and certain elements of learning will only arise if teachers bring that focus into the activity for the learner. For example, curriculum-wide learner-centred software has been shown to support cognitive engagement for certain groups of reluctant learners, but this has often happened in isolation, so the social aspect of learning has not been integrated and involved. Although learners may individually gain from the use of an ILS, without wider discussion of what they have learned, either with their teachers or with their peers or both, the consolidation and application of knowledge to reinforce its meaning and comprehension may be lost.
- Learner selection of activities can make a difference. For example, activities selected by a learner from an online resource bank supporting revision needs may well be supporting a greater ownership of learning, since the learner has selected to do these activities, rather than them being selected by a teacher.

Some aspects of learning are more strongly supported (given appropriate match to activity and learner needs, and involvement of teachers in focusing forms of interaction and questioning), by some forms of digital technology:

- Megacognitive elements by curriculum-wide teacher-centred software and by project and after-school club activities involving digital technologies.
- Cognitive elements by online resources supporting curriculum-wide needs.
- Metacognitive elements by online learner support and by project and after-school club activities involving digital technologies.
- Social elements by curriculum-wide teacher-centred software, software involving and supporting parents, online resources supporting curriculum-wide needs, online learner support and by project and after-school club activities involving digital technologies.
- Societal elements by online resources supporting curriculum-wide needs and by project and after-school club activities involving digital technologies.

The width of involvement is another factor to consider:

- Project and after-school club activities offer strong support for four aspects of learning.
- Online resources supporting curriculum-wide needs offer strong support for three aspects of learning.

Indeed, this picture suggests an appropriate combination of these two categories could offer support across all elements of learning. It is worth considering here the work of Mishra and Koehler (2006), in proposing the Technological

Pedagogical Content Knowledge (TPCK) model. As they said, TPCK can be a basis for effective teaching with digital technologies, but requires:

- An understanding of how digital technologies represent concepts, facts, ideas and knowledge.
- Adoption of pedagogies enabling teaching in constructive ways.
- An understanding of the difficulties learners face with concepts, facts, ideas and knowledge and how digital technologies help to overcome these challenges.
- An understanding of what learners know already and how knowledge is constructed.
- An understanding of how digital technologies can develop existing concepts, facts, ideas and knowledge and support knowledge building constructions.

The Roles of Formative Assessment

The intersection between technology, content, pedagogy and learning is also worth considering here through the lens of formative assessment. Wiliam (2010) reviewed impacts of teacher practices relating to formative assessment, and highlighted the importance of adopting certain forms and patterns of interventions if learning outcomes and impacts are to be fully realised. As he stated, features to consider from the literature are:

- The quality of formative assessment feedback is more important than frequency of feedback.
- Looking ahead at answers is associated with lower achievement levels.
- Feedback explaining answers is associated with higher achievement than feedback giving just a correct answer.
- Formative assessment needs to be undertaken regularly (learners taking at least one test every 15 weeks scored higher by 0.5 standard deviations).
- More frequent formative assessment was associated with higher achievement levels.
- Formative assessment more regular than once every two weeks gave no additional gains.

There are clearly implications here with regard to pedagogical integration of different categories of digital technologies. If, for example, teachers do not 'explain answers' (Wiliam, 2010, p. 139) when curriculum-wide learner-centred software is deployed, then results will be more limited. It is clear that intervention elements provided and highlighted in analysing learning effects of both project and after-school club activities and online resources supporting curriculum-wide needs can afford opportunities for teachers to regularly feed back in detail through formative assessment practices.

The difference in terms of impact measured by effect size, for different levels of feedback, is offered by Wiliam (2010, p. 144) based on Nyquist (2003). These are (and consider the definitions of these distinctive groups in terms of a match to criteria listed above):

- Strong formative assessment has an effect size of 0.56.
- Moderate formative assessment has an effect size of 0.39.
- Weaker formative assessment has an effect size of 0.26.
- Feedback only has an effect size of 0.36.
- Weaker feedback only has an effect size of 0.14.

Wiliam (2010, p. 154) goes further, highlighting 'key strategies' for formative assessment for "improving the quality of instructional decisions". These five key strategies he lists as:

1. Clarifying, sharing and understanding learning intentions and criteria for success.
2. Engineering effective classroom discussion, activities and tasks eliciting evidence of learning.
3. Providing feedback moving learners forward.
4. Activating students as instructional resources for one another.
5. Activating students as owners of their own learning.

The ways in which these five key strategies can be incorporated into pedagogical practices using each of the eight different categories of digital technologies is shown in Table 3.4. A description of the match is presented in each case, and those matches regarded as being strong are shaded.

From this analysis, the categories most easily matching the key strategies of Wiliam (2010) are project and after-school club activities, curriculum-wide teacher-centred resources, and online resources supporting curriculum-wide needs. In all other cases, it is clear that teachers are likely to need to take particular care in ensuring key strategies for formative assessment are in place if learners are to gain as far as possible from the use of digital technologies. A number of projects and studies have focused on ways that formative assessment can be undertaken or enhanced through uses of digital technologies. Wilson, Boyd, Chen, and Jamal (2011) examined uses of computer-based formative assessment in multiple-choice format with undergraduate students in geography and showed those using this practice gained higher grades (three levels higher on average) compared to those not using them. Yang (2010) reported on a different practice, in a study involving 95 undergraduate students, writing a reflective journal on their coursework, focusing on self-correction and peer review, and showed these practices supported monitoring, evaluation and amendments to their work (including organisational, stylistic and grammatical changes).

In terms of learners engaging with uses of formative assessment when using digital technologies, Timmers, van den Broek, and van den Berg (2013) studied factors influencing uses of formative assessment by learners, and found effort involved was predicted by beliefs about the task rather than about success, and seeking feedback was predicted by both these factors and by effort involved. This discussion will be picked up further in Chapter 5.

Table 3.4 Evidence of how key strategies of formative assessment practices are incorporated into each category of digital technology

Digital technology category	Key strategy 1	Key strategy 2	Key strategy 3	Key strategy 4	Key strategy 5
Topic-specific resources and software	Teachers and mentors usually identify clear learning intentions and outcomes with learners when they use this form of resource	Classroom discussions can be engineered if a teaching assistant is supporting a learner, but otherwise this happens more haphazardly	Teachers and teaching assistants often rely on the feedback from the software itself rather than providing additional feedback	Topic-specific resources and software is often used with individual learners rather than being used to stimulate peer interactions	Learners tend to complete activities that teachers or teaching assistants give them, rather than learners owning the learning
Curriculum-wide learner-centred	Learners are often asked to use the system to gain in terms of subject results, but specific criteria or intentions are often not set	Discussion of activities and outcomes is not often extended to classrooms	The systems provide feedback for learners as they move forward, giving them an idea of their progress	Often these resources are used to support individual learning rather than supporting peer interactions	The system usually provides a personalised route for learners, and they often gain ownership of their learning
Curriculum-wide teacher-centred	These resources are integrated into lessons where teachers often provide clear aims and objectives	The resources are often built into activities where teachers encourage discussion and sharing of ideas from learners	Teachers often use the resources in order to structure feedback that identifies how learners have moved forward	Teachers often use resources to encourage learners to share their ideas with others, and to ask learners to review strategies used	The teacher is still central to the activities, and the control is strongly with the teacher

Software involving parents	Teachers can set up situations where intentions and outcomes are clarified, but this is not always the case	Teachers can set up discussions with learners following home activities, but this does not happen as a matter of course	Feedback provided by the software and by parents may be supportive, but not all teachers follow this up in classrooms	These forms of software tend to engage interactions between learners and their parents rather than with their peers, although there are some exceptions (such as *Mathletics*)	Learners using these forms of software tend to engage with the activities strongly, and undertaking them in their own homes tends to enhance learning ownership
Online resources used in classrooms	These resources are integrated into lessons where teachers often provide clear aims and objectives	The resources are often built into activities where teachers encourage discussion and sharing of ideas from learners	Teachers often use the resources in order to structure feedback that identifies how learners have moved forward	Teachers often use resources to encourage learners to share their ideas with others, and to ask searching questions of learners	The teacher is still central to the activities, and the control is strongly with the teacher
Online revision resources	The learner selects activities to meet personal needs, and recognises success by numbers of correct answers	The learner is likely to be largely accessing these facilities outside the classroom	The learner is likely to gain immediate feedback, but this may not provide the learner with details of how to move forward	The learner is most likely to be doing this form of activity alone	The learner is selecting these activities, so ownership may well be high

(Continued)

Table 3.4 (Continued)

Digital technology category	Key strategy 1	Key strategy 2	Key strategy 3	Key strategy 4	Key strategy 5
Online learner support	Online mentors often clarify intentions and outcomes when running online activities	While mentors engage discussion as strongly as they can, this form of interaction is not always embedded later with other classroom activities	Mentors often identify key points and summarise learning outcomes so that learners are aware of how their learning has moved forward	While online activities can involve a range of learners, peer interactions do not necessarily arise	Online activities tend to engage interactions from learners who might not otherwise engage in classroom discussions, strengthening elements of ownership
Project and after-school club activities	Intentions and criteria for success, including deadlines and milestones, are usually defined clearly with project-based activities	Project-based activities usually offer and demand many opportunities for discussions and reviews of progress	Facilitators (teachers and external experts), as well as peers themselves, often review progress and identify subsequent needs	Peers are generally required to work collaboratively or in teams, so they act strongly as instructional resources for one another	The learning ownership of project-based activities is often strong across individuals and teams

Chapter 4

Groups of Learners and Impacts of Digital Technologies on Learning

Learners are Not a Singularity

In this chapter, we will turn to the learners themselves. There has been a concern learning should be 'personalised' to a much greater extent. In the UK, the then department for education (DfES, 2004) stated: "Personalisation is ... about putting citizens at the heart of public services and enabling them to have a say in the design and improvement of the organisations that serve them" (p. 4). The description went on to say personalised learning should accommodate a learner's individual needs, their interests and aptitudes, so they can gain to the greatest possible level. In terms of personalised learning practices, Robinson and Sebba (2010) found limited evidence in schools they studied, confirmed by Beauchamp and Kennewell (2010) who argued from their review of interactivity involving ICT resources in classrooms with group and individual work that learners need to have more opportunities to decide when and how to use ICT resources in classrooms. Some studies have explored aspects of personalisation with learner uses of digital technologies, including Cakir and Simsek (2010), who conducted a controlled study with 90 grade 7 learners, but identified no significant difference in scores achieved for learners using personalised materials or non-personalised materials, either in a computer-based medium or paper-based medium, and Alcoholado et al. (2012), who studied the use of single display groupware with learners in a grade 3 class in Chile, enabling them to solve mathematics problems individually but through a shared display, with benefits reported being greatest for those with lowest initial scores.

So, does this definition refer to development of practices focusing on processes and opportunities for learning, or does it refer to matching the attributes and characteristics of learners? In this book and in this chapter, the focus is on the latter—and a range of learner attributes and characteristics will be considered in the context of learning needs, interests and aptitudes for different groups of learners. The ways educational digital technologies might most effectively match and support these learning needs, interests and aptitudes will be discussed.

Learners certainly are different, and sometimes they are widely different. An entire population of learners at a national, regional or area level can be grouped in different ways—for example, by age, and by attributes. To illustrate difference in terms of some groupings used at a policy level already, categories and groups used in one of the states of Germany, Nord-Rhein Westfalen (NRW), will be used as an example. Schools in NRW are divided into nine main groups. In alphabetical order these are:

- Förderschulen—for learners from 2 to 19 years, with special educational needs.
- Gesamtschulen—for learners from 10 to 19 years, preparing vocationally as well as for university entrance.
- Grundschulen—for learners from 6 to 10 years.
- Gymnasien—for learners from 10 to 19 years, preparing intellectually for university entrance.
- Hauptschulen—for learners from 10 to 16 years, preparing at a minimum level of education for life.
- Kindergarten—for learners up to six years.
- Realschulen—for learners from 10 to 16 years, preparing at a general level of application and vocationally.
- Volkschulen—for learners from 6 to 16 years, preparing at a minimum level of education for life.
- Waldorfschulen—for learners from 2 to 19 years using a particular pedagogical approach (Steiner).

Considering the total numbers of learners in these schools in 2008 to 2009, numbers are considerable (see Table 4.1). A key question for those supporting these learners relating to the content of this book is: how many of these learners learn in particular ways, and how might educational digital technologies support them best?

Considering these total populations, it is possible to recognise at once that learners, even though they might be of the same age, are not all within the same institutions. Distribution by institution is concerned with learner differences and pedagogies, to provide learning opportunities that seek to match needs, interests and aptitudes of the populations in those different schools. However, even if teachers in any one of those institutions were asked whether all of their children learned in the same way, it would be highly unlikely they would say they do. Given that learner difference is being identified by teachers at a level that goes deeper than this form of taxonomy, it is clear that developing approaches to

Table 4.1 Numbers of learners in each school type in NRW Germany in 2008 to 2009

School type	Girls	Boys	Total
Förderschulen	38,545	70,309	108,854
Gesamtschulen	117,386	115,428	232,814
Grundschulen	342,158	353,178	695,336
Gymnasien	316,669	276,411	293,080
Hauptschulen	93,121	123,522	216,643
Realschulen	158,728	162,167	320,895
Volkschulen	233	283	516
Waldorfschulen	9,302	8,953	18,255

Source: Ministerium für Schule und Weiterbildung des Landes Nordrhein-Westfalen, 2009.

Table 4.2 Numbers of learners with specific educational needs in schools in 2008 to 2009 in NRW Germany

Specific educational need	Number in schools
Emotional and social	10,908
Intellectual development	17,560
Hearing and communication	3,439
Physical and motor	6,987
Hospital	2,326
Learning	45,773
Speaking	11,774
Sight	2,191
Total	100,958

consider differences and an appropriate personalisation will require an exploration of a potentially wide range of characteristics and features.

As an example of a taxonomy used already, within one of these school groups, Förderschulen, learners are divided into further groups, according to specific attributes. The groups, and numbers in each group, are shown in Table 4.2.

In this case learners are grouped in a way allowing needs, interests and aptitudes to be considered specifically, to explore how their learning might best be supported. Yet still, teachers recognise differences across learners in any one of these groups in terms of how they learn, why they learn, and what they learn. In this book, groups of learners will be considered and their learning will be explored separately, to look in more detail at how research evidence about uses of educational digital technologies might link more effectively to features concerned with learning.

Twelve groups will be considered separately, and, in some groups, a further sub-grouping will be used. Taking the categories of digital technologies identified in the previous chapter, the sections following will identify where learning benefits and outcomes arise when particular digital technologies are used with each group of learners. Each section will indicate evidence about different types of digital technologies, with their own specific affordances, and how these can support specific groups of learners.

The sections in this chapter are divided into four main but sub-divided groupings, concerned with:

- Cognitive challenges:

  o Learners with specific cognitive abilities or attributes.
  o Learners with limited opportunities.
  o Mainstream early learners.
  o Mainstream young learners.
  o Mainstream secondary school or college age learners.

- Physical challenges:

  o Learners with physical disabilities or attributes.
  o Learners not physically present in classrooms or lessons.

- Emotional challenges:

  ○   Learners with challenging emotional features and attributes.
  ○   Learners whose attitudes pose problems.
  ○   Learners with challenging behavioural attributes.
  ○   Learners with challenging social attributes and abilities.

- Geographic challenges:

  ○   Learners where geography poses problems.

Learners with Specific Cognitive Abilities and Attributes

Learners with limited cognitive abilities and attributes have been a focus for a wide range of research studies exploring benefits in terms of both engagement and achievement arising from using educational digital technologies. While this learner group is wide, it is certainly generally recognised that for learners across the group cognitive attributes affect levels of qualifications attained and the 'speed' with which they are gained (lowering achievement below national averages). Cognitive needs can cover a very wide spectrum—for those with specific, moderate, profound, severe, multiple, and communication difficulties, as well as those with dyslexia, dyscalculia, Asperger's syndrome, autism, Down's syndrome, and the gifted and talented.

Special Schools and Digital Technology Support

Digital technologies have been used in a variety of ways to support learners with specific (cognitive) needs. As new digital technologies emerge, it is common to see affordances being applied for learners in this group. Mobile devices, for example, are reported by Campigotto, McEwen, and Epp (2013) being used by a wide range of learners in grades 7 to 12 with cognitive needs in two schools in the Toronto area, allowing learners to link words and pictures with auditory output; this study showed the technologies could have wide application in special needs classrooms, enhancing self-confidence and perceptions of success in tackling activities. Similarly, Fernández-López, Rodríguez-Fórtiz, Rodríguez-Almendros, and Martínez-Segura (2013) described uses of mobile applications with learners with a variety of special needs, to support exploration, association, puzzle and sorting, finding, on average, language skills increased by 5.76%, mathematics skills by 5.56%, environmental awareness skills by 7.59%, autonomy skills by 7.26% and social skills by 4.23%. For those learners with special needs that might be associated with sensory impairment, Brown et al. (2011) reported a development combining elements of serious games with mobile location-based services to achieve independent travel to work and opening up educational opportunities online.

Using a different form of digital technology (curriculum-wide learner-centred software), Lewis (1997) looked at use of an ILS with numbers of learners with special needs in mainstream and in special schools in the UK. She concluded the facility "was liked by pupils with special educational needs and by their teachers; the reservations were about content. The enthusiasm it generated is a major asset for pupils who have had sometimes prolonged experience of school failure" (p. 117). Although the author questioned whether gains in learning demonstrated by system reports might have been procedural rather than strategic, she nevertheless concluded "Behavioural and attitudinal changes, towards greater autonomy and self-confidence in learning, may be particularly important bene-fits of an ILS for this target group" (p. 117). She also noted "The system required considerable skill and expertise . . . from specialist staff within the schools" (p. 117). Indeed, the author earlier in the chapter indicated adaptations needed to be made to ensure access for pupils within the special schools using "a glide-point (integral mouse/mat device), trackerballs, voice activated software (not fully developed), a big keys keyboard, various keyboard overlays, a touch window, and the variation of cursor size and maximising of cursor background contrast" (p. 105).

In a later study, looking at how digital technologies could affect access to learning by those with special needs across school and home learning settings, Passey (2011e) noted "teachers have not always found it easy to set homework for pupils, especially as parents are not used to working with their children on aspects of learning at home" (p. 379). In this study he found learners were gaining access to software such as *2Simple* and *2Design 4 Make*, applications allowing learners to continue their work on their designs at home. Similarly, some year 10 learners (14 to 15 years of age) continued discussion topics at home, and one of the 'top' users in this forum was a boy with quite severe behavioural difficul-ties, who would have found it more difficult to communicate in a face-to-face situation. The author noted that through this form of digital technology learners could gain in terms of:

• Megacognitive skills—engaging in independent learning.
• Cognitive skills—undertaking subject and topic work, practising media literacy skills.
• Metacognitive skills—planning learning, thinking about scheduling, thinking about ideas to explore later with teachers.
• Social skills—engaging with parents.
• Societal skills—practising and modelling working at home as well as in a specific school location.

Many learners with cognitive needs are supported in special schools, where specialist digital technologies may be provided. Infogroup/ORC International (2010) reported the median pupil:computer ratio in special schools in England was 3:1, but only 60% had assistive technologies to support cognitive access. They further reported 56% had a learning platform, but only 33% used it to communicate with learners, 29% used it for communication between learners, 19% used it for learners to download and upload homework, and 15% used it for live chat and discussion forums. Practices and the needs of learners in one school are not necessarily found in all schools. As the report stated, only 39% of these schools agreed ICT had supported them in engaging parents in supporting learning, and 22% agreed ICT had supported them in engaging parents with forthcoming lessons and homework. Teacher practice in schools supporting those with cognitive needs is not uniform; as the report stated, only 5% of teachers used ICT for learners to download and upload homework most days of the week, 34% rarely or never did this, 41% did not use ICT for this, and 0% of teachers set homework requiring pupils to use the internet every day, 41% did this rarely, and 36% never did this.

These data suggest there are schools and teachers who find digital technologies support learning for those with cognitive needs, but practice using digital technologies is not yet widespread and may be applied differently according to individual learner needs. Some of the reasons for this lack of wider use will be explored in this section, but one reason concerns the need for more development of affordances of digital technologies to engage with needs of specific learners. As Abbott (2007) noted, symbols and icons have been used increasingly to support engagement of ranges of learners with cognitive needs, and:

> A more recent publication (Abbott et al 2006) reflects upon the progress made with symbol use through the availability of desk-top publishing programmes, word processors and web browsers which make use of graphic symbols, and notes the widening of the groups making use of them.
>
> (p. 16)

Learners with mild levels of special needs are being supported through a wide range of uses of digital technologies. Ratcliff and Anderson (2011) in their case study looked at the use of *Logo* with learners in grades 1 to 6 with disabilities ranging from dyslexia, dyscalculia and dysgraphia, to attention deficit hyperactivity disorder (ADHD); all learners were able to use commands, apply geometrical knowledge to make designs and shapes, and create procedures. Kleemans, Segers, Droop, and Wentink (2011) involved 40 learners aged 7 to 12 years with mild learning difficulties in reading and mathematics in their study, in which learners used *WebQuests* with either ill-defined or well-defined assignments, and showed learning gains were higher for those working on ill-defined assignment tasks.

Dyslexia

In terms of a more specific cognitive need, Aubrey and Dahl (2008) refer to research indicating uses of digital technologies to support those at risk of dyslexia. They refer to the work of Regtvoort and van der Leij (2007), who compared the effects of 31 trained 'at risk' five- to six-year-old learners of dyslexic parents with using a computer-based phonemic awareness programme with those of 26 control learners who were not trained. Their tests showed those who were trained gained more in terms of both phonemic awareness and letter knowledge. But, this advantage was not sustained; the advantage was not displayed when the learners moved into grades 1 and 2, according to their reading and spelling tests at those later times. The authors referred to the work of Magnan and Ecalle (2006), who explored the effects of an audio-visual computer system. Again, those 65 learners five years of age who were trained in using the system to distinguish phonetic features for recognition of written words gained more in phonological skills and recoding than those who were untrained in the control group. Abbott (2007) also referred to uses of digital technologies to support learners with dyslexia, and to the work of McKeown (1992), who said "Technology will not provide all the answers to the problems of specific learning difficulties but it can be effective in reducing the number of hurdles that children have to cross at any one time" (p. 100).

While digital technologies could provide positive support for learners with dyslexia, some forms of digital technologies might be less useful in their current forms. Habib et al. (2012) found that undergraduate and college students with dyslexia found VLEs could be particularly challenging, in terms of presenting materials in ways leading to overload, having limited word processing and search function, and forcing learners to work and integrate materials across different systems.

Low Literacy Levels

Although young people are recognised as using digital technologies readily, it should not be assumed learners with low levels of literacy skills will access and use digital technologies at the same levels as other learners. Conti-Ramsden, Durkin, and Walker (2010) studied 17-year-old learners with language impairment and found them more anxious about use of computers than a control group, especially females. In terms of uses of mobile devices, Durkin, Conti-Ramsden, and Walker (2011) in a controlled study involving 94 17-year-old learners, found those with language impairments were less likely to reply to text messages, or replied with shorter messages; the authors concluded texting is a medium that does not ensure those with low literacy will engage, with longer-term implications.

There are wide reports of digital technologies supporting learners with low levels of literacy skills, however. Potocki, Ecalle, and Magnan (2013) reported positive effects of a CAI program on enhancing text comprehension for those having difficulties in comprehending when learning to read, and Rodríguez, Filler, and Higgins (2012) showed computer-based language resources for grade 1 learners with limited English language skills supported reading comprehension particularly. Abbott (2007) referred to uses of specific digital technologies to support their learning, to "the use of handheld text-reading pens to enable people with learning difficulties to use the web more easily (Harrysson, A Svensk and Johansson 2005)" (p. 18). Considering ways to explore literacy skills development for this group of learners, Carnahan, Williamson, Hollingshead, and Israel (2012) reported a study of a teacher using technologies to support a "Balanced Literacy Approach"; "In everyday instruction, such an approach connects reading, writing, and word study activities" (p. 22). Their article lists a range of technological resources the teacher can use (categorising them as electronic books, technology tools and comprehensive resources). Their conclusions emphasised the need to align digital technology resources with learner needs and teacher requirements, saying "Although all of these resources are valuable, they are only effective insofar that they align with the needs of each learner and support the concepts being taught" (p. 28).

In terms of writing, MacArthur (2009) reviewed the literature looking at uses of digital technologies with 'struggling' or weak writers. As he said, "Struggling writers can benefit from a wide range of computer applications for writing. Word processing, spelling checkers, word prediction, and speech recognition offer support for transcription and revision" (p. 93). He went on to say word processors support publication that is more authentic for learners, concept or mind-mapping software can support planning of learning, but "New forms of writing, including Internet chat, blogs, multimedia, and wikis, have not been studied extensively, but they may offer both opportunities and challenges to struggling writers" (p. 93). He concluded from his review that "the one area where there is sufficient research to draw fairly confident conclusions is word processing" (p. 101). He stated word processing has been shown to have a 'moderate' positive effect on writing, particularly for weak writers. He cautioned, however, that teachers need to provide sufficient time and access for learners to develop drafts and revise their work, and this might depend on their speed of input through the keyboard. He went on to say that "although the research on assistive technology for writing is limited, sufficient research exists to establish that applications like word prediction and speech recognition can be beneficial at least for some students" (p. 101). But, as he said, the research is not yet specific in terms of identifying learners who will benefit most (whether weak writers, those slow with a keyboard, those with limited vocabulary, or those with low levels of engagement or motivation, and at what ages, for example), and the settings or landscapes in which this might best occur. He also highlighted the limited research done on concept or mind-mapping devices and on devices offering automated scoring of text.

In terms of reading, Soe, Koki, and Chang (2000), in their meta-analysis of effects of CAI on reading, stated the possible very wide level of this issue: "While the actual number of children who are poor readers is being debated, one widely accepted indicator is that 40 percent of all U.S. nine-year-olds score below the 'basic' level on the National Assessment of Educational Progress" (p. 1). From their meta-analysis, the authors concluded "computer-assisted instruction has a positive impact on reading achievement. However . . . the results given here must be interpreted with caution" (p. 13). In another meta-analysis, Torgerson and Elbourne (2002), this time focusing on random-controlled trials to identify the extent of impact of CAI on spelling when compared to traditional instruction, found that "When six of the seven studies were pooled in a meta-analysis there was an effect, not statistically significant, in favour of computer interventions (Effect size = 0.37, 95% confidence interval = −0.02 to 0.77, p = 0.06)" (p. 129). After controlling for background factors, they concluded that "using computer software may be as effective as conventional teaching of spelling, although the possibility of computer-taught spelling being inferior or superior cannot be confidently excluded due to the relatively small sample sizes of the identified studies" (p. 129).

In terms of e-books and the facilities now available to support reading through a digital environment, Daniel and Woody (2013) in their study showed e-books were read for longer than traditional texts (and increasingly at home), and multi-tasking occurred more frequently in those readers. Chen, Teng, Lee, and Kinshuk (2011) explored ways to supplement text-based reading with access to both supplemental digital materials and questions to scaffold reading strategies, and found online scaffolding questions significantly improved reading understanding. Karemaker, Pitchford, and O'Malley (2010) studied 17 beginner readers five to six years old who found it hard to read, and found there were significantly greater gains in written word recognition and enjoyment of instruction following use of *Clicker* compared to using *Big Books*.

However, a significant note of caution is raised here. Santoro and Bishop (2010), in their review of software resources available to support early learners finding it hard to read, found many resources rated poorly on their educational criteria measures, and those more highly rated for interface design tended to rate low in terms of content.

Those on the Autistic Spectrum

There are limited research findings about uses of digital technologies with learners on the autistic spectrum, including those with Asperger's syndrome. Abbott, Detheridge, and Detheridge (2006) referred to a study looking at uses of virtual reality (VR) environments supporting learners with autism, saying results "showed some benefits for developing imaginative play following the use of VR scenarios (Herrera, Jordan and Vera 2006). The researchers set up shop and classroom scenarios and found that students with autism began to play more imaginatively after using these" (p. 16).

Other studies have looked at uses of this form of digital technology. Cheng and Ye (2010) stated limited social competence and reciprocity were key features of learners on the autism spectrum, and their study used a virtual learning environment with a 3D avatar, an animated scenario, and verbal and text communication features. It involved three learners, in uses related strongly to their daily lives, and the researchers found significant effects on performance, both from performance in the VLE as well as beyond, in terms of reciprocal social interactions such as greater eye contact and listening to others. Cheng, Chiang, Ye, and Cheng (2010), in another study, explored how 3D animations were used to support developments of empathic thinking and understanding with three boys 8 to 10 years of age over a five-month period, showing the system had significant positive effects on empathic understanding and practice, again both within the system and beyond. In a study by Lorenzo, Pomares, and Lledó (2013), how an immersive virtual reality system could accommodate the needs of learners with Asperger's syndrome (10 from primary schools and 10 from secondary schools in Spain) was explored, and while major difficulties were found at the outset of the study, most learners were able later to use the system and tackle tasks, leading to more positive social competencies and functional abilities.

Using mobile digital technologies, Mintz, Branch, March, and Lerman (2012) described the use of an application on smartphones to support social and life skills of learners on the autistic spectrum in four special schools, and their uses were shown to impact social and life skills in some cases. Mintz (2013) in a further study explored the use of a mobile application for smartphones by 15 teachers and 26 learners (with average age of 15 years), and found some learners were better suited to this technology, especially those recognising they had difficulties and seeking to address them.

Using digital technologies to involve and support parents and carers with learners on the autistic spectrum, Doyle and Arnedillo-Sánchez (2011) described multimedia software used to construct social stories, and how this helped carers and parents to understand their learners more, which subsequently led to enhanced responses.

Those with Down's Syndrome

Similarly, there is limited research literature referring to uses of digital technologies supporting learning for those with Down's syndrome (DS). Aubrey and Dahl (2008) referred to a study in Spain by Ortega-Tudela and Gomez-Ariza (2006) exploring how multimedia computer-assisted teaching supported learning of basic mathematical concepts and skills. Their study involved 10 six-year-old learners in the experiment, and compared outcomes with eight six-year-old learners in a control group. The authors stated "The experimental group showed a higher performance on post-test, following training on a multi-media software programme" (p. 41). The experiment provided counting activities in the form of games, and the control group did these with paper copies. Aubrey and Dahl (2008) concluded: "The results showed clearly that teaching using multimedia materials facilitated the acquisition of basic mathematical knowledge and ability of young DS children" (p. 41).

Those with Severe Learning Difficulties

Digital technologies have been used to support learners with severe learning difficulties. Stephenson and Carter (2011) studied uses of multi-sensory environments in schools to support learners in this group. As the authors said, while multi-sensory environments (MSE) are increasingly used in schools to support learners with severe disabilities, how teachers use them has not been explored widely. This study gathered evidence from five teachers in two special schools, who were interviewed and observed using these systems in their classrooms. The authors reported that "Most teachers seemed to believe that use of the MSE or the equipment in it would have automatic and remarkably wide ranging benefits for their students" (p. 339). The researchers, however, found limited evidence of how teachers were focusing the use of the environments with instruction, and how they were using monitoring to identify outcomes. The researchers were not able to find empirical evidence to validate teacher claims, and called for more research in this area.

Gifted and Able Learners

In terms of gifted and able learners, Rodrigues (1997) looked at the use of two ILSs. She found that while learners found the *SuccessMaker* system enjoyable over a period of two months, "for some able students the novelty was beginning to diminish. Though the students were still keen to work with ILS, none of them said they would extend the time they spent on the ILS system" (p. 118). Able learners using the other system, however, showed wide dissatisfaction and felt it did not meet their needs. As the author concluded, such systems need to challenge learner needs "more effectively and present new learning in a manner which is intelligible, plausible and fruitful for the student. It is difficult to provide contexts which are appropriate to able students which they will consider relevant to their age and maturity" (p. 125). This is a point raised in the report of Passey, Rogers et al. (2004), who found able learners tended to prefer information-rich environments provided through digital technologies, rather than communication-rich environments.

In a study specifically involving gifted and able learners, Simon, Johnson, Cavell, and Parsons (2012) looked at uses of a graphical tool to stimulate inter-actions between learners about specific topics, and showed a teacher with nine gifted and talented learners in a primary classroom was able to use the system with a concept cartoon to engage learners in discussion and argumentation about the topic of electricity.

In Summary

Evidence of uses of digital technologies and outcomes arising for those with specific cognitive needs can be summarised as follows:

- Topic-specific resources and software are often used to support specific elements of topic and subject learning with learners with cognitive needs. The ways teachers and teaching assistants build on the outcomes is clearly important.
- Curriculum-wide software has been used effectively to support some learners with cognitive needs, but ILSs tend to be of more value for those with lower starting levels rather than those at higher starting levels.
- Teaching-wide software has been used effectively with some groups with cognitive needs, although the outcomes of multi-sensory environments for those with more severe needs are not fully established.
- Parent-involved software is being used with children with cognitive needs, although learning outcomes are not yet fully established.
- Curriculum-supportive online resources are being used effectively in some instances to support learners with dyslexia, those across the autistic spectrum, and those with Down's syndrome.
- Online learner support for those with cognitive needs is an area not commonly reported within the research literature, but outcomes for gifted children have been recognised.
- Project and after-school club activities involving digital technologies are not commonly reported in the literature, although outcomes for gifted children are recognised.

Learners with Limited Opportunities

Some learners experience limiting opportunities when accessing educational and training events and facilities. In discussing issues for this learner group, it should be recognised there is potential overlap with discussions about learners not phys-ically present and those where geography poses challenges. Nonetheless, qualities described here are concerned with limitations in engagement: lack of timely physical access (not being present when opportunity arises); limited width of awareness (understanding whether something might be of interest or value); and timeliness (of knowing when opportunities arise).

Limited Physical Access

One way suggested to address the issue of lack of timely physical presence when opportunities arise is to increase uses of alerts and interactions through mobile and non-mobile devices. In a study in Malaysia, Ismail and Azizan (2012) explored needs of distant learners using mobile devices, and ways they perceive interactivity. Views of 61 distance university-based learners about the importance and forms of interactivity deemed useful were gathered and analysed. The authors found learners generally believed interactivity was an important element to support their learning and: "Overall, these findings suggested that the respondents need an interactive m-learning system that allows them to not only ask questions by their demand (query), but also provide answers instantly to their questions (query auto-reply system)" (p. 125). These responses concur with outcomes of a study (Passey et al., 2010) looking at how young people could develop an online curriculum vitae; the results indicated young people had concerns about lack of feedback, speed of feedback and regularity of feedback, from both their counsellors and from potential employers. There are potential implications here for those setting up important alert systems.

Limited Width of Awareness

There is limited research available focusing specifically on how uses of digital technologies might help to enhance width of awareness, although uses of digital resources to widen and deepen topics in schools is recognised (Passey, 2011a), and ideas of using mobile texting or applications with dispersed learners has also been highlighted (Passey, Williams, & Rogers, 2008). Learners with low literacy levels from refugee backgrounds would certainly be considered likely to fall within this group of learners. Even though evidence shows digital technologies can support the development of literacy from low levels (see the sub-section in this chapter on this topic), Windle and Miller (2012) in a survey of teachers supporting this group of learners, from across the State of Victoria in Australia, found use of digital technologies in pedagogic practices was not consistent or at a level that might be considered regular or high. Indeed, only 37% used ICT resources on a regular basis, and 40% wrote texts with the class on a traditional board, an interactive whiteboard, or an overhead projector.

However, some developments and studies suggest that uses of certain digital technologies could support learners with limited awareness in gaining key skills to address challenges they face. For example, Kim and Pedersen (2011), in a controlled study, looked at uses of a digital problem-based learning program, with 172 grade 6 learners, and found those using the metacognitive scaffolding significantly improved in terms of their hypothesis-development.

Timeliness as a Factor

Timeliness is a related factor that can influence learners in terms of identifying opportunities, choices and involvement in activities. Timeliness can be related to physical location (limiting access), but it can also be related to an understanding of how to tackle and act within given time periods. It can be argued timeliness in this sense is a skill needing to be used by learners, and learners need to be both aware of the influence of timeliness and how to act appropriately. This relates to the need for learners to have skills in decision making, and some learners are known to have limited abilities in these respects (see Passey et al., 2008).

In terms of developing such skills, Carnahan, Basham, Christman, and Hollingshead (2012) explored how video modelling had been used as a concept and practice to support awareness and development of certain skills by learners with specific needs. They referred to development of practices using mobile devices, so that learners physically removed or isolated could still gain access to skill development through specifically designed video models. This form of practice could certainly be related to skill development of timeliness. As they said, "Video modeling offers a way to provide multiple means of representing information and an alternative to teacher-led instruction by providing students concrete examples and support, thus decreasing dependence on adult prompts" (p. 53). In developing video models for use by learners they emphasised certain design needs as "Some learners truly enjoy or benefit from seeing themselves as the model [video self-modeling] whereas others prefer not to see themselves in the video" (p. 54). These authors identified three factors to consider when designing these forms of online support models: learners' needs; the level or extent of support or reinforcement needed; and affordances of the device to help to engage and integrate practice.

While digital technologies can provide opportunities and enhancements to support learning for a wide variety of learners, specific skills needed by those learners need to be identified carefully and themselves supported, perhaps through uses of digital technologies, as well as with tutor and teacher support as appropriate. Research into uses of digital technologies to support this group of learners and with these forms of skills is clearly at an early stage.

In Summary

Evidence of using digital technologies with learners with limited opportunities can be summarised as follows:

- Topic-specific resources and software have been used to support learners with limited opportunities, sometimes through local or community centres, but increasingly uses of mobile devices coupled with specific applications are being considered in this context.
- Curriculum-wide software has been used in the past to support learners in these contexts, but this is not found to be widely used currently.
- Teaching-wide software, parent-involved software, and curriculum-supportive online resources are not evidenced in terms of supporting needs of this group of learners.
- Online learner support has been used, and its use through mobile devices is being explored more widely (see Passey, Davies, & Rogers, 2010, for example).
- Project and after-school club activities involving digital technologies have been used with this group of learners, but evidence about their involvement and outcomes is not clear, as they tend to be included within wider groups of learners (such as those involved in *First Lego League* projects).

Mainstream Early Learners

Mainstream early learners are defined here as young people up to five years of age. The period up to five years of age is a time when a child is developing physically, socially and emotionally, with a particular focus on active engagement with their surroundings and those in their surroundings. As Bee (1997) says, children by four years of age can generally climb stairs one foot at a time, kick and throw a large ball, "understand false belief", improve uses of past tense and plurals and passive sentences, be at Erikson's stage of initiative versus guilt, at Freud's phallic stage, show attachment behaviour under stress, begin signs of individual friendships, and display more and more verbal aggression (p. 214). Educational digital technologies can play important and increasingly prominent roles in the lives of many children of this age (see, for example, Plowman et al., 2008). However, their interactions with educational digital technologies are limited often by physical abilities such as their motor skills, and low levels of reading abilities (although use of icons and imagery are used across a range of digital technologies to support their access).

The importance of access to digital technologies at a young age is argued from findings of studies such as that of Saçkes, Trundle, and Bell (2011). In their study of 8,642 children from kindergarten to grade 3, they identified availability of a computer at home and high socio-economic status as statistically significant predictors of baseline computer skills, while having access to a computer in a kindergarten prior to going to school was a statistically significant predictor of computer skill development by grade 3, with no differences noted between girls and boys.

Some studies have looked at digital technologies to support reading awareness with early learners. Shamir and Shlafer (2011) looked at use of e-books to support literacy of 136 early learners, and found that concepts about print were enhanced by the use of the digital resources.

Toys and Digital Devices

Children of this age can use a number of specific forms of digital technologies, including educational toys developed for young learners, and assistive technologies to develop motor and co-ordination skills. The literature highlights uses of topic-specific resources and software, as well as resources broadcast through a television medium, and software involving and supporting parents in developing children's learning abilities at those young ages. Aubrey and Dahl (2008) offered a useful overview of the range of digital technologies that are encountered by and used by this age group: "barcode scanners, calculators, camcorders, cameras, cash machines, computers, console games, dishwashers, laptops and tablet PCs, ICT-based 'smart' toys, microwave ovens, mixers, mobile phones, networked desktop PCs, photocopies, scanners, televisions and washing machines" (p. 3). They went on to list digital technologies specifically developed for use by children in their early years: "Bee-Bot programmable floor robots, Roamers or Pixie Robots, digital audio players (DAPs), CD or cassette players, digital cameras, Digital Blue Computer Microscopes, mini DV camcorders and Digital Blue Movie Creators, DVD or video players, iPods, interactive whiteboards"

(p. 3), and they mention how some devices aimed at older audiences have been modified to accommodate use by this age group—laptop computers, mobile telephones, photocopiers, scanners and televisions.

The authors highlighted a number of studies where learning benefits arose when digital technologies were used with early learners. They reported three- and four-year-old children could make greater developmental gains when they learned using ICT, and that "Haughland (1990; 2000b) demonstrated that . . . US preschool children's use of computer software led to gains in intelligence, non-verbal skills, structural knowledge, long-term memory, manual dexterity, verbal skills, problem solving, abstraction and conceptual skills" (p. 38). They reported another study, indicating that "Grubb (2000) has also affirmed the greater increase in concept age of US kindergarten children in a twenty-first century classroom than students in a traditional kindergarten classroom" (p. 39).

The importance of teacher interventions when digital technologies were used and where gains were identified was stressed: "As Haughland (2000a:2) noted, however, teacher training is essential as 'relatively few teachers in a relatively small number of schools have been trained to maximise technology use in classrooms'" (pp. 38–9). They emphasised the importance of parental interventions in this respect, reporting work of Plowman and Stephen (2006), identifying ways parents support learning for those in early years, going beyond a technically-based learning: developing positive attitudes to learning, whether in personal, social or emotional terms; providing an understanding of forms of learning existing in the wider world, such as communication, language, literacy, solving problems, numeracy, creativity, reasoning or recreational interests; and gaining operational ICT skills.

Television Programmes

One form of digital technology receiving a great deal of research interest and focus has been broadcast television. The role of television programmes in widening understanding was noted by Aubrey and Dahl (2008), referring to the work of Linebarger and Walker (2005), who explored television viewing of 51 early years' learners to language outcomes, starting at an age of six months, and reviewing three-monthly logs of language and programmes watched. Aubrey and Dahl (2008) reported that "At thirty months of age, certain programmes resulted in greater vocabularies and higher expressive language scores when parental education, home environment and children's cognitive performance were statistically controlled" (p. 40). The Metiri Group (2006) similarly reported that "A great body of research shows that children can learn from viewing and interacting with video and television" (p. 5). In an early evaluation of impacts of the *Sesame Street* programme, Ball and Bogatz (1970) reported children watching the programmes gained more in terms of scores on letter, number and classifica- tion tests. They also claimed the more programmes the children watched, the more knowledge they gained.

The Metiri Group (2006) noted long-term effects and impacts of television programmes on early learners also, reporting that watching *Sesame Street* was associated with higher levels of vocabulary, letter and number recognition, as well as having higher levels of "verbal and quantitative readiness" (p. 6), more positive attitudes to school, more positive relationships with other children, with these effects persisting through to 15- to 20-year-old learners, who gained higher scores in English, mathematics and science, higher levels of self-esteem, and had more positive attitudes towards teachers. The authors reported these outcomes had been replicated in studies beyond the US, in Mexico, Portugal and Turkey.

In terms of impacts on early years' learners, as Fisch and Truglio (2001) said, "More than 1,000 studies have examined Sesame Street and its power in areas such as literacy, number skills, and promoting prosocial behavior, as well as formal features pertaining to issues such as children's attention" (p. xvii). Fisch (2004), in his later review of impacts of educational television, balances this view, by saying "Nevertheless, even those negative effects that are supported by data do not present the entire picture. Often, far less attention has been devoted to the positive effects that carefully crafted, developmentally appropriate television programs can hold" (p. 3). He goes on to argue that if a medium can influence negatively, it can also influence positively "if product commercials can inform, then also can science concept programmes; that if programmes can influence aggressive behaviours, then programmes can also influence co-operative behaviours" (p. 3).

Some research studies have explored ways educational media might support needs of those with poor socio-economic backgrounds. A study by Vandewater and Bickham (2004) reported educational media could account for limiting effects of poor family backgrounds. Their study looked at impacts of educational media on reading and pre-reading skills, with learners from two to five years of age, in families with what they termed "family stressors" having "lack of economic resources, family conflict, and maternal depression" (p. 717). They reported findings indicated "all family stressors were negatively related to the quality of the home learning environment, which was in turn directly related to children's reading skills" (p. 717). But, as they went on to say, "only family conflict was negatively related to educational media use, though media use was positively related to reading skills" (p. 717). Because of relative strengths of relationship, they concluded "Results suggest that educational media use is less prone to disruption by family stressors than other influences on young children's reading and pre-reading skills" (p. 717). Wright et al. (2001) reported a related study. Their study involved two different cohorts of early learners, in middle to low socio-economic groups, where diaries of television programmes watched were completed across the period from two to five years of age in one cohort, and four to seven years in another. Tests were used and completed each year, to identify levels of reading, mathematics, vocabulary (receptive), and readiness for school. Their analyses controlled for both quality of the home environment and primary language in the home. The authors reported that viewing "child-audience informative programs between ages 2 and 3 predicted high subsequent performance on all four measures of academic skills. For both cohorts, frequent viewers of general-audience programs performed more poorly on subsequent tests than did infrequent viewers of such programs" (p. 1347). The authors noted previous viewing affected later viewing choices, stating that "Children with good skills at age 5 selected more child-audience informative programs and fewer cartoons in their early elementary years. Children with lower skills at age

3 shifted to viewing more general-audience programs by ages 4 and 5" (p. 1347). The authors concluded that development of early learning can be dependent largely on content of programmes watched by children in their early years.

Computer Use by Early Learners

Early learners are often routinely exposed to uses of computers by older children, young people and adults, and some are gaining early access to digital technologies that are computer-based rather than television-based. Aubrey and Dahl (2008) looked at impacts of specific computer-based software on early learners. They reported the work of Calvert, Strong, and Gallagher (2005), who looked at how early learners around four to five years of age handled and gained from access to a computer story. They reported that "Children who controlled the computer demonstrated more attention and involvement than those who watched an adult control the experience. Control, however, had no effect on children's memory of visual or verbal content" (p. 40). They also reported the work of Weiss, Kramarski, and Talis (2006), who looked at how 116 early learners around four to five years of age used different forms of software (individually-based and collaboratively-based) as well as non-computer based materials, to support learning of mathematics. They reported that "both computer groups outperformed the control group in mathematical achievement. With respect to disposition, the co-operative learning group increased its positive attitude about co-operative learning and the individual learning group improved its mathematical skills at a higher level" (p. 40). Aubrey and Dahl (2008) also reported a study (Li, Atkins, & Stanton, 2006) exploring school readiness and prior computer use with 122 early learners 3.5 to 5 years of age, randomly assigned to an experimental group (using a computer 15 to 20 minutes each day) or a control group (using standard materials). They reported that "The experimental group performed significantly better than the controls on the school readiness test. The effect was strongly enhanced by children's home computer experience. Findings were inconclusive regarding the potential effect of computer use on motor skills" (p. 40).

In Summary

Evidence (from this sub-section, as well as in Chapter 3) about uses of digital technologies and outcomes with early learners can be summarised as follows:

- Topic-specific resources and software can support literacy, numeracy, but also motor skills, and widening understanding in the short term and the long term.
- Parent-involved resources can support literacy, numeracy, affective and social attitudes, when appropriate interactions are coupled with effective content in television programmes such as *Sesame Street*.
- There is more limited evidence of uses or outcomes with curriculum-wide software, teaching-wide software, curriculum-supportive online resources, online learner support, or project or after-school club activities involving digital technologies.

Mainstream Young Learners

Mainstream young learners are defined here as young people between 5 and 11 years of age. The development of cognitive skills, including verbal and reading skills, mathematical and scientific knowledge, is recognised as often being rapid for this age group. As Bee (1997) says, they have gained a variety of concrete skills, are developing inductive logic, as well as understanding and using conservation of weight and volume, are increasingly "less tied to appearance", describe others with more "enduring qualities", friendship is "based on reciprocal trust", they play in separate gender groups, "enduring friendships appear", continuing "throughout these years", and puberty begins for some boys by the age of 11 years (p. 267). At this age, children often engage with educational digital technologies in their homes as well as in school environments (see, for example, Lewin, 2004; Valentine, Marsh, & Pattie, 2005).

Young learners from 5 to 11 years of age increasingly use specific forms of digital technologies. Livingstone (2012) offers an overview of evidence applying to primary school age learners, saying that "Equivocal findings such as these led a pan-European literature review to conclude that ICT impacts positively on educational performance in primary schools, particularly in English and less so in science and not in mathematics (Balanskat et al., 2006, p. 3)" (p. 12).

Home Access and Uses in Primary Schools

In terms of average levels of access to digital technologies of this age group, Ofcom (2012) indicates that in the UK: home access to the internet grew from 85% to 90% between 2011 and 2012; the average monthly hours online for 2- to 11-year-old boys is 4.5, and for girls is 4.2; and the most popular sites for 2- to 17-year-olds are *YouTube*, *Google*, *Facebook* and the BBC.

These generally high levels of access are found in many primary schools. Infogroup/ORC International (2010) reported the median pupil:computer ratio in primary schools in England was 6.9:1. However, only 67% had a learning platform, 59% used it to communicate with learners, 51% used it for communication between learners, 53% used it for learners to download and upload homework, and 40% used it for live chat and discussion forums. Across the same primary schools, 48% agreed ICT had supported them in engaging parents in supporting learning, and 45% agreed ICT had supported them in engaging parents with forthcoming lessons and homework. But the divide between access and use to support learning is clear when it is considered that in the same report, across these schools, only 1% of teachers used ICT for learners to download and upload homework most days of the week, 27% rarely or never did this, 55% did not use ICT for this, 1% of teachers set homework that required pupils to use the internet every day, 47% did this rarely, and 22% never did this.

Digital Technology Skills and Learning Outcomes

Evidence from the literature and from practice suggests the level of digital skills for this age group of learners is not a limiting factor in terms of abilities to access digital resources. Aubrey and Dahl (2008) reviewed evidence of how readily this age group can use a mouse, and pointed to the work of Donker and Reitsma (2005), who set up a study in the Netherlands to look at how proficient learners six and seven years of age were in using drag and drop, and click, move and click features on screen. Their study involved 104 learners, and they found that while six-year-old learners moved items more slowly than seven-year-old learners, nearly all learners could undertake the activities with the same degree of accuracy. They found drag and drop led to a greater level of accuracy than click, move and click features, and vertical accuracy was less than horizontal accuracy. Aubrey and Dahl (2008) concluded by saying that "five- and six-year-olds are well capable of using a mouse to operate educational software" (p. 41). Lane and Ziviani (2010), from a study of 221 5- to 10-year-old learners, found speed and accuracy of using a mouse developed with age as well as visual-motor proficiency, but fluency was more influenced by tasks, so their recommendation was to not expose young learners to tasks requiring speed testing, but regular practice is important.

In terms of whether digital technologies support learning for this age group, STEPS (2007) reported a cross-European project, saying "ICT strategies have resulted in improved learner outcomes (creativity, competence development and motivating lifelong learning), higher levels of teachers' digital competence, increased access to and use of ICT in schools and change and innovation in primary school education" (p. 6). On the other hand, the Metiri Group (2006) reported that while learning impacts have been identified in the short term, longer-term impacts and the transfer of learning have not necessarily been evidenced. They highlighted the work of Vanderbilt University (Cognition and Technology Group at Vanderbilt, 1997), showing "middle school students viewing a story in an interactive video format recall more information than those reading a text version of the story" (p. 6). However, they pointed out that while understanding and remembering can be identified, applying it to other situations has not been evidenced. As they said about transfer of learning measures used, "Students taught with Jasper showed a small but insignificant improvement over control students on standardized tests, but performed better on word problems—and significantly better on subscores of planning problems than did students in control classrooms" (p. 6). However, evidence from Somekh et al. (2007) and Passey (2011d) suggests uses of some digital technologies, supported by appropriate teacher interventions and parent interventions, can lead to learning across contexts and at least some aspects of learning can be impacted.

Reported Levels of Impact

Identifying levels of impact of digital technologies on learners of this age range has been reported through a number of studies in the previous chapter. Additionally, Underwood (2009, p. 3), from across the range of studies conducted in the UK, reported impacts on attainment:

- At the end of Key Stage 1 (seven years of age):
  - 4.75 months of progress for high attaining girls in mathematics.

- ○ Improved progress for girls, as well as average and high attaining boys in science.
- ○ Improved progress for average and high attaining pupils in English.

- At the end of Key Stage 2 (11 years of age):
  - ○ A term of additional progress in English.
  - ○ 2.5 months of progress in writing for low attaining boys.
  - ○ 2.5 to 5 months of progress for some groups in mathematics through effective use of interactive whiteboards.
  - ○ 7.5 months of progress for some groups in science through effective use of interactive whiteboards.

Other studies have looked at uses of specific hardware devices. For example, Torff and Tirotta (2010), in a controlled study with 773 learners in upper elementary schools, showed those using interactive whiteboards reported more motivation, but the effect was weak, even when teachers were more positive, and McDonald and Howell (2012) in their study in Australia involved a class of 16 learners aged five to seven years in using a robotics tool, and identified outcomes in areas of literacy, numeracy, digital skills and engineering concepts during six weeks of use.

Other studies have explored digital technologies focused on digital resources. Chen, Liu, Shih, Wu, and Yuan (2011), in their study involving 33 grade 5 learners, explored uses of blogs and peer review, and found this combination led to enhanced quality of writing, offered practical advantages, aided editing and amendment, and offered scope to enable deeper and wider qualities and details to be included. Korat (2010) involved 40 learners aged five to six and 50 learners aged six to seven years in a controlled study in Israel showing reading an e-book led to significant gains in word meaning and word reading (especially for younger learners) when compared to the control group. Wood, Pillinger, and Jackson (2010) found early learners using talking books gained more in phonological awareness than learners in adult-led sessions, but adult tutoring appeared to suit more able readers better.

There are studies that have looked at other subject uses of digital technologies. Gallardo-Virgen and DeVillar (2011) in their study with 24 grade 4 learners showed collaborative work on science tasks using a single screen and an individual mouse led to higher levels of science knowledge and written work. Sung and Hwang (2013) explored the way a grid-based tool could support learners in science, enabling them to organise and share their knowledge and ideas leading to enhanced learning outcomes, while Fessakis, Gouli, and Mavroudi (2013) explored how five- to six-year-old learners tackled problem-solving tasks involving a Logo-based environment accessed via an interactive whiteboard, finding these learners could engage with mathematical, problem solving and social skills through this activity. Manches, O'Malley, and Benford (2010) studied how physical blocks affect the development of four- to eight-year-old learners' strategies in numerical partitioning, and found manipulation of groups of blocks is important but might be constrained by graphical interfaces. Korallo, Foreman, Boyd-Davis, Moar, and Coulson (2012) in their study involving 127 learners eight to nine years of age in the UK and the Ukraine, focusing on learning about historical chronology within a virtual environment, found the addition of active challenge to the environment had positive impacts, but only when learners were familiar with using the ICT.

In Summary

Evidence (from details in this section and in Chapter 3) about uses of digital technologies and outcomes for young learners can be summarised as follows:

- Topic-specific resources and software are used by teachers to support learners across this age range, but as age increases, so the choice of software moves more towards learner-centred use and away from teacher-centred use, especially when this relates to online games-based exercises.
- Curriculum-wide software is not used widely with this age group, but when it has been used in the past, some benefits have been identified over some time periods.
- Teaching-wide software, when planned to support appropriate activities, focusing on aspects of wider and deeper learning, and benefiting from appropriate teacher interventions, can lead to positive outcomes and benefits at megacognitive levels.
- Parent-involved software is being used increasingly with this age range of learners, and supportive forms of involvement of parents are being seen to enhance elements of learning and learning outcomes, in terms of understanding particularly.
- Curriculum-supportive online resources, when planned to support a long-term curriculum, focusing on aspects of wider and deeper learning, and supported with teacher interventions bringing out learner dialogue and discussion, have been shown to support megacognitive outcomes and impacts measured through levels of understanding and subject attainment.
- Online learner support has not been a strong focus with learners of this age range, but some schools are using these forms of activities through learning platforms and environments to enhance opportunities for learning, to reinforce and prolong engagement with activities undertaken initially and taken back to classrooms.
- Project and after-school club activities involving digital technologies are beginning to be explored with learners of this age range. Some projects evaluated have been shown to offer benefits at a megacognitive level, and to enhance awareness, understanding and engagement with learning.

Mainstream Secondary School or College Age Learners

This group, defined here as those aged 11 to 19 years of age in schools or colleges, generally attend classroom lessons or workshop sessions, and enjoy a full social life and a state of positive emotional well-being. As Bee (1997) says, puberty has been completed for young people by 19 years of age, some have consolidated formal cognitive operations, some have reached Kohlberg's stage 4 of "law and order", self-esteem has risen, and perhaps half of the young people have achieved a clear identity (p. 329).

Learners from 11 to 19 years of age are increasingly using specific and different forms of digital technologies, in both school and wider educational settings. Learner attitudes towards and skills with ICT have been shown to affect learning. Reed, Drijvers, and Kirschner (2010) studied 565 grade 7 and 8 students, aged 12 to 14 years, in 23 classes from one Belgian and seven Dutch secondary schools, and found learner attitudes accounted for a 3.4 point difference in test scores on a 10-point scale when using computers to learn the concept of function, but learners concerned about the tool rather than the mathematical aspects gained less.

There is increasing evidence reported of the long-term impacts arising from uses of digital technologies on this age group. For example, Huston, Anderson, Wright, Linebarger, and Schmitt (2001) reported that 15- to 19-year-old learners who had watched *Sesame Street* when they were up to five years of age, compared to those who had not, were gaining in terms of higher levels of attainment in English, mathematics and science. They were spending more of their own time reading books, and their self-perceptions of competence were higher.

Home Access and Uses in Secondary Schools

The commonly high levels of digital technology access and use by this age group of learners is demonstrated by a report from Ofcom (2012), indicating in the UK: home access to the internet grew from 85% to 90% between 2011 and 2012; average monthly hours online for 12- to 17-year-old boys was 15.8, and for girls was 14.5; and average monthly hours online for 18- to 24-year-old boys was 34.1, and for girls was 26.3. The same report indicated the most popular sites for 2- to 17-year-olds to access online were *YouTube*, *Google*, *Facebook* and the BBC, and the most popular sites for 18- to 24-year-olds were *YouTube*, *MSN/Windows Live/Bing*, *Facebook* and *Wikipedia*. Interestingly, while 98% of 16- to 24-year-olds owned a mobile telephone, and 66% of these were smartphones, 41% of 16- to 24-year-olds said they were addicted to the smartphone. Additionally, 91% of 16- to 24-year-olds had accessed the internet via some form of electronic device in 2011, and 78% of 15- to 24-year-olds used a social networking site.

Clearly home access for many young people is high. In terms of school access, however, a report from Infogroup/ORC International (2010), providing data about learners in secondary schools in England (11 to 18 years of age), provided a somewhat different picture. This report indicated the median pupil:computer ratio was 3.4:1, and while 93% of schools had a learning platform, 70% used it to communicate with learners, 55% for communication between learners, 81% for learners to download and upload homework, and 38% for live chat and discussion forums. Some 58% of schools agreed ICT had supported them in engaging parents in supporting learning, and 57% agreed ICT had supported them in engaging parents with forthcoming lessons and homework. But, only 19% of teachers used ICT for learners to download and upload homework most days of the week, 27% rarely or never did this, and 10% did not use ICT for this. Similarly, only 5% of teachers set homework requiring pupils to use the internet every day, 13% did this rarely, and 3% never did this.

By contrast, when evidence about impacts of using digital technologies with this age group is considered, the picture is positive. Livingstone (2012) offers an overview of evidence across OECD countries applying to secondary age school learners, saying "there is a positive association between the length of time of ICT use and students' performance in PISA mathematics tests. Particularly, broadband access in classrooms results in significant improvement in pupils' performance in national tests taken at age 16" (p. 12). So, in spite of learners who might want to use ICT to support their learning, and forms of ICT can support aspects of learning, teachers appear from the evidence above to be limiting uses of ICT. Nevertheless, uses and outcomes are reported widely.

An issue raised by teachers often is the concern that digital technologies are not supporting learners when preparing for examinations. Indeed, Liao (2007), who adopted meta-analysis as an approach to explore impacts on learning, found an effect size of 0.55 for impact of CAI compared to teacher instruction overall, but "the smallness of the ES associated with high school subjects (10th–12th graders) is probably due to the fact that these students have to study very hard for a nationwide college-entrance-examination in Taiwan" (p. 226). The author argued in this context CAI might not be accepted as a sensible or most beneficial approach, but he also suggested these learners might be involved in different pedagogical approaches.

Subject Level Outcomes

In the same article, Liao (2007) indicated subject impact (impacts of uses of digital technologies according to subject) can vary, and this factor needs to be considered when exploring outcomes arising from uses of digital technologies. Some studies have highlighted affordances supporting and enhancing subject learning for those in this age group. Hathorn and Rawson (2012) found reading of computer-based text by undergraduate students improved mental models of topics when prompts supported monitoring and 'big' picture views, while questions about the topic were less effective. Broma, Preuss, and Klement (2011) explored use of a micro-game following a lecture with five classes of learners in four high schools across the Czech Republic, and found while there was no immediate gain in knowledge compared to those using digital media accessible online, longer-term retention was significantly improved. Yilmaz and Kiliç-Çakmak (2012) in their study involved four grade 8 classes of learners 13 to 14 years of age, and found interface agents in digital programs worked best and led to higher achievement and retention of science and technology facts and understanding if they were in human form. Bertacchini, Bilotta, Pantano, and Tavernise (2012) in their study involved 30 high school students aged 16 to 18 years in using a 3D interactive learning environment offering instruction and enabled them to create theatre-style displays about chaos using a range of artefacts; results showed they gained more knowledge than those involved in traditional lessons.

Some studies have looked at literacy skills and their development with this age group. Woody, Daniel, and Baker (2010) studied university students and found they did not prefer e-books to textbooks, and this was irrespective of gender, levels of computer use or ease of using computers. However, Yang and Wu

(2012), in their study involving 110 grade 10 learners in senior high schools, found digital storytelling led to gains in terms of language test results, critical thinking and positive motivation when compared to learners involved in lecture-style sessions.

Studies have looked at other subject areas also. Hauptman and Cohen (2011), in a controlled study involving 192 10th graders in the learning of geometry and enhancement of spatial thinking, indicated the virtual environment used decreased the gap in performance between visual and kinaesthetic learners, and highlighted the importance of virtual environments for those with emotional and kinaesthetic styles. In this context, Wengenroth et al. (2010) in their study explored uses of four virtual patients to alert learners 13 to 16 years of age to facts and issues concerned with occupational diseases and prevention.

In terms of impacts arising, Underwood (2009), from across a range of studies conducted in the UK, reported uses of digital technologies provided:

- At the end of Key Stage 3 (by 14 years of age):
  - Gains equivalent to a term of additional progress in science.
- At the end of Key Stage 4 (by 16 years of age):
  - An average gain in national science examinations equivalent to 52,484 students moving from a 'fail' grade of D to a 'pass' grade of C.
  - Gains in the overall percentage of learners gaining highest level national subject examinations the year after broadband was introduced.
  - For those with a computer at home, a positive association between national examination results, amounting to an equivalent of some two examination grades.

In the context of subject gains, Shieh (2012) described how a pedagogical approach using digital technologies enhanced learning of physics. The author described the approach as provision of media-rich resources in the forms of simulations and visualisations to support topic aspects of learning. The instructional approach involved small-group work, active learning and discussion. Interactions and discussions were supported through uses of an interactive response or voting system, so the tutor could ask questions, and immediately gain answers picked up with learners individually or as a group. The aim was to adopt a method to deepen understanding, at conceptual and analytical levels. The author (Shieh, 2012) described the findings of the study, saying "the TEAL class outperformed the two control classes . . . the TEAL students, in general, appeared to be interested in attending the physics class, and were also more active in participating in science activities outside the class" (p. 212). Additionally, it was found teachers were affected in terms of their ideas for teaching by practices they experienced.

This study highlights the importance of teacher interaction and pedagogical approaches on learner outcomes, and suggests needs for a match between digital technological potential to learner expectations if impacts are to arise in ways to support learning and measureable through standard test instruments. Geer and Sweeney (2012), for example, argue that wide experiences and access of learners in schools in Australia means they "have preconceived ideas of what technologies they can expect to use in the classroom and how they will learn. Our schools are slowly changing but are struggling to understand what a contemporary learning environment might look like" (p. 294).

Focusing on Higher Order Skills and Critical Thinking

In terms of learning gains at secondary school level, McMahon (2009) argued digital technologies should be used widely across schools to develop critical thinking and higher order skills. His study explored the relationship in one school between a technology-rich environment and higher order (or critical) thinking skills developed in learners. Correlation analyses allowed factors where relationships existed to be identified. He found statistically significant correlation results associated with a number of factors: "Length of time spent in the environment has a positive, non-linear effect on the development of critical thinking skills. Students with better developed computing skills scored higher on critical thinking activities" (p. 269). He found in the latter case significant association related to those learners with higher levels of computer programming skills, and abilities to manipulate Boolean logic. He argued that "schools should integrate technology across all of the learning areas. This will allow students to apply technology to the attainment of higher levels of cognition within specific contexts" (p. 269). His conclusion was based on a key finding: "Students with better computing skills demonstrate a higher level of critical thinking" (p. 280). Findings from other studies, and indeed from meta-analyses and second order meta-analyses, indicate measurable test outcomes are enhanced when digital technologies are used—although, as an important rider, studies also indicate the nature of teacher interactions and pedagogies used are important contributing factors.

Other studies have highlighted how digital technologies can be involved in supporting higher order thinking and metacognitive skills. Chen, Lambert, and Guidry (2010) found learners accessing internet-based resources tended to score higher in traditional achievement measures, but were more likely to be involved in higher order thinking, reflective practices, and to integrate knowledge and ideas more. L.-H. Chen (2010) showed with 105 university students in central Taiwan the important differences between field-independent learners who focus on online content and analyse its use, and field-dependent learners who like to see a 'big picture' in order to understand the learning content in context. Laxman (2010) involved a class of 25 first-year polytechnic students in Singapore, and found information searching skills played an important role in problem solving, especially as information needs to address ill-structured problems were often complex, so learners needed more advanced information searching skills. Zhang and Quintana (2012) found grade 6 learners using a software tool to scaffold online inquiry gained in terms of efficiency, focus and metacognitive approaches. Snodin (2013) found, in a study of 28 university students in Thailand, that a course management system could support autonomous learning, especially once initial ideas about practices had been provided by a teacher. Ellis, Goodyear, Bliuc, and Ellis (2011) in their study of responses from 300 learners in high schools in Australia, exploring ways they used the internet, indicated the importance of integrating sources of information, and highlighted the need for pedagogic and learning focus on the knowledge handling processes of synthesis.

In Summary

Evidence (from details in this section and in Chapter 3) of uses of digital technologies with secondary school age learners can be summarised as follows:

- Topic-specific resources and software have been used in many subject areas such as algebra, geometry, historical events, geographical locations, art awareness and appreciation, and musical activities, to support learners.
- Curriculum-wide software has been used in the past, more widely than currently, consequently perhaps as other forms of software such as learning platforms have become more prevalent and have offered wider forms of activities.
- Teaching-wide software has been used in some subject areas (largely in mathematics) to support subject learning, and benefits have been shown in the literature.
- Parent-involved software is less in evidence with this age group. As the roles of learners and parents shift during adolescence, so the involvement of parents often becomes shifted, and there is less connection and use of technologies demonstrated (although parental involvement tends to increase when learners approach examination time).
- Curriculum-supportive online resources are accessed by many teachers across a variety of subject areas. The influence of these resources on learning, and their impacts on learning effectiveness, has been demonstrated across many subjects.
- Online learner support has been increasingly used by learners across this age group. Some impacts have been demonstrated. The increasing take-up by learners outside the school system will be considered further within the next and concluding chapters.
- Project and after-school club activities involving digital technologies have been used with this age range of learners, and have led to important outcomes of a social and team-working nature, as well as of a cognitive or metacognitive or megacognitive nature.

Learners with Physical Disabilities or Attributes

Learners with physical disabilities and attributes may be limited in terms of a full range of sensory or physical engagement open to them, but educational opportunities can be widened or more accessible through uses of specifically-designed assistive or access technologies (see, for example, Abbott, 2007). Although the focus on assistive technologies is not the main focus of this book, this does play a significant role in the overall engagement of many young people in this wide group. Many young people with physical disabilities gain access to learning in special schools or in specifically designed or supported training sessions; in these settings they may use assistive technologies such as switches, a switch-adapted mouse, keyboard converters, text-to-speech software, voice recognition and word prediction software, text-to-Braille convertors, screen readers, screen magnifiers, or amplification systems.

Special Schools and Assistive Technologies

Schools specialising in the support of young people with physical disabilities often have digital technologies accessible to their learners. Infogroup/ORC International (2010) reported that in all special schools in England (covering emotional and behavioural as well as physical needs), 67% had assistive technologies to support physical access, and 65% had assistive technologies to support sensory access.

Uses of some technologies are wider than others. As Abbott (2007) argues, "Switch access is well established, although still under-researched, with much of the literature dealing with switch use in everyday life rather than specifically for learning" (p. 17). He goes on to say that "switch control of a computer can be very time-consuming, but for some users it is the only route to relatively independent control" (p. 17), but also provides an example of a digital technology addressing this issue: "Innovative software can enable switch users to develop surprisingly rapid text output; Dasher (www.inference.phy.cam. ac.uk/dasher), for example, uses prediction, colour and movement to enable writers" (p. 17).

Emerging digital technologies are being applied as assistive technologies in some cases. Standen, Camma, Battersby, Brown, and Harrison (2011) explored the development of a *Wii Nunchuk* to replace traditional switches, trialled with 23 learners 17 to 21 years of age, leading to improvement in access for some learners, making this a potentially important alternative device.

Other studies report applications of digital technologies to support learning in specific cases of physical need; uses of digital technologies to support learning for those with acquired brain injury, for example. Montero, López-Jaquero, Navarro, and Sánchez (2011) explored use of a computer-based tool to support relearning basic motor, sensory and cognitive skills, and found it was accepted by younger people, improved their motivation, and reduced activity times. In supporting development of physical features such as balance, Vernadakis, Gioftsidou, Antoniou, Ioannidis, and Giannousi (2012), in a study involving 32 undergraduate students at a university in Greece, showed that a *Nintendo Wii* training programme was as effective as a traditional training programme.

Limited Access and its Implications

It is important to recognise that beyond access to digital resources enabled through assistive technologies, learners with physical disabilities also need ICT skills to use digital technologies to provide access to learning opportunities. A recent study in Sweden (Lidström, Granlund, &Hemmingsson, 2012) indicated while learners with physical disabilities might be supported through assistive digital technologies (ATD), they might also have lower levels of access to activities involving computers when compared to other mainstream users and "used the computer for less varied educational activities than the reference group" (p. 21). The authors identified four important factors positively affecting levels of access to computer-based activities: attendance at a mainstream school that had resources available; their age (16 to 18 years); regularity of using a computer within a school; and frequency with which teachers used computers in their teaching. They concluded: "regardless of whether they use a computer-based ATD or not, students with a physical disability have restricted participation in some computer-based educational activities in comparison to students from the general population" (p. 21).

Learning Support for those with Hearing Impairment

Some studies have looked at how forms of digital technology might support learning for those with hearing impairment (HI), and have shown benefits arising. Yang and Lay (2005) reported findings from a study exploring use of a computer-based system to support learning of pronunciation of phonemes in Mandarin. As the authors stated (Yang & Lay, 2005), "Deaf or hearing-impaired people have difficulty hearing their own voice, hence most of them cannot learn how to speak" (p. 537). The authors looked at impact of a voice-recognition system to support learners with HI, describing affordances of the system as follows: "The system analyses the spoken Mandarin phoneme of a hearing-impaired person, compares it with the phonemes database, and shows the results on the computer monitor . . . the system automatically gives the learner a percentage score for each phoneme" (p. 537). The authors explored uses with high school students, and found: "After five months, most learners can pronounce 95% of the phonemes correctly" (p. 537).

Using a different form of digital technology, Liu and Hong (2007) studied uses of smartphones to support learning beyond classrooms for those with HI. As they outlined: "A significant challenge for teachers is to provide after-class learning care and assistance to hearing impaired students that sustain their motivation to participate in continuous learning activities" (p. 727). The authors created a system using smartphones and the General Packet Radio Service (GPRS) network. Both teachers and parents welcomed the system, and from their study of outcomes the authors concluded: "Most student parents considered after-class student–teacher interaction and strategies effective in improving student learning at home . . . students achieved a better homework completion rate when the teacher used smart phones and the GPRS ubiquitous network to provide learning support" (p. 740).

In another area of development, Hussein, Abo-Darwish, and Al-Atiat (2010) reported uses of an e-dictionary translating "online any text or paragraph into multiple modes of communication (sign language with lip movement and finger spelling)" (p. 646). Although there were clear limitations in terms of the facilities offered at that stage of development, the authors concluded such a facility could help learners who were HI, particularly if "real voice, his sign language action and lip movement can together" be provided for the learner (p. 651).

In terms of enhancing access to sound for those with partial hearing, Dockrell and Shield (2012) evaluated uses of sound-field systems on learning and attention in primary schools. As they said, "Both teacher ratings and student performance on standardized tests indicated that sound-field systems improved performance on children's understanding of spoken language. However, academic attainments showed no benefits from the use of sound-field systems" (p. 1163). As the authors went on to say, learners who were in classroom settings with poor acoustics gained in terms of listening comprehension when the sound-systems were used, but for those classrooms with better acoustics the sound-systems did not offer any advantage.

Digital technologies have also been developed to support music learning needs for those with HI. Yang, Lay, Liou, Tsao, and Lin (2007) explored use of a computer-aided music-learning system (CAMLS) for the HI, stating: "This system can be a computer-supported learning tool for the hearing impaired to help them understand what pitch and tempo are, and then learn to play songs thereby increasing their interest in music classes and enhancing their learning performance" (p. 466). The authors indicated their system provided an "instant feedback mechanism for hearing impaired students in the form of automatic assessment of their learning performance. This allowed the hearing impaired students to not only custom-tailor their learning conditions, but also provide[d] immediate, comprehensive information about their learning performance" (p. 474). The authors used experimental and control groups to test impact of the system, and found those "who received learning guidance by CAMLS made significant progress compared with the traditionally instructed T group . . . Further, a t-test . . . was applied and found a significant learning difference between the two groups" (p. 474).

An alternative approach has been to support more text-based interactions for those with hearing impairment. Al-Bayati and Hussein (2009) studied effects of e-tutorials on the motivation of learners who were HI. Their results indicated e-tutorials could be beneficial for learners who were HI, but "HI students are not comfortable with finger spelling as mode of communication in teaching process particularly HI students at primary level standard school" (p. 196) and "it is very hard for HI student to use e-lessons alone without the help of teacher" (p. 197). Snoddon (2010) reported a study looking at "the production of ASL [American Sign Language] identity texts by elementary students in grades two, three, and five (approximately seven to ten years of age)" (p. 197). In this study the ASL curriculum used in the Ontario provincial schools for deaf learners was used as a basis for project activities developed and used in classrooms with learners. Digital technology was integrated into curriculum activities in order to support both engagement and ASL literacy skills. The author concluded from the study that having older deaf adults in a classroom as storytellers, having the teacher supporting discussions about culture and identity concerned with deafness and language, and having the teacher guide and explore ideas and concepts through the storytelling "fostered students' identity investment and cognitive engage-ment in their own stories. These conditions also reveal the benefits of technology as a learning tool for ASL literacy" (p. 210).

At a broader level, El Emary and Hussein (2012) explored a taxonomy of learners who were HI, to look at ways different e-learning resources might be presented to better match their specific needs. These authors classified HI learners as follows:

- HI 1—able to hear only partially and to speak at a low level or early stage.
- HI 2—able to hear only partially and to speak at a higher level or later stage.
- HI 3—not able to hear but able to speak at a low level or early stage.
- HI 4—not able to hear but able to speak at a higher level or later stage.
- HI 5—not able to hear and not able to speak.

The authors usefully detailed the ways different forms of e-learning resources could be provided in order to meet the needs of these five categories. They detailed specific design needs for tutorials, drill and practice resources, problem-solving resources, tests, instructional games, and simulations. They also explored ways teaching strategies could match learner needs and categories, and forms of communication and learning processes matching the needs and characteristics of each group.

Learning Support for those with Visual Impairment

In terms of those with visual impairment (VI), far fewer studies have been reported, especially those focusing on enhancing learning. Some studies have explored uses of digital technologies including learners with VI, rather than focusing entirely on this group. As Ko, Chiang, Lin, and Chen (2011) said, "it is difficult for learners with special needs to read effectively due to their limitations or disabilities, such as dyslexia, intellectual disability, visual impairment, visual perception difficulties, or palsy" (p. 88). They went on to describe the range of assistive technology devices available to learners to support reading: "e-readers, screen-magnifying software, and adaptive computer devices" (p. 88). As they said, e-readers can read out a text, screen-magnifying software can enlarge characters, and a switch with scanning facility can support those with motor impairment, but "However effective these methods may be, they are of little use for the cognitively challenged, especially for those lacking lexical knowledge" (p. 88) and the authors argued for those learners: "Extra support should include the following: presenting important concepts with pictures, audios, and videos; or teaching students to read concept maps instead of drawing" (p. 88). They argued bottom-up and top-down support approaches are both needed: "The supports of the bottom-up approach include pictures, speeches, texts, and videos for key words; adjusting attribution of text; and supplying alternative representations for the text" (p. 88), while "The top-down approach provides concept maps, text summarization, and background knowledge" (p. 89).

In their study, the authors explored use of a system to support key needs of a range of learners: "This experiment aimed to explore whether the cognitive support features in the TriAccess system could assist students with learning disabilities in comprehending articles. . . . A two-factor within-subject experiment was conducted" (p. 94). Their results from the study "indicated better reading performance when the students employed cognitive supports" (p. 96). As they went on to say, the effects were based on a degree of personalisation—learners could choose preferred font size, spacing and colour. But the study did not explore specific effects on individuals as a result of choices by learners.

In another study looking at challenges for those including learners with VI, Stewart II, Choi, and Mallery (2010) investigated "whether academic outcomes (course grades) differ when taking online and traditional courses, among students with and without disabilities" (p. 27). In this study, 3,078 undergraduate and graduate students, largely of Black ethnic background, attended a college on the east coast of the US. The authors used linear modelling to analyse their results, and to look for relationships between impairment and outcomes, controlling for background factors such as socio-economic status. Their results indicated that "students with disabilities may perform better in online courses than traditional courses" (p. 27). The authors drew a number of conclusions: "These findings run contrary to the implication of the intercept as outcome model, which indicated that the average student—not accounting for disability status— is more than likely to achieve higher scores in traditional courses" (p. 36), but "this is not indicative of poor performance in traditional settings" (p. 36) and they would suggest online provision as an option "among individuals whose physical and environmental challenges (e.g., limited public transportation in a rural area) have historically hampered post-secondary options" (p. 36).

Those with VI clearly face a range of significant challenges with regard to learning. As Siu and Lam (2012) said: "Although computer assisted learning (CAL) is becoming increasingly popular, people with visual impairment face greater difficulty in accessing computer assisted learning facilities. This is primarily because most of the current CAL facilities are not visually impaired friendly" (p. 295). The results of their case study in Hong Kong showed "children with visual impairment often need to spend more time and take special care in learning because learning materials only tend to be provided in visual format" (p. 302). They argued extending access to CAL facilities would be of value to those with VI, as they would not then need to spend time accessing facilities that were only accessible in public settings. They also highlighted the need for a balance between personal access to CAL facilities and support and learning happening within wider social settings, saying "It is not helpful to isolate children with visual impairment from other learners, as they need to be able to share their knowledge and experience. It is particularly important for young children to learn under guidance and sharing" (p. 302). The authors raised the issue of high costs of equipment designed for a specific small market, and value gained from publicly accessible facilities.

The evidence indicates learners with VI require more support through uses of digital technologies than is being provided for currently. Kelly and Wolffe (2012) studied patterns of access and use of the internet by learners with VI. They concluded from their study that "an average of 43% of the transition-aged youths with visual impairments used the Internet regularly for online communication" (p. 597). Their study also showed this level did not shift significantly as the learners matured, and those learners who used the internet regularly were more likely to be engaged after school in work ($p = 0.01$), in further education or in training ($p = 0.01$), or in volunteer work or community service ($p = 0.01$). The study found learners at the youth transition with VI were not progressing in the same way as learners without VI. Indeed, using the measures of performance in the study, the highest performance for learners with VI was 49%, compared to a 93% performance level for those without VI. The authors concluded: "Transition-aged youths with visual impairments who had worked at a paid job since high school or volunteered in the community were about two times as likely to have used the Internet as were youths who did not" (p. 604). They compared levels for those who were engaged in further education or vocational training, and in this case the difference was five-fold rather than two-fold. Engagement with digital technologies is clearly a predictive indicator; supporting engagement as well as associated attitudes and skills for those with VI could clearly support later engagement in a range of societal interests and endeavours. In this context,

Freire, Linhalis, Bianchini, Fortes, and Pimentel (2010) described how a mediator provided descriptions of a software resource displayed on an interactive whiteboard to support learners who were blind, and Levy and Lahav (2012) looked at how a sound-based mediation system could support learning for blind people, showing for four people studied there was a gain in terms of greater connections of representations, conceptual knowledge and detail about the topic. In terms of enhancing independence, Abbott (2007) highlighted how "Handheld devices that help blind people to know where they are, for example, are now being used in pilot research to assist people with learning difficulties in Gothenburg, Sweden, to become more independent when away from home (Lindstrom 2007)" (p. 18), and Sánchez and Sáenz (2010) described a mobile tool designed to help people who were blind to use the Metro system in Santiago de Chile and, using control groups with five learners in each group, found the system supported cognitive and sensory skills as well as psychomotor skills enhancing orientation and mobility.

In Summary

Evidence of uses of digital technologies and outcomes for those with physical impairment or features can be summarised as follows:

- Topic-specific resources and software have been used to support learners with HI and physical disabilities, but are less frequently identified in the literature for those with VI.
- Curriculum-wide software has been shown to be less successful when used by learners in settings where they are isolated or working alone.
- Teaching-wide software has been used effectively with all groups of learners, but the forms of e-learning activity may need to be carefully considered and matched to more specific learner needs and characteristics.
- Parent-involved software has been explored with learners with HI on smartphones, with some success.
- Curriculum-supportive online resources have been used more with learners who are HI, while issues of access have been identified more for learners with VI.
- Online learner support and project and after-school club activities involving digital technologies have not been identified from the literature with these groups of learners.

Learners Not Physically Present in Classrooms or Lessons

Learners not physically present in classrooms or lessons can face particular and wide challenges accessing educational opportunity. Non-presence may result from home schooling, absenteeism (either temporary or permanent, being hospitalised, in motherhood, involved in family care or homeless), or exclusions from schools (for behavioural reasons, where alternative provision for continuing learning is often offered, or perhaps being in prison). In terms of home schooling, digital technologies are used routinely in some instances to support home learning (through Schools of the Air in Australia, for example). Other examples of educational digital technologies enhancing educational provision for those who are home-schooled are reported by Lines (2001): "Alaska sponsors the Alyeska Central School, where teachers in Juneau work with students all over the state via mail, the Internet, telephone, and occasional home visits. In California, children can enroll in a public school's independent study program" (p. 2). The author, in reviewing results of attainment of home-schooled learners compared to traditionally supported learners, concluded, from data available (which might not present an entire picture), that "homeschoolers do well. For example, in Alaska, the state's Alyeska Central School has tested its homeschooling children for several decades. As a group they usually score above average in any subject area and at all grade levels" (p. 2).

Learners Excluded from Schools

For those young people whose periods of exclusion may start with levels of truancy from school, Underwood (2009), from across a range of studies conducted in the UK, reported young people with computers at home played truant less: "For example, having access to a computer at home is associated with a 5.8% reduction in the likelihood of playing truant at age 16" (p. 3).

In the UK, learners excluded from a school (due to behavioural issues, perhaps arising due to unforeseen home or personal circumstances), are often referred to a centre called a pupil referral unit (PRU) (also termed an alternative school or short-stay school). This centre supports a small number of learners, working with teachers or tutors sometimes on a one-to-one basis. These centres often use digital technologies to help to engage learners in subject or topic work. Passey, Rogers, Machell, and McHugh (2004) found teachers in one PRU were using digital technologies to engage learners, and found effects were positive, both on learning engagement and in enhancing social engagement with others. This was also found to be the case in a PRU using a virtual learning environment (VLE), reported by Passey (2011e), and in the case of a PRU enabling groups of learners to create video-game levels (Passey, 2012b). In the latter case, social outcomes were identified particularly strongly; the teacher in this school took the project forward to support specific needs of the learners—developing social skills and sharing practices, which learners found difficult. The learners were recognised as having low self-esteem, and they did not easily work in groups, even when using ICT. The project was run in one-hour-long ICT lessons, with learners spending half the time playing the video game, and half the time researching and planning. The teacher found the project generated a great deal of speaking and listening; the learners were found to express themselves more easily, took turns playing the game and helped each other, rather than taking control. One learner who took a lead role, for example, demonstrated the control of the game to another student—a practice not previously seen in lessons.

In contrast, Cranmer (2010), however, also studying learning in PRUs, found that learners said they lacked motivation in general, and "this is reflected by a corresponding lack of motivation to learn technologies, such as the internet, to support either school work or to enhance their own hobbies and interests" (p. 191). Cranmer also found informal learning was not an aspect appealing to all young people, and use of the internet to extend their learning or interests was not a direction appealing to all.

Young Offenders

For young offenders, some prisons provide learning support through forms of digital technologies. Schuller (2009) reported on all age groups in the UK, rather than young offenders in particular, stating: "The Prisoners' Education Trust (PET) estimates that at least 4,000 prisoners are studying by distance learning" (p. 22). He went on to say PET funds over 2,000 prisoners alone every year for distance education courses ranging across more than 200 subject areas. Most of these are concerned with vocation and employment, and the major provider is the Open University (with over 1,000 prisoners studying their courses). Schuller (2012) also stated: "Distance learning, along with e-learning, is a recognised element in the OLASS [Offender Learning and Skills Service] policy document, The Offender Learning Journey, yet distance learning is not available other than to a tiny minority or through charitable funding" (p. 22). LearnDirect, another course provider, maintains secure internet access in a number of prisons, enabling access for some 3,000 prisoners to learning. This provider ran a pilot from 2005, for two years, offering over 400 courses and online access to tests and examinations. The report highlighted the need for more qualified staff to support learning in prisons through this route, and for wider access to ICT across more prisons.

The content and discussion included in a sub-section on learners involved in criminal activity, in the next section, relates also to this group.

Those who are Hospitalised

Those who are hospitalised face two major challenges with regard to learning: access to learning provision distant to them and located in classrooms; and access to those who can support learning through tutoring or mediation. Janssens, Brijs, and Van den Branden (2010) described a project in Belgium seeking to link learners who were in hospital with their classrooms: "Bednet is an organisation that enables children and youngsters with a long term or chronic illness to connect to their mainstream school from hospital or home" (p. 179). The system relied on a broadband internet connection, offering communication between the classroom or school and the young person in the hospital. Specific hardware and software was used for this purpose, and linked the young person with classmates outside and inside lessons. As the authors said: "This limits or even avoids not only school retardation, but it also contributes to the child's healing by supporting a goal-oriented motivation and diverts the child's focus from illness and its consequences to a more 'normal' life" (p. 179). The authors highlighted the avoidance of isolation and exclusion through use of this system. The interface used aimed to mirror the learner's home work-desk, and supported access to "IT-based learning resources, the IP-videoconferencing tools, and the remote access by teacher and child of scanners and printers at the school and the child site for the exchange of documents, assignments and exercises" (p. 180). As the authors said, young people attending large hospitals may be able to attend a hospital school, but for those in smaller hospitals or receiving treatment at home, this form of provision is not available. The system had been running for four years when the authors reported their study, and, at any one time the system supported some 120 learners, although the number of applicants to use the system was greater than the number able to be supported. The authors reported findings showing the system contributed to social inclusion, allowing learners to maintain their courses of study and attainments, and allowing contacts between them and their classmates to be maintained during school time.

In the State of Victoria in Australia, the Department of Education and Early Childhood Development set up a pilot study using iPads in the Royal Children's Hospital (iPads for Learning, n.d.). Their website detailed the pilot through a number of case studies. One case study described how a 16-year-old young person had been in a ward for more than 200 days; with limited physical and communication capabilities, she was not able to easily make contact with other young people, and was constantly supported by staff in the ward. Having an iPad supported her therapy, by encouraging her to apply pressure to the screen through her fingertips, and supported communication with staff through the text to speech facility. Two applications, *Doodle Buddy* and *Scrabble*, enabled her to access school work. Additionally, she used email to communicate with her classmates, and used an application enabling her to continue a course in Mandarin.

In this example digital technology is being used to support at a range of levels—in cognitive terms, through engagement, providing distance connection with courses and materials, and in social terms, as a means to connect to support staff, other young people and school. In other examples provided on this website, one important factor discussed is the way involvement with learning through digital technologies takes the child's mind away from their direct concerns about their health, and this itself is reported as having a positive effect.

Young Mothers and those Involved in Family Care

For young mothers, or girls pregnant at school, the literature does not offer clear examples of how digital technologies have been used to support engagement with education and learning. While there are few references also to digital technologies being used to support young people who are involved in family care, one article (Hanson, Magnusson, & Sennemark, 2011) described a study looking at uses of a blended learning environment with older people cared for by family members and care providers. The study described was "Blended Learning Networks (BLNs) whose aim is to enable older people, their families, and care providers to exchange knowledge, learn together, and support each other in local development work so that care is improved for older people" (p. 561). The authors highlighted particular impacts on shared practices, leading to wider awareness and understanding, concluding that "BLNs act as a useful model for knowledge exchange concerning a complex topic and involving a wide range of stakeholders" (p. 570). The authors stated shared understanding allowed all involved to explore areas of fruitful developments locally, and particularly enabled both care providers and the elderly people to 'have a voice', so their views were valued and used by others involved.

Those who are Homeless

For young people who are homeless, an alternative form of technology to support their needs was reported by Hendry, Woelfer, Harper, Bauer, Fitzer, and Champage (2011). They described the project, specifically for young people aged 13 to 25 years, designed through a curriculum called *New Tech for Youth Sessions*. As they said, "Motivated by the ordinariness of digital media and its importance in communicating with society's institutions, the primary goal of the curriculum was to develop students' life skills for information technology and digital media" (p. 774). The authors described how a community technology centre was used, where homeless young people could drop in and be guided through the curriculum through a series of activities, related to employment, but also "A crucial secondary goal was to position students to recognize their self-worth, through meeting challenges, positive communication with adults, and reciprocal peer support" (p. 774). The authors concluded that "based on extensive professional experience we are cautiously optimistic: We do believe that instruction in information technology and digital media can be used to position young people to experience feelings of self-worth" (p. 781). The authors recommended programmes to support homeless young people should consider how digital technologies can support "ordinary communication, personal development, education, and access to information and services held by institutions" (p. 781). The authors argued community technology centres with drop-in facilities can both be recognised by those on the street as being accessible to them, while at the same time providing a link back to a mainstream.

In Summary

Evidence of uses of digital technologies and outcomes by learners who are not physically present in classrooms can be summarised as follows:

- Topic-specific resources and software have been used in a range of situations to engage young people not physically present, more through the use of CD-ROMs in the past and more through the use of specific online resources currently.
- Curriculum-wide software has been used in the past to support engagement with young people who are in short-stay or PRUs, but this practice appears to have diminished somewhat, while courses to support those in prison, for example, have been used in a range of cases.
- Teaching-wide software is not generally accessible to these groups of young people.
- Parent-involved software can be used, and particularly by those who are home-schooled.
- Curriculum-supportive online resources are not commonly accessible (except through projects or pilots) to these groups of young people, but, with support from community centres or online tutors, it would be possible for young people to gain access to resources such as *Mathletics* or *Khan Academy*.

- Online learner support is used effectively with some of these groups of young people, while others (such as those who are teenage mothers) appear not to have been involved in projects focusing on uses of these digital technologies.
- Project and after-school club activities involving digital technologies have been used to effectively engage and benefit some groups of young people who are in PRUs rather than in mainstream schools.

Learners with Challenging Emotional Features and Attributes

Learners exhibiting emotional features and attributes will be considered in this section: shyness; withdrawal; emotional distraction; choosing to be elective mute; and those with mental illness. These learners can experience similar challenges (sometimes linked to or associated with those facing social or cognitive challenges) when engaging with education.

Some studies have indicated positive emotions generally are supported through uses of digital technologies. For example, Chen and Sun (2012) in their study explored uses of different digital media with learners identified as visualisers and verbalisers, and found video-based materials supported learning outcomes and positive emotions for verbalisers, while visualisers worked better with video and animation.

Anxiety

In terms of learners across the whole group, lowering of anxiety may be a key need, which could possibly be supported by appropriate uses of digital technologies. In the context of dental anxiety, Salam, Yahaya, and Ali (2010) posed the problem as follows: "Lack of confidence is one of a common factor of children's dental anxiety and potentially distressing problem for both the children and the dental practitioner" (p. 173). So, "Based on the issues posed previously, we developed a persuasive technology application named a persuasive multimedia environment (PMLE) which provides a self-mechanism for children to overcome their anxiety with assisting from their parents or teachers" (p. 176). From the study, they found positive results, stating the test taken before and after the intervention session showed, by comparison, "statistic difference, indicating that PMLE was effective. Participants changed their anxiety feelings in the intended directions, reducing anxiety feelings in children dental anxiety test result, with the opposite pattern for the baseline test" (p. 180).

Shyness

Learning environments and online discussion forums have been shown (Passey, 2007) to be used more by and to benefit learners who exhibit traits of shyness, evidenced both from self-reports and reports from teachers. On the other hand, Öztürk and Özmen (2011) concluded from their study of university-level students studying education, in the context of developing problems with internet use such as addiction or problem behaviours, that "lying, neuroticism and shyness were significant predictors in terms of problematical Internet use" (p. 1806).

In terms of primary school age learners who might be shy, Higgins, Mercier, Burd, and Joyce-Gibbons (2012) in their study looked at uses of multi-touch tables by 10- to 11-year-old learners engaged on a history task, and found interactions and collaborations between learners were effectively supported. Across a wider age range, Gamage, Tretiakov, and Crump (2011), from feedback from teachers using multi-user virtual environments, reported shy students were more likely to engage in interactions online with both teachers and peers. In terms of affordances supporting this engagement, AbuSeileek (2012) in a study involving 216 undergraduates at a university in Jordan showed, when using collaborative facilities to support language learning, students preferred to make their identities anonymous in order to reduce anxiety.

Withdrawal

In terms of the attribute of withdrawal (manifest through low engagement or attendance), many studies have identified enhancement of engagement with learning through different forms of technology (for example, Passey et al., 2004). In terms of attendance, even in the context of a university, with students studying business courses, Lavin, Korte, and Davies (2010) concluded from their study: "Overall there are certain aspects of student behavior (the amount of time that students study, the quantity of notes they take, their attendance, and their interaction with the instructor) which appear to be technology neutral" (p. 1). However, they went on to say that there were identifiable impacts in cases of "student preparation for class, attentiveness, quality of notes taken, student participation in class, student learning, desire to take additional classes from the instructor or in the subject matter, and the overall evaluation of the course and the instructor" (p. 1). But, other studies offer quite different perspectives. Zavarella and Ignash (2009), for example, looking at retention of students in a university mathematics course, concluded: "Students in the computer-based format were more likely to withdraw from the course compared to those in the lecture-based format, and personal reasons for choosing a specific format appeared to influence completion rates" (p. 2). The authors suggested more detailed information should be given to students prior to their involvement in courses, particularly if they involve online learning.

The relationship between engagement with literacy and longer-term success has been pointed to in a number of studies, and withdrawal has also been considered in contexts of low literacy engagement. As Sheng, Sheng, and Anderson (2011) said, "ELL students [English language learners for whom English is not their first language] scored consistently lower in reading and in mathematics than non-ELL students . . . The relationship of poor academic achievement and high dropout rates has been well documented empirically" (p. 99) and "academic achievement, typically assessed with standardized achievement tests or grade point average (GPA), has consistently been one of the strongest predictors of dropping out of high school" (p. 100).

Emotional Distraction

In terms of affective attributes, effects of digital technologies in supporting engagement of learners emotionally distracted, perhaps due to certain home or personal circumstances (which might range from having parents who are substance abusers to having just fallen out with a best friend), is documented in a number of reports and studies. For example, Dangwal and Sharma (2013) reported on women surviving violence and living in sheltered homes in India, and the effects of them being provided with computer-based informal learning; within six months of access being provided, the women were engaging in uses for both recreational and educational purposes, enabling them to develop interests beyond their immediate situations and circumstances.

In the context of nursing education, and emotional distraction relating to using online environments, Reilly, Gallagher-Lepak, and Killion (2012), reported that "Pedagogical strategies that foster a sense of community in online courses between students and faculty enhance cognition through affective engagement of students" (p. 100). As the authors went on to say, "Four themes uncovered in this study—aloneness, anonymity, nonverbal communication, and unknowns—were described in both positive and negative terms. Only the theme of trepidation dealt solely with negative affective experiences" (p. 104). The authors highlighted emotional distraction being associated with learners concerned both with the need to keep up (clearly potentially increasing anxiety) and from intimidation by others. As the authors said, "Emotion is interwoven into all learning experiences as illustrated in the rich words participants used to describe their frustrations and fear, as well as feelings of connectedness and enjoyment" (p. 104). The authors offered clear recommendations for those running online courses: "Instructors need to recognize the emotional processes that students experience in online courses and design strategies to buffer the negative affective experiences that can impair learning" (p. 104).

Elective or Selective Mute

Learners who are elective (or selective) mute (SM) are capable of speaking, but they choose not to. In terms of its context, as Bork (2010) said: "It is believed that this paralyzing condition is an anxiety related disorder that is best described as 'the fear of being seen or heard speaking'. Successful treatments of SM incorporating technology in the intervention process have been documented" (p. 37). The author described a digital technology used to support an intervention of learners with SM: "iSpeak++ is a psychoeducational software program designed to assist educators to facilitate SM intervention inside school" (p. 41). The programme asked learners to perform daily activities, concerned with coping with anxiety, and encouraging self-monitoring or self-modelling. The programme used game-style activities to perform these tasks, and allowed peers to join in the games. From the study of the intervention, the author concluded that "educators play an important role in the intervention process. Effective SM intervention demands expert knowledge and time, both of which educators often lack". But the author also reported the software used could be of value, and the success of other programmes such as Clicker 5 suggested further research and development should be focused in this area.

Those with Mental Illness

How digital technologies can support the learning of those with mental illness is not well represented in the literature. Wichers et al. (2011) discussed use of digital technologies by those with depressive disorders as a means to help them monitor their own levels of depression. Whilst interventions and projects in schools to support learners with mental illness have been detailed in the literature (see, for example, Boyle, Lynch, Lyon, & Williams, 2011), digital technologies were not used and involved.

In Summary

Evidence of uses of digital technologies and outcomes for learners with challenging emotional features and attributes can be summarised as follows:

- Topic-specific resources and software have been used in some instances, but ways in which counsellors or teachers have interacted with this software has been crucial in terms of outcomes.
- Curriculum-wide software has been used with some learners in this group, but more in the past than currently.
- Teaching-wide software may be used, but there are no known reports where specific studies have looked at outcomes or impacts with this group of learners.
- Parent-involved software has been used in some instances, but reports involving learners in this group with these forms of digital technology are limited.
- Curriculum-supportive online resources may be used, but there are no known reports of specific studies looking at outcomes and impacts with this group of learners.
- Online learner support has been used with learners in this group, but outcomes have varied considerably. The roles of forms of interaction and development of ownership are clearly important with this group of learners.
- Project and after-school club activities involving digital technologies are not clearly reported for learners in this group, although it is known some learners with these attributes have been involved in project-based activities such as *First Lego League*.

Learners where Attitudes Pose Challenges

Learners where learning attitudes pose challenges, particularly affecting those around them, including their teachers or mentors, have been the subject of many projects seeking to support learners' specific needs through uses of educational digital technologies. In this section different attributes will be considered: disaffection (loss of interest and trust in teachers or those around them); dissatisfaction (loss of interest in subject content or the practices in classrooms); disenfranchisement (loss of ability to trust forms of engagement with others); disengagement (having low levels of engagement in learning activities generally); and low literacy engagement.

Engagement

Harcourt (2012) argues engagement with learning does not currently take account of learners' perspectives enough. From her study of early years' learners, she concluded that although engagement involves interactions involving a learner, peers and adults in a learning setting, it "has consistently been conceptualised, observed and often measured only from the adult perspective. Ways of knowing whether a young learner is engaged appear to be reliant upon adult observations and inferences in relation to the child's behaviour and internal state" (p. 76).

In terms of when disengagement initially arises, when it manifests itself, and its relationship to other personal characteristics and attributes, as Joffe and Black (2012) stated, from a study of 352 mainstream secondary school learners, "Adolescence is a time of transition when young people with language difficulties are at increased risk of experiencing social, emotional, and behavioral difficulties (SEBD)" (p. 461). The authors found learners with lower attainment and poor language abilities also showed significantly higher levels of social, emotional and behavioural difficulties when compared to a normative sample.

In terms of using digital technologies to support engagement with learning, Blood et al. (2011) reported uses of handheld devices to support engagement with learners with negative attitudes towards learning. They reported: "Handheld devices appear to be effective at reducing the amount of prompting and assistance from teachers during task-engagement and have been used to encourage time management and scheduling among students with disabilities" (p. 301). They also reported findings of studies indicating uses of handheld devices had supported the instigation and completion of activities on a daily basis for those with ADHD. They argued that as handheld devices are comparatively inexpensive and used widely by young people their use should be encouraged with this group as they would be recognised as socially acceptable.

Considering the use of another form of digital technology, Ciampa (2012) reported a study looking at impacts of e-books on reading engagement of young learners aged seven years in Ontario, Canada. The study used e-books to support reading and listening comprehension. Outcomes were identified by the researcher using listening comprehension tests, motivation questionnaires, behavioural checklists, and reading logs. Oral responses were coded according to levels of literal, inferential and evaluative questions asked during each reading session. The author reported that "all of the participants increased their comprehension scores from pretest to posttest after using the online e-book reading program, enjoyed the e-book reading experience, and frequently read the online e-books at home in their free time" (p. 27). Findings indicated engagement and interest went beyond access to single volumes or the online medium itself. The author concluded that "a wide variety of reading choices and the opportunity to select books may have an impact on reading engagement and ultimately listening comprehension" (p. 51). As the author said, a crucial finding was "the strong correlation between enjoyment of the online e-books that the children read and their preference for a choice of books" (p. 51). The author emphasised the important role the teacher has in building engagement through this medium, recommending that "As primary teachers begin to incorporate electronic reading into their instructional programs, they must also give strong consideration to the quality, quantity, and purpose of the e-books they provide for children to read" (p. 54). He stressed the need for e-books to be considered beyond entertainment, and integrated into regular reading practices.

In terms of learning engagement at secondary school age, Delialioğlu (2012) studied ways blended learning environments can support engagement. The author argued that low levels of engagement have been identified as a main reason for dissatisfaction, for negative experience and for school drop-out. The author detailed the design of the study, comparing different forms of learning environment and their effects on engagement: "The study used a repeated measure research design to compare student engagement. A third year computer networking course in a pre-service teacher education program was implemented as a blended learning course in spring 2008 and spring 2009 semesters" (p. 312). The design involved integrating an online learning environment initially with lecture sessions, and then with problem-based sessions. Learners involved completed surveys on three occasions across the two-year period of the study. The author discussed the findings, saying "No significant differences for Level of Academic Challenge and Course Satisfaction could be explained with the use of online materials in a blended learning environment" (p. 320). The author argued that instructional material used was known to be challenging for learners, and learners started with low levels of technical and operational skills. But the author found that "Regardless of the utilized instructional strategy, students were highly satisfied with the course configured as a blended learning environment" (p. 320). The author argued this might well have been due to the variety of resources provided—in multimedia format, as simulations, involving hands-on activities, and using games and online sessions. The author identified advantages of using the blended learning environment, as "students had the freedom to study at their own pace, they also had the opportunity to discuss the online material and laboratory activities with their peers and the instructor to perform the hands-on activities" (p. 320). Highest levels of engagement were associated with elements involving active learning strategies and problem-based learning. In terms of the possibility of engaging learners in online interactions for those learners displaying low levels of engagement in classroom activities, Zacharis (2011) in a study involving 161 undergraduate students, found engagement and achievement in online courses was not related to learning styles as defined by Kolb (concrete experience; reflective observation; abstract conceptualisation; or active experimentation). So uses of online engagement might match a wide learner group in this respect.

Involving another form of digital technology, Nakamura (2012) studied effects of using a wiki on enhancing the engagement of 47 US college students who were in remedial classes for English as a second language. These learners had generally low engagement with literacy (reading and writing), and the aim was to move them from remedial classes to mainstream classes. The author noted that "repeated out-of-class engagement over the course of the semester was positively associated with successfully exiting remediation. However, average level of engagement was low, suggesting that, in this context, technology-mediated learning activities do not necessarily lead to increased engagement" (p. 273). The author went on to say, "As in other mandatory remedial programs, morale can be low, and many (though not all) students are disengaged and even resistant. Instructors are eager to implement innovative teaching techniques and create a motivating classroom environment" (p. 274). The author highlighted the need for more research looking at effects of digital technologies in these classroom and subject contexts. In terms of findings from the study, the author explained "almost half of the students either missed class on one or more computer lab days or spent the lab time doing something besides the assigned wiki contributions" (p. 286). For those learners who did move from the remedial to the mainstream classes, the author found "successfully exiting remediation was much more strongly associated with out-of-class edits and number of editing occasions" (p. 287). As the author said, the features concerned with success related to when and how activity was undertaken rather than how much. The author stated: "This was true despite wide variation in the substantive kind of editing activity students engaged in (e.g., formatting changes, adding text, revising text, inserting emoticons, inserting greetings to other students, etc., as determined by the initial coding of each edit)" (p. 287).

Disaffection

Disaffection is a characteristic explored by Hartas (2011). She reported on disaffected learners, gathering evidence using focus group sessions and interviews about their experiences and their views of education and learning practices, reporting that "the young people expressed concerns about participation in school matters and critiqued the curriculum as irrelevant to their aspirations and employment needs" (p. 103). She stated these young people sought participation to involve them working in more informal ways, so their views could be listened to. She argued that "The findings suggested that to enable young people's participation in learning and other aspects of school life, the curriculum, learning and pastoral support and the school-to-training transition require re-thinking" (p. 103).

Disaffection as a feature of learners is certainly not something that can be addressed necessarily quickly or only with the use of digital technologies. However, there do appear to be a number of young people who are disaffected and for whom digital technologies enhance engagement quite strongly (see Passey et al., 2004; Passey, 2012b). Nevertheless, research into ways digital technologies might support those who are disaffected, dissatisfied, disenfranchised or disengaged is not currently very extensive. As stated in an earlier sub-section, Waxman, Lin, and Michko (2003) from their meta-analysis of existing studies found "teaching and learning with technology has a small, positive, non-significant ($p > .05$) effect on students' affective outcomes when compared to traditional instruction" (p. 12).

Dissatisfaction

Shahriar, Pathan, Mari, and Umrani (2011) studied factors affecting dissatisfaction among learners in a higher education institution in Pakistan. Even for these high-level learners, features they identified with dissatisfaction were clear, and highlighted issues leading to what the learners described as boredom: "Some blamed teacher for repeating the same ideas and others for giving long lectures instead of allowing them to do something, sometimes, which creates boredom" (p. 103). Interestingly, the authors found one learner felt dissatisfied when not having prepared for the session beforehand, and they remarked on ways teacher interactions affected learner levels of satisfaction: "The students wished their teachers were more cooperative, friendly and helping. . . . The students also have hard feelings for the teacher for keeping favourites. One even, remarked that the teacher's continuous attention to some students discourage him" (p. 104). The learners commented on their perceptions of resource quality, and "one student said that the course book is dry and boring; he attends the class as a compulsion" (p. 105).

Disenfranchisement

In more severe cases, disenfranchisement and drop-out from school or classes can result. However, a large-scale national study in the US (Vaughn et al., 2011, p. 202) suggested drop-out (termed disengagement in this study) is strongly associated with non-educational background factors:

- Increased disengagement was associated with increased anti-social behaviours and comorbid psychiatric disorders.
- Increased disengagement was associated with increased substance abuse and anti-social personality disorder.
- The anti-social behaviours associated with disengagement included physical interaction and assault, property vandalism, lying, animal cruelty, stealing, and physical and emotional harassment.
- The comorbidity disorders associated with disengagement included disorders concerned with alcohol, cannabis, nicotine and drug abuse, as well as major depression and bipolar disorders, and specific phobia.

In this context, clearly an issue for uses of digital technologies is how they fit appropriately into a range of intervention stages—early identification, early prevention, or later addressing of issues. Studies reported in this section and other sections of this book indicate ways that different stakeholders are beginning to explore this range of options.

In Summary

Evidence of uses of digital technologies and outcomes for learners where attitudes pose challenges can be summarised as follows:

- Topic-specific resources and software have been used to support learners in this group, but the relationship of the teacher or tutor is clearly vitally important.
- Curriculum-wide software has been used in the past (see, for example, Passey, 1997), but currently there are few reports of uses of this form of software to support learners in this group.
- Teaching-wide software is not reported to be used specifically with learners in this group, although some has certainly been used with some learners in this group (those who are displaying early stages of negative attitudes to learning in mainstream classrooms) supported by teachers in wider class groups.

- Uses of parent-involved software with this group are not evidenced widely, but there is some use in cases where learners have low levels of literacy.
- Curriculum-supportive online resources have been used with learners in this group (see Passey, 2011a).
- Online learner support for this group of learners is an aspect that has not been evidenced to any great extent.
- Project and after-school club activities involving digital technologies are known to support some learners in this group (see Passey, 2012b).

Learners with Challenging Behavioural Attributes

Digital technologies have been used to support learners with different behavioural attributes and have been the focus of a number of research studies, and many projects have used educational digital technologies to support specific needs of this group (see, for example, Passey et al., 2004). In this section the attributes considered are: disruption; aggression; physical assault; Tourette syndrome; and abuse or bullying.

In terms of overall impacts on positive behaviours, Waxman et al. (2003) from their meta-analysis of 42 existing studies found a

> mean study-weighted effect size for the three study-weighted comparisons that contained behavioral outcomes was −.091, (p > .05), with a 95-percent confidence interval of −.142 to 1.243, indicating that technology had a slight, negative, nonsignificant effect on students' behavioral outcomes.
>
> (p. 12)

However, considering the impact of digital technologies on learners with behavioural challenges, Crawford (2010), exploring uses of digital technologies in music lessons in a school in Australia, concluded that "technology used in such a way can overcome serious behavioural issues of students caused by cultural diversity and or socioeconomic situations" (p. 34). The author attributed impacts to higher levels of interest and engagement, and associated higher perceptions of value arising from the learning.

Using Video Modelling

In terms of this group of learners as a whole, Blood et al. (2011) reported uses of video modelling to support positive behaviours and attitudes. The authors stated that, while many research studies had focused on learners with developmental disabilities or those on the autistic spectrum, "Baker et al. (2009) recently conducted a review in which they identified sixteen empirical studies in which video-modeling had been used successfully with students with emotional and behavioral disorders" (p. 300). Within these 16 studies, the authors indicated video modelling had been shown to impact by improving social interactions between peers, enhancing levels of on-task behaviours, and reducing behaviours considered inappropriate.

In terms of learners using video digital technologies, Kennedy and Swain-Bradway (2012) described how home-made videos had been used in schools to support a range of positive school behaviour practices and policies. The authors concluded that "Videos can introduce and illustrate practices for faculty, teach and remind students of behavioral expectations, and celebrate successes" (p. 21). They stated videos could support positive behaviours by offering learners models of expectations of behaviour in certain locations (such as in a classroom, or on a bus, or in a corridor), or of ways to address certain behaviours (such as bullying). However, the article did not offer research evidence on effectiveness of these videos.

For more specific forms of behaviours, particular digital technologies are sometimes advised. For example, while Tourette syndrome can be manifest in a very wide range of ways, Christner and Dieker (2008) advise the learner to "videotape presentations ahead of time, use a computer or word processor for writing tasks, use a classroom FM system to amplify teacher's speech directly to the student, and use a sensory seat to help with attention issues" (p. 46).

Disruptive Behaviour

There is a literature exploring methods to identify, analyse and appropriately intervene with disruptive learner behaviours (see, for example, in a primary school context, Shumate & Wills, 2010). However, the literature indicating how digital technologies have been used in interventions is much slimmer. There are examples of learners within PRUs where digital technologies have been used in cases of disruption (Passey, 1997; Passey et al., 2004). In these cases curriculum-wide software was used (in the former case), while topic-specific resources and software was used in the latter case. In both cases positive outcomes were reported by teachers; the ways the software provided regular positive or neutral feedback was identified as a key element in supporting positive behaviours with these learners. A similar picture in terms of the literature is presented for aggression and aggressive behaviours. Van Acker (2007) provided an extensive review of forms of interventions and uses of alternative education settings to support those displaying aggressive behaviours, but no specific reference was made to uses of digital technologies within those settings. As he said, "Prevention strategies that keep youth from engaging in antisocial and delinquent behavior often involve educating youth about the dangers of antisocial behavior. Intervention strategies divert youth from crime, providing appropriate alternatives to meet their social, emotional, and economic needs" (p. 7). He went on to list common intervention programmes—after-school interventions, counselling, work-study sessions, social skill courses, and conflict resolution sessions. He also raised the roles of suppression strategies as well as "procedures, rules, and statutes to identify, monitor, isolate, punish, and rehabilitate criminal offenders" (p. 8). There are clearly potential areas where digital technologies could be used across and integrated within this framework of intervention strategies.

Anti-social Behaviour

In terms of anti-social behaviour, in their report on uses of digital technologies and effects on motivation, Passey et al. (2004) reported some police officers in the UK indicated uses of mobile technologies could reduce levels of anti-social behaviour if personal issues could be handled and resolved at a distance rather than face-to-face. Evidence to support this conjecture has not been identified specifically, but influences through other digital technologies have been referred to elsewhere. For example, the research of Huston et al. (2001) stated young people 15 to 19 years of age who had previously watched *Sesame Street* when they were five years of age or younger were expressing low levels of aggressive behaviours compared to those who had not.

From a different perspective, Ibañez, Playfoot, Fabregat, Costa, and Torres (2010) described a project development aimed at reintegrating young people with anti-social behaviour, stating its aim was to "develop a gaming technology platform to provide young people who have become marginalised in society as a result of anti social behaviour with a learning environment to facilitate their reintegration into society" (p. 29). The authors described details of how their gaming technology development would do this, saying "Current assessment tools, aimed at understanding the motivations and feelings of individuals through an interview or question and answer session, could be transposed highly effectively into game contents" (p. 32). The design involved learners being presented with scenarios showing issues or dilemmas, they would respond to choices, and these would be seen by their counsellors and used as points to instigate discussions. They believed the game scenarios could elicit more open responses from learners, which would take learners outside the normal more adult setting in which discussions of this nature take place.

The literature on abuse or bullying relating to access and use in a digital environment is emerging increasingly strongly, and offers another perspective on this issue. Von Marées and Petermann (2012), from a review of the current literature, concluded that: "To date, little research has been published on effective preventive measures and interventions to reduce cyberbullying. Based on empirical evidence, researchers suggest that programs for the prevention of cyberbullying should be incorporated in school curricula" (p. 472). The authors recommended school curricula should cover elements of internet safety and conduct, and offered details about "reactive (e.g., delete, block or ignore messages) and preventive strategies (e.g., increased security and awareness). Students who experience cyberbullying also need effective coping skills (e.g., seeking social support) to reduce the associated stress and negative emotions" (p. 472).

While published research into effective measures might be limited, there are certainly a wide range of online and offline resources and publications providing teachers, parents and learners with advice and guidance in this area. In the context of bullying as a whole, which includes cyberbullying, the importance of whole-school and whole-community approaches are highlighted in a number of reports. Cross et al. (2011), who explored effectiveness of a bullying programme, found in their control study, "students in the intervention group at the end of the first study year were significantly less likely than comparison students to report being bullied versus not bullied" (p. 120). They found that while there was no difference in these control and test groups with regard to being bullied regularly by the end of the second year of the study (when learners were in grade 5), this had again changed by the end of the third year (when learners were in grade 6) so test groups were less likely to be bullied regularly. The authors reported that

"Importantly, however, at every posttest the intervention group students were approximately one and half times less likely than the comparison students to report seeing another student their age or younger being bullied" (p. 120). They concluded the programme's effectiveness was higher in grades 4 and 6 than in grade 5. However, the authors did emphasise that effect sizes were small. In terms of preventing and increasing awareness about bullying, Rubin-Vaughan, Pepler, Brown, and Craig (2011) in their study gathered evidence about uses and outcomes of a well-known computer-based bullying prevention program, designed for learners in grades 2 to 5, with between 226 to 438 learners involved in any one module, and showed their knowledge of bullying and selection of strategies to prevent bullying had been enhanced significantly.

One aspect of particular concern in this area is related to sexual misconduct and 'grooming'. But, as Agosto, Forte, and Magee (2012) said, "Although the risks of encountering sexual predators via social media are relatively small, a much more widespread threat to teens' online security is online aggression by their peers, or 'cyberbullying'" (p. 39). The authors highlighted the effects of cyberbullying on lower academic attainment and performance, on anxiety and distress, on self-esteem, and mental and physical health side-effects. They also stated cyberbullying had been linked to increased levels of suicide in young people, advising "Widespread education about the kinds of dangers that young people are likely to encounter online is a critical need, and librarians, parents, educators, and teens themselves need to be a part of this conversation" (p. 40).

In Summary

Evidence of uses of digital technologies and outcomes for learners with challenging behavioural attributes can be summarised as follows:

- Topic-specific resources and software have been used to support learning for some learners displaying challenging behaviours. However, it is the integration of these resources into wider interventions that is identified as being most useful and beneficial.
- Curriculum-wide software has been used in the past with some learners in this group, but is now less widely used.
- Teaching-wide software is not highlighted as being used with this group of learners.
- Parent-involved software is used within some whole-school behaviour practices and policies, and is accessible online to inform about, as well as to support and prevent, bullying and cyberbullying.
- Curriculum-supportive online resources are used to support learning in areas such as positive behaviour practices, bullying intervention, and addressing cyberbullying.
- Online learner support has been used with some learners in this group, particularly for those who find social interactions difficult, but who want to interact without the confrontational issues associated with physical presence.
- Project and after-school club activities involving digital technologies have been involved with learners in this group, leading to the production of videos

looking at certain behaviours, modelling them positively, and focusing on positive behavioural aspects of monitoring, as well as on developing online resources focusing on bullying and cyberbullying.

Learners with Challenging Social Attributes and Abilities

Learners with different social attributes and abilities will be considered here: social deprivation; marginalisation; criminal activity; drug and alcohol abuse; and low social or communicative engagement. Some studies have looked specifically at impacts of digital technologies in enhancing social engagement and inclusion (see Haché & Cullen, 2009), while others have focused on more specific issues.

Those in Areas of Social Deprivation

A number of national and regional projects in the UK, for example, have focused on support for learners in areas of social deprivation (see, for example, Passey, 2011d). Identifiable impacts and outcomes, particularly where there has been access to topic-specific resources and software and to internet-based resources and online support, have been shown. Details are provided in Chapter 3 of findings from a range of reports and studies focusing on this group, which are not repeated here.

In terms of considering the concept of a 'digital divide', Hollingworth, Mansaray, Allen, and Rose (2011) argue that material differences in digital technologies at home need to be considered alongside parallel differences concerned with social and cultural capital, experiences from work and employment, and relationships and beliefs in education and learning. Countries and communities have looked at ways to address these concerns. Hohlfeld, Ritzhaupt, and Barron (2010) looked at how schools, families, and community members were using ICT across the State of Florida and showed within a few years prior to 2010 all school sectors and socio-economic groups significantly increased their ICT access and provided education for families and communities, but high schools in the most economically advantaged areas supported their families and communities most. The authors argued schools must take a lead in supporting the development of social capital with ICT. The reasons for this are highlighted in findings from other studies too. Vekiri (2010b) in a survey of 345 grade 5 and 6 learners in one private and six public elementary schools in Greece, found learners generally had positive views about ICT and its uses, but those from lower socio-economic status homes indicated less confidence in their ICT skills. The longer-term implications were highlighted by Berger (2010), who found in a group of first-year university students in South Africa learning mathematics using a CAS, those who were non-computer literate at earlier stages performed at the same level as others, but were less able to interpret representations. It was argued this was due to differences in earlier mathematics teaching (and presumably, concerned as much with pedagogical approaches as individual characteristics). Similarly, Rauh (2011) found across users of a virtual school, learners in more socially disadvantaged areas on average performed less well in online courses compared to those in other areas. Kim and Lee (2011), on the other hand, across

1,043 students and 915 underprivileged students using online learning in Korea, found underprivileged students were more satisfied with online learning, but they preferred online tutors rather than working on their own.

Those who are Marginalised

Those who are marginalised can be so for a number of reasons. For example, as Leman, Trappers, Brandon, and Ruppol (2008) state: "Throughout Europe, migrations and ethnic diversification have become a matter of fact. The new post-guestworker (Gastarbeiter) migrations are characterized by diversification and fragmentation" (p. 238). These authors refer similarly to parallel challenges facing young people, but state digital technologies could be used more effectively to address some of the issues young people face. They argue currently recognisable issues have not led to an education strategy at a European level, and interventions to date have tended to be top-down, patchy, and not integrated into widening practice. The authors argue there is a need to put a policy in place enabling young people to "decode interethnic discourse, helping to structure interethnic dialogue—including the intra-European socialization of distant partners, and 'in vivo' language training are just some of the obvious examples of educational measures in which the Internet could play a prominent part" (p. 249).

Fredrikson and Tikkanen (2010) described one development to address aspects of marginalisation with young learners using music. They described how five- to six-year-old learners supported the design of activities in *Open Source (OS)* software where music would support social activity and provide intervention. The system was called *JamMo*, and provided singing and composition games in which learners could engage. As the authors said: "There is a growing body of neurological and related research evidence that the promotion of early compe-tences in music and language are interwoven" (p. 41). In the project they described how "music is used to also help children to develop language skills whilst positively affecting children's emotional, social, and intellectual develop-ment" (p. 41). They described how the facility was developed as follows: "JamMo is a ubiquitous product (i.e. application), which provides sound synthesis, sampling, sequencing and touch-screen virtual musical instruments in an educative form for children in different age groups and learners with specific needs" (p. 412). As they said, this facility sought to engage learners in creative aspects of music, whilst at the same time supporting social cohesion and handling emotional needs. At the time the article was written, a singing and composition game had been trialled with four immigrant learners five to six years of age, as well as a range of learning materials. Issues (particularly technical issues) had arisen, but the authors recognised value had arisen from the fact learners were able to be involved in the trialling and evaluation of this facility.

In another project, de Vicente Gutiérrez and García (2010) described a devel-opment using mobile technologies to engage young people who were margin-alised: "ComeIn is developing a networked media platform for the deliverance and exchange of this type of interactive media content, specifically aimed at marginalized youth" (p. 49). The aims of the project were to provide a mobile online community with which marginalised young people could associate, to provide content to support social inclusion across a range of geographical regions and groups with different interests, to help marginalised young people create these facilities themselves, and to analyse impacts of this network and identify recommendations for the future.

Development of digital technologies to support learners who are marginalised is clearly at an early stage. While projects have been instigated, reports of impacts will necessarily arise at later stages.

Those with Language Barriers

To support those with language barriers, Harrison (1997) reported findings from a study using curriculum-wide software with learners whose first language was not English (E2L). In this UK study, mixed results were found. However, as the author emphasised, "it is very difficult to make generalisations about the learning needs of E2L pupils" (p. 127). He went on to conclude the use of this form of software (from two different providers) was "very good for slow learners because they fail privately and can go over work again . . . excellent for developing confidence . . . develops concentration span (for most children) . . . develops personal organisational skills and independence in learning" (p. 134). The author concluded it improved knowledge in both mathematics and English.

In a later review of studies focusing on uses of digital technologies to support language learning for non-native speakers, Zhao (2003) reported "the limited number of available studies shows a pattern of positive effects. They found technology-supported language learning is at least as effective as human teachers, if not more so" (p. 7). He went to say "availability and capacities of information technologies have not been fully taken advantage of by language students or educators. To truly capitalize on modern information and communication technologies to significantly improve language learning, a number of issues must be addressed" (p. 22).

Language barriers can arise for a number of reasons, and how these might be supported through uses of digital technologies varies. López (2010), in a controlled study with two student groups in grades 3 and 5 mathematics and reading, showed interactive whiteboards could help to close an achievement gap between early English language learners and other students by enhancing pedagogical interactions. Chiu, Wu, Hsieh, Cheng, and Huang (2013) in their study indicated using a structured communication facility with predetermined utterances could lead to enhanced communication competencies, as well as strategic and discourse competencies for primary aged learners. Ponce, López, and Mayer (2012) in their controlled study involving 1,041 grade 4 learners in 21 schools across three regions of Chile, used a program to support reading comprehension through features of highlighting and outlining types of texts, paraphrasing, self-questioning and summarising, and found it led to higher gains for those using the program, particularly for lower achieving learners. Liu (2011) in a controlled study looked at the impacts of using concept mapping (individual and collaborative) on writing performance of 94 university undergraduates, and found both forms of concept mapping had positive impacts on low-level and middle-level writers.

Those Facing Ethnic and Cultural Barriers

For those who face ethnic and cultural barriers, uses of digital technologies may assist, but may also at times constitute a barrier. As Migliorino (2011) said in an Australian context, a number of groups facing ethnic and cultural barriers (Cald Australians who are ageing, refugees who have arrived recently, and skilled migrants) have "medium level English language literacy, all of which are at risk of being excluded by new technologies that require either, or both, high level English and digital literacy" (p. 107). The author recommended libraries and community centres should support access to facilities to promote inclusion and address the barriers currently leading to exclusion.

Whether digital technologies provide for ethnic and cultural neutrality is not simply answered. For example, Richardson (2012) in his study looked at attainment of different ethnic groups engaged in online courses, and concluded online tuition is viable for all ethnic groups, differences in attainment might arise, but these are probably not due to the quality of interactions with tutors or their peers. Gyabak and Godina (2011), however, reported on uses of digital storytelling to support learners in remote rural areas in Bhutan and found these had limited success, due to language and cultural issues raised by the nature of the resources used.

But there are cases where digital technologies are being used to support learners who face ethnic or cultural challenges. Y. Yang et al. (2013) carried out studies in rural public schools, minority public schools and migrant schools in China, and found computer-based learning could assist both boys and girls equally across those areas and schools. Levy (2011) in a longitudinal case study looked at how five children of migrant parents involved in land work in southern New Mexico used laptops for learning both in high school and at home, and found the learners felt supported in overcoming challenges of language, family commitments and travel, and were able to access courses online, and complete them.

Those Involved in Criminal Activities

With regard to uses of digital technologies to support those involved in youth crime, Barn and Barn (2010) stated that whilst engaging those involved in youth crime, enhancing social inclusion and engaging those who are marginalised through this activity was clearly a key priority and policy need, the development of social capital is seen as an important way to consider addressing this need. The authors suggested that "two groupings of technologies have the potential to support such activity: Social software and its integration with mobile devices and CRM [customer relationship management]; and secondly the use of virtual worlds" (p. 204).

Young offenders involved in criminal activity have been the subject of some trials and projects using digital technologies. In a study of one project, Levesque, Johnson, Welch, Prochaska, and Fernandez (2012) reported: "Studies assessing the efficacy of juvenile justice interventions show small effects on recidivism and other outcomes" (p. 391). In their article, these authors described the development of a multimedia form of intervention called *Rise Above Your Situation*. The development concerned behavioural change, which could be supported through assessments, appropriate feedback, reports from the system itself, and reports from counsellors. Impacts from a study involving 60 young people using the system showed "91.7% of youths agreed that the program could help them make positive changes, and 86.7% agreed that the program could give their counselor helpful information about them" (p. 392). The authors detailed their findings further, and indicated ways the learning landscape or environment had helped the young people, their counsellors and the interactions and interventions between both parties. As the report stated, online facilities supported inter-actions positively: "The reports put a number of important topics on the table for discussion—topics counselors might not have considered or felt comfortable addressing otherwise. Counselors also learned about youths' personal goals, providing more opportunities for engagement and collaboration" (p. 403). The environment provided opportunities for shared and joint interpretation of key points, clarification of points that might not be fully understood, and detailing information more fully. The element of collaboration was highlighted as being particularly important. The authors provided one example, saying the system offered an idea enabling a young person and a counsellor to work together and the consequential level and quality of interactions arising was enhanced: "'We did it together, discovered the info together. Because the report said to do it, it took the argument out of it'" (p. 403).

Content and discussion in this sub-section relates to that in a previous section, which considered learners who are in prison.

Those Involved in Drug and Alcohol Abuse

Young people involved in drug and alcohol abuse have been involved in projects using digital technologies to support learning, and research has identified posi-tive benefits arising. Interestingly, again in these cases, benefits arise clearly from ways counsellors or parents are involved, rather than benefits arising from a digital technology facility divorced from concepts of social interactions. Schinke, Fang, Cole, and Cohen-Cutler (2011) reported findings from a study of a project involving 546 adolescent girls (with Black and Hispanic American ethnic and cultural backgrounds) and their mothers (from New York, New Jersey and Connecticut). Those involved provided self-reported evidence, and the subse-quent analysis of results showed "the experimental intervention reduced risk factors, improved protective factors, and lowered girls' alcohol use and their future intentions to use substances. The study supports the value of computer-based and gender-specific interventions that involve girls and their mothers" (p. 35). The programme focused specifically on substance abuse in a single gender—girls—and sought to improve qualities of communication between mothers and daughters, as well as to help mothers to monitor the behaviour of their daughters, and to "build their daughters' self-image and self-esteem, establish rules about and consequences for substance use, create family rituals, and refrain from communicating unrealistic expectations" (p. 39). At the same time, the programme sought to support the girls with "skills for managing stress, conflict, mood, and anxiety; refusing peer pressure; and enhancing body esteem and self-efficacy" (p. 39), and they found out detailed information about levels of substance abuse of their peers. The programme was delivered through 10 sessions, in homes, at times to suit those involved, with most using online internet access and some using CD-ROMs. The authors identified positive benefits arising: "girls showed improvements in their communication with their mothers, in their understanding of family rules regarding substance use, and in their awareness of parental monitoring of their social activities and friendships" (p. 40). The authors reported the girls "improved their normative beliefs about the extent of substance use among their peers, were less depressed, and expressed higher levels of self-efficacy regarding their ability to not smoke, drink, and use drugs" (p. 40). The girls reported reductions in alcohol use, and they expected to use lower levels of tobacco, alcohol and drugs in the future. Mothers reported improved communication with their daughters, family rules about substance use being in place more, and they were more able to monitor activities of their daughters and friends.

In terms of assessment, treatment and research of drug addiction, Bickel, Christensen, and Marsch (2011) reviewed research literature detailing how digital technologies had been used in these practices, and concluded that "New technologies appear to produce better or similar results in detecting, informing, and educating individuals with substance use disorders relative to traditional counselor-facilitated methods" (p. 7). But they identified four important prerequisites if effects of digital technologies are to be used more widely:

- Effective innovations in practice need to be disseminated so that key organisations are aware of them.
- Evaluation evidence needs to show the innovations are not only effective but also feasible in terms of integration into practice.
- Resources available in key organisations need to accommodate the needs of the innovations.
- Innovations need to show how organisations and those working in the organisations can bring about appropriate change.

Those who are Reluctant Communicators

Young people who are reluctant talkers, with low social or communicative engagement, have been seen to be supported through uses of online discussion, where they can engage without fear of others being physically present within the same space. Impacts of uses of online discussion forums within a learning platform environment with 'quiet' learners were discussed by Passey (2007). The report stated: "Many teachers during interviews suggested that those learners who are quiet in classrooms are not quiet in community areas within *Virtual Workspace*" (p. 5). Evidence from teachers and learners themselves indicated this group was benefiting in certain respects more than other learners (more details are given in Chapter 3 in the section on 'Online support'). Teachers in this study indicated quiet learners were not easy to support, but clearly an online learning environment such as *Virtual Workspace* provided opportunities extending the potential for learning for reluctant communicators in classrooms.

In Summary

Evidence of uses of digital technologies and outcomes for learners exhibiting challenging social characteristics and behaviours can be summarised as follows:

- Topic-specific resources and software have been used to support learners with challenging social attributes, and although software has been focused on specific aspects of social challenge, it is nevertheless important to recognise it is also the ability of interaction between the young person and the counsellor, teacher or parent that contributes to impact.
- Curriculum-wide software has been used to support these groups of learners, but more commonly in the past than currently.
- Teaching-wide software has been used, and teachers have been able to focus its use in terms of engagement, particularly encouraging discussion or involvement in whole-class games-style activities, with learners who might otherwise be more reticent in class.
- Parent-involved software has been used to support learners in these groups, and to enhance communication between learners and parents.
- Curriculum-supportive online resources have been used to support learners in these groups, particularly where teachers have been able to engage learners who normally display low levels of social communication in classrooms.
- Online learner support has been used to engage learners who normally display low levels of social communication in classrooms.
- Project and after-school club activities involving digital technologies have supported some of this group of learners.

Learners where Geography Poses Challenges

Some learners live in areas and localities where geography poses challenges; geographical features can mean individuals are easily isolated or remote from others. Isolation and limited travel choice can lead to learning exclusion and limited education or training opportunities. In some instances young people are unwilling to travel from their localities, which can clearly severely reduce opportunities. Interestingly, of course, some young people in some countries have experienced these issues for many decades, and digital technologies have been used to support their needs and reduce their educational isolation (using radio with remote learners in Australia in the 1950s, for example).

Geographical Isolation and Rural Locations

In terms of geographical isolation, the situation in some areas of Australia is well known, both in terms of extents of isolation but also in terms of ways adopted to address the issue as effectively as possible. The Australian Bureau of Statistics (2010) reported in 2010 there were 6,357 primary schools, 1,409 secondary schools, 1,286 combined primary and secondary schools, and 416 special schools across the country, but, as stated in an Australian Government document (2012), the country contains a number of highly remote areas, where travel for children is difficult. In these areas alternative provision is available to parents in the form of the School of the Air (first trialled in 1950 and now managed through 11 different bases across a number of States), schools of distance education (managed through five different bases) and Community Schools (managed through a single base). A document from the Commonwealth of Australia (Questacon, 2012) reports the number of students involved is now 1,000; the Australian Bureau of Statistics report (2010) states there were, in 2008, 3,457,000 students in schools across Australia, so the proportion involved in distant managed provision is small (some 0.03%).

In terms of those in rural localities, and considering how digital technologies might help to address some of the issues they face, Kim et al. (2011) conducted a study comparing outcomes arising from uses of mobile digital technologies in rural and urban settings. As they said, mobile devices could provide ideal affordances to support education in remote locations; they can be easily carried and transported, their cost is not high comparatively, and they can supplement and complement other education resources and practices available. The authors adopted mixed methods approaches for their study, aiming to identify implications of using "a mobile learning technology-based learning model in two public primary schools near the Mexico-USA border in the state of Baja California, Mexico. One school was located in an urban slum and the other in a rural village community" (p. 465).

The populations were detailed by the authors: "About 15% of the students in both schools were migrant indigenous children who followed their parents throughout the southern part of Mexico (i.e., Oaxaca mountain regions)" (p. 469). As the authors stated, parents often moved to gain jobs as farm workers or manual labourers, so learners often did not attend school for even a one-year-long period. Additionally, many parents did not speak Spanish, the language used in schools. The authors detailed the socio-economic backgrounds:

> The socio-economic status of the students in the urban school was lower than that of the rural school . . . The urban school, like other schools in the low-income area in the border city, had very poor infrastructure that consisted of a half-classroom size library facility.
>
> (p. 470)

Parents worked in factories, but many were unemployed. The rural school was in a higher socio-economic status area, but although "the rural school had a computer lab, the computers were stacked up under dust, not arranged to be used and there was no Internet access at the school, leaving the school without single functioning computer and Internet access" (p. 470). Both schools reported high levels of drop-out.

Control and trial groups were involved in both schools. Learners in the trial groups were given a *TeacherMate* mobile device. The authors found the mobile devices were adopted easily, quickly, and learners drove ways to use them. The ways the mobile devices were used was largely decided by the teachers: "They indicated that they had the students use the devices mostly twice a week for an average of 20 min each, amounting to at least 640 min of individual mobile learning time in class for the span of 16 weeks" (p. 472).

The authors collected empirical and ethnographic evidence, using a school district Spanish literacy assessment test completed by all learners pre- and post-test for both control and experimental groups, observations in the different contexts, surveys of stakeholders involved, and interviews with all 160 grade 2 learners involved. The authors analysed their results using a mixed-model Analysis of Variance (ANOVA), and identified all three main factors—location, technology and time—as having significant main effects on literacy result differences.

The findings suggested that "students in the rural village, seriously lacking educational resources and technology exposure, may have benefited substantially more from mobile technologies than urban school students possibly due to their relatively higher socioeconomic status and higher parental involvement and interest in education" (p. 465). The authors found outcomes were not associated with factors such as the levels of parents' education, the previous experiences of teachers and school managers, or the perception of teachers to the mobile devices or their training in its use. The authors concluded that "the use of mobile learning devices significantly contributed to higher literacy achievement levels in contrast to the control situation where only existing educational materials were used for literacy development and enrichment" (p. 473). Further analyses revealed literacy scores for learners using the mobile devices in the rural school (M=0.70, SD=0.11) were significantly higher than those in the urban school (M=0.57, SD=0.23), t(46)=2.80, p=0.007. The authors summarised their results, stating the mobile device "as a supplementary learning tool had a fundamentally different effect in the rural school compared to the urban location. The students from the rural village benefitted more from the technology than their respective peers in the urban slums" (p. 475).

Further data supported identification of differences according to location. From interviews "parents from the rural school appeared to be more involved in their children's education with 90% of them being aware of the mobile learning project in the school" (p. 476). By contrast, the researchers found only 13% of parents in the urban school knew about the project. The amount of time parents spent supporting their children at home with homework also varied considerably: "94% of rural school parents spent more than 5 h a week helping their children. In contrast, 74% of urban school parents spent less than 2 h a week working with their children" (p. 475). Although parents in the rural school had higher expectations of their children, this was not markedly different from expectations of parents in the urban school.

The authors considered in some detail how their findings could be reasoned, suggesting there could have been a difference in pedagogical approaches taken, the rural school teachers used the mobile devices to support individual remedial and personal self-directed literacy learning, the lower level of resources in this school could have been supplemented greatly by the facilities afforded by the mobile devices, or small differences in test achievement between groups might have been extended more over the period of the project, leading to significant differences at the end of the trial period. Additionally, they suggested drop-out effects might have been different in the different groups, or indeed the effect would be a short-term novelty effect rather than being sustained. However, it is clear from other studies that long-term effects are not due just to the technology effects, but also the effects of teachers and others in building longer-lasting and sustained outcomes. The fact that, in this case, there were differences in terms of school resourcing, pedagogical approaches and parent involvement, are all clearly important. Evidence elsewhere suggests these are vitally important factors likely to determine longer-term outcomes, but, the digital technology is a factor through which these other factors can interact, intervene and build.

Those Living in Remote Areas

Learners in remote areas face challenges that can lead to lower levels of attainment in some subjects or topics. Li and Ranieri (2013) studied four schools in China, involving 658 learners 10 to 14 years of age, and found learners from rural or migrant schools scored lower in terms of digital access, autonomy in using devices, social support when using devices, and width of applications to purpose.

Access through online resources, online courses and online tutoring has been suggested as a way to support these learners. Certainly study findings would suggest this range of digital technologies has the potential to support learners in remote areas. Yu, Tian, Vogel, and Kwok (2010) found, from a survey of 187 university undergraduates and focus group discussions with 14 students, that online social networking supported social learning processes and outcomes, influencing social acceptance and adaptation to culture. O'Bannon, Lubke, Beard, and Britt (2011) looked at pre-service teacher preferences for lectures or podcasts, and found achievement was not affected by either medium, but found a preference for a balance rather than one or the other. Some studies have pointed to the need to consider individual learner characteristics within this group, however. Rienties et al. (2012), in their study involving 143 high school students using a computer-supported collaborative online learning environment, found increasing online support and scaffolding enhanced engagement for control-oriented learners but decreased engagement from autonomous learners, indicating the need to balance or consider how to address the needs of each group separately. But studies have also pointed to benefits and learning outcomes arising for learners widely. Hansen et al. (2012) in their study involving 413 children from grades 5 to 7 using a laptop in areas in Ethiopia showed significantly higher scores were gained for learners in grades 6 and 7 in the field of categorisation in abstract reasoning, for example.

In Summary

Evidence of uses of digital technologies and outcomes with learners where geography poses challenges can be summarised as follows:

- Topic-specific resources and software have been used to support those who are isolated by geography, either in the form of radio or television broadcast programmes, or online resources accessible as and when required.
- Curriculum-wide software has not generally been made accessible online to support these learners, but evidence suggests that without appropriate supportive social interactions, such facilities might not be found to be particularly useful in the long term.
- Teaching-wide software has not been used due to the particular circumstances involved where teachers are not necessarily located with learners, but

parent-involved software has been used, and uses of online resources supported by parents are now increasingly accessible and encouraged.

- Curriculum-supportive online resources are becoming increasingly available, as forms of digital resources, at one time only accessible in classrooms, now become available online.
- Online learner support has been used widely with this group of learners, and has been shown to be successful.
- Project and after-school club activities involving digital technologies have not been widely developed or reported for this group of learners at this stage, but there is clearly opportunity for this area to be developed further.

Future Concerns and Possible Areas of Focus

At this point an overview of findings, to show how different forms of digital technologies have been used and outcomes have been evidenced with specific groups of learners, also shows where evidence points to current strengths or weaknesses. In Table 4.3, shaded cells show those categories of digital technologies used commonly or where evidence currently demonstrates outcomes or impacts, while un-shaded cells show more limited use or weaker levels of evidence, and diagonally shaded cells indicate gaps in the picture, particularly relating to levels of evidence available.

It is clear from this review that more is reported and known about uses and outcomes of certain categories of digital technologies with specific groups of learners than it is with others, a point picked up further in the concluding chapter. From this review, there are two focal areas emerging, highlighted here and subsequently discussed in more detail:

- The first is the concept of lifelong learning. There is need for individuals to consider lifelong learning increasingly; digital technologies provide ways to enable lifelong learning practices.
- The second is the concept of intergenerational learning. Knowledge, skills and attitudes of young people in certain subject or topic areas (such as abilities to use certain social networking sites) is often more advanced than those in older people; practices to support uses of digital technologies across communities and societies need to integrate intergenerational learning practices.

Lifelong Learners

Lifelong learning is a concept increasingly affecting approaches being taken to education provision, and is likely to continue to affect concepts of learning and those engaged from early ages. Although effects of this concept will continue to emerge over time, evidence shows people increasingly need to take on board knowledge, attitudes and skills to enable them to engage with a series of vocations, as well as to continue to increase on-going development of communication and certain technical skills in their lifetime (see, for example, Sissons & Jones, 2012). The need for lifelong learning is clearly widening; how educational digital technologies might be used to support these practices, and the effects they have, are issues explored and described in policy areas, such as those

Table 4.3 Overview of how categories of digital technologies are being used with specific groups of learners

	Digital technology category							
	Topic-specific resources and software	Curriculum-wide learner-centred	Curriculum-wide teacher-centred	Software involving parents	Online resources used in classrooms	Online revision resources	Online learner support	Project and after-school club activities
Learners with limited cognitive abilities or attributes	Often used with evidence across a range of learners	Used more widely in the past than currently	Used with some groups but evidence is limited	Used with some groups but evidence is limited	Used with some groups with some evidence	Not commonly reported or evidenced	Not commonly reported or evidenced	Not commonly reported or evidenced
Learners with limited opportunities	Used in some cases but evidence is limited	Used more widely in the past than currently	Limited reports of use and evidence	Limited reports of use and evidence	Limited reports of use and evidence	Used in some cases but evidence is limited	Used in some cases but evidence is limited	Used in some cases but evidence is limited
Mainstream early learners	Often used with evidence across a range of learners	Limited reports of use and evidence	Limited reports of use and evidence	Used with evidence across a range of learners	Limited reports of use and evidence	Limited reports of use and evidence	Limited reports of use and evidence	Limited reports of use and evidence
Mainstream young learners	Often used with evidence across a range of learners	Used more widely in the past than currently	Often used with evidence across a range of learners	Used with evidence across a range of learners	Often used with evidence across a range of learners	Used in some cases but evidence is limited	Used in some cases but evidence is limited	Used with evidence across a range of learners
Mainstream secondary school or college age learners	Often used with evidence across a range of learners	Used more widely in the past than currently	Used with evidence across a range of learners	Limited reports of use and evidence	Often used with evidence across a range of learners	Used in some cases but evidence is limited	Used with evidence across a range of learners	Used with evidence across a range of learners
Learners with physical disabilities or attributes	Used in some cases but evidence is limited	Used but evidence is not always positive	Used in some cases but evidence is limited	Used in some cases but evidence is limited	Used in some cases but evidence is limited	Limited reports of use and evidence	Limited reports of use and evidence	Limited reports of use and evidence

Learners not physically present in classrooms or lessons	Used with evidence across a range of learners	Used in some cases but evidence is limited	Limited reports of use and evidence	Used in some cases but evidence is limited	Limited reports of use and evidence	Used in some cases but evidence is limited	Used in some cases but evidence is limited	Used with evidence across a range of learners
Learners with challenging emotional features and attributes	Used in some cases but evidence is limited	Used more widely in the past than currently	Limited reports of use and evidence	Used in some cases but evidence is limited	Limited reports of use and evidence	Used but evidence is not always positive	Used but evidence is not always positive	Used in some cases but evidence is limited
Learners where attitudes pose problems	Used in some cases but evidence is limited	Used more widely in the past than currently	Limited reports of use and evidence	Limited reports of use and evidence	Used in some cases but evidence is limited	Limited reports of use and evidence	Limited reports of use and evidence	Used with evidence across a range of learners
Learners with challenging behavioural attributes	Used in some cases but evidence is limited	Used more widely in the past than currently	Limited reports of use and evidence	Used in some cases but evidence is limited	Used with evidence across a range of learners	Used with evidence across a range of learners	Limited reports of use and evidence	Used with evidence across a range of learners
Learners with challenging social attributes and abilities	Used with evidence across a range of learners	Used more widely in the past than currently	Used with evidence across a range of learners	Used with evidence across a range of learners	Used with evidence across a range of learners	Used with evidence across a range of learners	Limited reports of use and evidence	Used with evidence across a range of learners
Learners where geography poses problems	Used with evidence across a range of learners	Limited reports of use and evidence	Not generally used	Not generally used	Used in some cases but evidence is limited	Used in some cases but evidence is limited	Used in some cases but evidence is limited	Limited reports of use and evidence

stated in the European Commission (EC) strategy document (EC, 2012): "in a rapidly changing world, lifelong learning needs to be a priority—it is the key to employment, economic success and allowing people to participate fully in society."

Digital technologies are increasingly supporting digital participation across age ranges. They are increasingly providing facilities, such as access to online courses, driving and supporting some lifelong learning practices. The development of appropriate and effective lifelong learning practices to sustain individual involvement has been the focus of a range of reports and studies. de Freitas et al. (2006) reported the development of an online system to support lifelong learning, which took a social network perspective in terms of its conceptual development, encouraging learners to consider how they might move along a lifelong learning pathway. As the authors said, "our user studies indicated that social networks (eg, parental influence, advice from friends and other learners) were extremely important for helping learners to make their educational choices and career decisions" (p. 878). They went on to say social networks were identified as being crucially important in situations where advice from tutors or careers advisors was not available. Their focus was, therefore, "to provide e-collaborative support for these informal social networks through online support and open access to communities of learners and practitioners" (p. 878).

The internet itself has been seen as a means to support social networking for lifelong learning purposes. As Wei and Chen (2006) said, "The Internet has recently been identified as a potential enabler of lifelong learning. Web-based learning systems enable learners easily to access rich resources and actively participate in learning activities without time and distance limits" (p. 917). These authors recognised a key challenge was to provide systems to support discussion as well as enabling collaborative forms of knowledge construction. They identified the application of knowledge in different contexts as being a vital need for a system to effectively support lifelong learning needs. Although they raised the importance of ways in which communities of lifelong learners could operate in this context, they argued that "Most online collaborative learning communities use Web text-based discussion forums for knowledge sharing. However, such discussion forums are separated from the context of learning activities" (p. 917). They argued further that effective dialogue requires roles of mentors, as facilitators and guides, concluding that "Students were satisfied with the means of posting contextual questions from e-books and the answers given by the adaptive mentors. Students accepted the mentors and benefited considerably from collaborative mentor support. Students preferred the supported forum to non-support discussion forums" (p. 929).

Digital technologies are being developed to support wider lifelong learning practices. For example, Gu, Gu, and Laffey (2011) reported how mobile lessons were being developed to support access on the move for lifelong learners in China. It is worth noting that while the study of Wei and Chen (2006) was undertaken with first-year computer studies students in a university environment, nevertheless, it is known that an increasing number of learners are accessing materials online, whether provided in bespoke forms by schools, or by businesses and companies, or as freely accessible material, from universities or organisations such as the *Khan Academy*. A message emerging from the reviews of lifelong learning practices is increasing numbers of online tutors or mentors are likely to be needed in the future, or, as an alternative, 'intelligent tutors' will be developed within background online management systems.

Evidence of uses of digital technologies and outcomes for lifelong learners can be summarised as follows:

- Topic-specific resources and software are increasingly being accessed by learners through the internet, and increasing ranges of free material as well as commercially accessible resources are becoming available online.
- Curriculum-wide software, teaching-wide software, parent-involved software, curriculum-supportive online resources, and project and after-school club activities involving digital technologies are not highlighted commonly for use in this context. This does not mean, however, they are not used, or resources in these categories will not be developed in the future.
- Online learner support has been used increasingly to support lifelong learners, and it appears this form of digital technology is likely to be developed further in the immediate future, alongside support provision practices integrating facilitation from online mentors and tutors.

Intergenerational Learners

A concept that should be considered in the context of learning enhanced through digital technologies is that of intergenerational learning. The concept often refers to older people supported in their learning by younger people. In a digital age, where concepts of 'digital natives' and 'digital immigrants' are raised as ways to define and consider what is being observed in practice (Prensky, 2001), it is important to recognise younger people often have skills older people do not. Young people may well have more time to practice and try out different ideas with digital technology devices, and consequently, young people are now in some cases supporting older people through intergenerational learning practices.

How digital technologies support intergenerational learning across different age groups, including children supporting their families, and older people being supported by children and other family members, has been explored in a range of studies (see Milligan & Passey, 2011). Exploring this concept from the learner perspective, certainly some learners have different views and concerns from teachers and tutors. For example, in considering the design of an online learning environment, Palaigeorgiou, Triantafyllakos, and Tsinakos (2011) reported on design features identified through 25 design sessions by 117 undergraduate information systems students, saying that "they extracted a great breadth of needs which are not met in their totality by any current system. Students evaluated 40% of their proposals as innovative" (p. 155).

At this time, few studies have explored concepts or models through which learners might support intergenerational learning practices. Passey (2011d) looked at this within the context of primary school learners supporting their parents using internet access and computer technologies in homes. In terms of the background of the parents and families receiving a computer and internet connectivity, "Most had used a computer before; 140 had not used a computer before, but 654 had. . . . 445 reported they did not have a computer or laptop in the home previously, while 340 reported they did" (p. 26). Similarly, 567 reported they had used the internet before while 216 had not, but nevertheless most felt they did not need help from their children, with 581 indicating they did not need training, while 194 said they did. In all these cases the primary aged children had wide experience of using computers and the internet in their schools. Training sessions were set up where family members could explore uses of the facilities with their children, encouraging family members to then explore these uses in their own homes, supported by their children. In many cases parents became involved in working with their children when they were set online homework activities, or when the children chose to do online learning activities. This form of intergenerational practice not only supported family members in terms of their understanding and skills, but also supported their children's learning through parental encouragement and involvement.

There is clearly scope for exploring the area of intergenerational learning with digital technologies more, especially perhaps in terms of how these practices themselves can support and enhance learning. Although the enhancement of ICT and digital skills is a clear focus, evidence also indicates certain models could support much wider and longer-term learning outcomes, especially through interactions with the primary or elementary school age group.

Evidence of uses of digital technologies and outcomes for intergenerational learners can be summarised as follows:

- Topic-specific resources and software have been used by learners involved in intergenerational learning practices, with primary age children and their parents. Some schools have supported their children in creating video clips about specific subject topics so these can be shown to parents at home to increase their awareness and understanding of 'new' topics, such as chunking in mathematics (see Passey, 2011e).
- Curriculum-wide software and teaching-wide software have not been reported to be used in this context.
- Parent-involved software has been identified and focused on specifically by some teachers in some projects.
- Curriculum-supportive online resources have been used by learners in the context of home learning and intergenerational learning, including uses of *Education City, Mathletics* and *Espresso Education* resources.
- Online learner support has been involved in some projects, and university level students have been involved in providing advice about the design of online environments.
- Project and after-school club activities involving digital technologies have been used in the sense of training sessions for family members involving their children, to develop awareness of online learning resources and how family members can be involved with their children in supporting their learning.

Chapter 5

Groups of Mediators and Uses of Digital Technologies in Supporting Learners

An Introduction

Learning arises often through a socially mediated process. This is as true when digital technologies are involved as it is without their involvement. Indeed references throughout the preceding chapters have often referred to the importance of mediation and its qualities when digital technologies are used, as well as the fact that measures of impacts when digital technologies are combined with effective mediation are greater (see, for example, Tamim et al., 2011). In this text and in others, the importance of recognising that digital technologies play a part within a wider learning landscape is itself an important concept—removing or isolating the digital technology from its landscape can have effects and implications. This concept is considered in more depth by Luckin (2010), who articulates this in terms of a learning ecology.

Learning landscapes (or ecologies), however, by their definitions, are likely to be both complex and diffuse. Indeed digital technologies add complexity to the landscape of learning, rather than creating a single, clear pathway. For example, a learner may be using a desk-top digital system within a school, but at home will be using a laptop system, and in a visit to a museum will be using a handheld or mobile system. Some authors have referred to issues raised by this complexity as being 'disruptive' (see, for example, Hedberg, 2011, who discusses disruptive impacts of mobile technologies on pedagogical concerns and practices of teachers in Australia). Mediation also adds complexity; mediation is not always confined to one mediator, but results from a combination of interactions through a range of mediators. Mediators can span different forms of focus for different learners: for example, teachers in schools and further education colleges, career support workers for young people who are seeking education, employment or training, or targeted youth support workers. Each of these groups has their own focus of concern; ways digital technologies can support their needs and the needs of those they in turn support are clearly often quite different and specific. This chapter considers these mediators, and looks at ways digital technologies have been used to support their specific remits, focusing on learning.

Mediators Support Different Groups of Learners

Ways mediators work in terms of a learning landscape vary; there are mediators providing support in quite informal settings (parents and guardians), or in quite formal settings (teachers), or in non-formal settings (youth workers at organised youth centre events). Some mediators do not meet learners face-to-face (such as online mentors), while others meet them for very specific purposes (such as youth offending workers). To explore ways educational digital technologies match support needs of different mediators, six groups are considered here.

Teachers are supporters within schools or colleges, working within classroom or workshop environments, within formal settings generally, and within specified time slots with certain groups of learners. A wide range of manuals and texts have been written about and for this group, considering ways digital technologies can be integrated into teaching and learning practices (for example Newby, Stepich, Lehman, & Russell, 2006; Beetham & Sharpe, 2007; Sharpe, Beetham, & de Freitas, 2010).

Teaching assistants are those working alongside teachers, within classroom or workshop environments, in formal settings. They are not teachers, but support the work of teachers, and often are asked to work on specific curriculum aspects with smaller groups of, or individual, learners. Some are asked to search for or to generate digital resources. A limited range of manuals and texts have been written about and for this group (for example Fox, 2001; Balshaw & Farrell, 2002), while guidance and advice on using digital technologies is available online (for example, Classroom Assistant, n.d.).

Parents and guardians work in quite different environments, supporting children in informal settings, varying from emotional support to technical support. Often parents support children in indirect rather than direct ways, encouraging and praising their learning, rather than giving advice or guidance on subject or content matter. Research has shown that the form of involvement of parents is important, and when focused in particular ways, gains are positive (for example, Desforges & Abouchaar, 2003; Harris & Goodall, 2007).

Support workers and youth workers are those often working with young people in their adolescent years, in informal as well as non-formal settings, particularly in social environments or community centres (to support emotional and social needs, as well as career needs, for example). In some cases, learning is focused on specific areas of concern, when, for example, young people are seeking employment. Few manuals and texts have been written about this group, although some reports have focused on careers, support and youth workers using educational digital technologies with young people (for example, Bimrose, Barnes, & Attwell, 2010; Passey & Davies, 2010).

Counsellors are those who have a specific support agenda, normally affiliated to an agency concerned with a social or emotional need, such as mental health and well-being, housing needs, or to support and monitor in circumstances concerned with drug, alcohol or criminal activities. Although counsellors do not have a specific educational remit, they are often involved at least in indirect ways, in supporting young people in moving towards a more stable or socially acceptable lifestyle, through which they offer educational advice as well as support through educational programmes addressing specific social or behavioural issues. Few manuals and texts have been written for this group about using digital technologies, although some reports have focused on counsellors supporting those involved in drug or criminal-related activities using educational digital technologies (for example, Haché et al., 2010).

Online tutors are supporters working at a distance, maybe using a range of different digital technologies in order to engage with young people (facsimile machines were used the past, whereas Skype, online learning platforms and environments, email and video-conferencing tend now to be the media most used). Many studies have focused on this group of supporters, and have identified a variety of outcomes from different perspectives, and a range of manuals have been published also (for example, Higginson, 2001; Murphy, Walker, & Webb, 2001).

Teachers

Teachers have important roles in supporting learning influenced through digital technologies. Vekiri (2010a) surveyed 301 grade 8 and 9 learners (135 boys and 166 girls) taught by seven teachers (four females and three males) at four schools, showing both boys' and girls' beliefs about computers and information science were differentially affected by parents, teachers, and school information science teaching. Luu and Freeman (2011) highlighted the implications; using data from the Programme for International Student Assessment (PISA, 2006), the authors found scientific literacy was predicted by a number of ICT-related variables, including student prior experience with ICT, frequency of browsing the internet, and confidence with basic ICT skills, and these were all associated with gaining higher scores in science.

Levels of Use in Supporting Teaching

In terms of teachers engaging with uses of digital technologies to support their teaching, studies have often shown they engage in more ways than might be expected. In the UK context Infogroup/ORC International (2010) reported, in at least half their lessons, 63% of teachers used ICT to help learners be creative, 56% used ICT to gather information, 47% used ICT to analyse information, 50% used ICT to problem solve, 55% used ICT to enable learners to work with others, and 27% used ICT to share information between learners. From the same survey, at least fortnightly, over 75% of teachers in primary, secondary and special schools used ICT for assessment purposes; 93% of ICT teachers used ICT for assessment purposes, and 69% of other subject teachers used ICT for assessment purposes. The teachers in the survey reported using a variety of digital resources in their lessons, most frequently via interactive whiteboards, using image and text-based documents.

By contrast, studies from countries around the world indicate concerns with low levels of use of digital technologies. In India, for example, a study by Kulkarni (2012), taking data from 300 teachers across 45 secondary schools, looked at factors contributing to low levels of use. The author found there were no significant differences in terms of attitudes on the basis of gender, but there was on the basis of home ownership.

There has been increasing evidence, however, that impacts on attainment can arise when digital technologies and teaching practices effectively work together. Waxman et al. (2003), from their meta-analysis of prior studies, found that "The mean study-weighted effect size for the 29 study-weighted comparisons containing cognitive outcomes was .448, (p < .01), with a 95-percent confidence interval of .171 to .724" (p. 12). They concluded teaching with digital technologies had a small but positive effect on learners and their cognitive attainment, when impact was compared to traditional forms of teaching. They also found this level of effect held, independently of other factors. Using a series of ANOVA tests, exploring 57 independent variables, they found and concluded "the results do not differ significantly across categories of technology, instructional characteristics, methodological rigor, characteristics of the study, and subject characteristics" (p. 12).

Appropriateness of Applications

Some teachers raise concerns about forms of digital technologies used in schools, and their appropriateness to age group. Teacher concerns about using digital technologies might be international, but differences across countries are also recognised. Joshi, Pan, Murakami, and Narayanan (2010) in their study of kindergarten teachers in the US and Japan found different beliefs about roles of computers in their classrooms, with the Japanese teachers sharing more concerns. As Aubrey and Dahl (2008) stated, "Chang, Mullen and Stuve (2005) argued that the frequency and form of computing for young children was still open to definition at the classroom level" (p. 42). They reported the case where five- and six-year-old learners in a classroom were using PDAs, and from ways in which learners were able to access and use them, concluded "the PDA operating system requires simpler steps in overall manipulation and may be more suitable for young children. It is noted, however, that whether a PDA is an appropriate technology for young children depends largely on its implementation" (p. 42). As the authors went on to say, although the learners relied on adult guidance, they easily handled the devices through uses of icons and keys.

Some researchers have identified how pedagogy and uses of digital technologies can support specific topics or subject learning. As Soe et al. (2000) said: "Reading instruction aligned with computer-assisted instruction can serve as a powerful teaching tool to assist teachers in helping students reach their potential in reading" (p. 14). But, teachers have also noted difficulties in shifting their pedagogies when they use digital technologies. As Looi et al. (2011) found when looking at the introduction of mobile devices into a classroom, "the teacher felt pressurized to cover the essential learning points through a teacher-centred approach (teach to textbook). She was task oriented and aimed to finish the predefined drill-and-practice activities in the conventional curriculum in the stipulated time" (p. 279). Following the use of the mobile devices in the classroom with learners, however, the researchers saw from observations of teaching practice "a transition from didactic teaching to student-centred learning. She was inclined to give students more time to construct their own understanding rather than feed them with information" (p. 279). The researchers also noticed the teacher gave learners more time to answer questions, rather than providing them quickly with answers.

Some authors have studied and described differences arising in terms of pedagogical approaches. For example, Ejiwale (2012) found that "The reformation of the instruction of subjects across STEM fields has changed the role of

STEM educators from being 'dictators' in the classroom/ laboratory to being facilitators of students' activities" (p. 87). The author emphasised that the change in pedagogy was concerned with how the teacher saw their role within a wider educational environment or learning ecology or landscape. The author went on to say this meant the level of certain pedagogies in classroom practices had shifted, and "This is enhanced by instructional strategies and delivery that synergize diverse students, strategies, technologies, societies, and subjects" (p. 87).

Matching Pedagogies

Other authors have studied differences in pedagogy arising when digital technologies are used, and have identified specific learning aspects supported as a consequence. For example, Rosen and Beck-Hill (2012) found, when they compared pedagogies in classrooms where digital technologies were used with those where they were not, "the experimental teachers commented that they had a differentiated curriculum available at their fingertips through the program, which made planning and implementing differentiation more feasible and more consistently functional" (p. 237). Further, the researchers noted the differentiation took content, process and product into account, leading to varied pedagogical approaches and strategies. They also commented that "The areas of differentiation that include rigor, teacher feedback, collaboration, and instructional scaffolding were also apparent more often in the experimental classrooms than in the traditional classrooms of the control schools" (p. 237). Shifts in pedagogies are being identified in different subject and topic areas. Felvégi and Matthew (2012), for example, highlighted ways that e-books are shifting a signature pedagogy—reading literacy instruction.

The literature does identify pedagogies that are not only subject or topic specific, but that are effective. Ucar and Trundle (2011), in a study looking at the development in 96 pre-service teachers of science conceptions of tides following access to different forms of data, found 72% having inquiry-based instruction with archived online data held scientific conceptual understanding, 46% having traditional instruction supported with a simulation held scientific conceptual understanding, but only 43% having traditional instruction held scientific conceptual understanding. Similarly, Savage et al. (2010) in a controlled study involving 60 learners six to seven years of age using a technology-based literacy intervention program called *ABRACADABRA*, when compared to learners using a non-technology program, delivered through three different teaching approaches, found the largest impacts were associated with adaptation, where technology-based content was linked clearly and regularly to other wider learning themes. In another subject and topic context, Watson, Mong, and Harris (2011) in their study indicated how a teacher in a high school using a video game designed to teach about the topic of the Second World War shifted his pedagogy to a learner-centred approach, moving around the classroom, asking and answering questions, and picking up on key points with the class. In a recent report, Luckin et al. (2012) used a taxonomy for learning activities matching pedagogical approaches with uses and applications of digital technologies closely. They used the following categories, and illustrated clearly teachers were using these forms of activities through adapted pedagogies: learning from experts;

learning from others; learning through making; learning through exploring; learning through inquiry; learning through practising; learning from assessment; and learning in and across settings.

In Summary

Uses of digital technologies and outcomes for learning mediated by teachers arise through a number of forms of mediational interactivity, summarised in Table 5.1.

Additionally, teachers can use resources to develop caring thinking in learners, which can be appreciative (of needs and concerns of others), active (asking them to participate in discussion), normative (providing examples of acceptable practice), effective (in terms of those found to be most positive), and empathetic (concerned with feelings and attitudes of others). Teachers can also use digital resources in lessons focusing on citizenship (the role and behaviour of individuals in society), work (examples of how subject topics are used within work), recreation (making learners aware of resources to support their own interests outside lessons), and for personal, social and health education.

Teaching Assistants

Their Roles

Feiler and Watson (2011) described the often vitally important role teaching assistants (TAs) play, stating they work in situations where they can "develop such close relationships, which can result in a level of involvement that is immensely valued by children and families. This is recognised in the UK Audit Commission's (2003) report on services for children with disability" (p. 118). In spite of this recognised important role, the literature on teaching assistants and practices, and how these involve digital technologies, is sparse; there is more discussion about the role of the teaching assistant in general. Their role in inclusion (of learners with special needs, managing those with behavioural issues, or supporting integration), for example, was described by Tucker (2009) as "central to the role of many TAs by managers, teachers and parents alike. Yet at the same time there are indications offered through research that the contribution of TAs to inclusion is not always viewed as necessarily positive" (p. 293). Devecchi, Dettori, Doveston, Sedgwick, and Jament (2012) outlined main aspects of support provided by teaching assistants (called classroom assistants and support teachers in some countries) and by higher level teaching assistants (HLTAs) "facilitating instruction and access to the curriculum by providing differentiation or carrying out intervention programmes; supporting the assessment of children and monitoring their progress; managing children's behaviour and attending to their emotional needs; carrying out varied administrative tasks" (p. 176). Some differences do occur across countries, and the authors highlighted ways support teachers in Italy and teaching assistants in England work: "In Italy, by law the collaboration between classroom and support teachers should be between equals. In England, TAs and HLTAs work under the management and supervision of classroom teachers and/or the SENCO." They also pointed out

Table 5.1 Mediational interactions used by teachers to support learners

Mediational interactivity	Digital technology involvement
Instruction	Many teachers globally now use interactive whiteboards to instruct, using these facilities for presentational purposes, using visual, auditory and textual media available
Explanation and illustration	As above, teachers are using interactive whiteboards for these purposes, but are also using handheld and mobile devices, including electronic calculators and geometry and algebra facilities
Direction	Teachers do use interactive whiteboards to direct learning, but also use laptops, desk-tops and online systems to support this form of interaction
Demonstration	Teachers use add-on devices to project images and magnified items, as well as accessing video material online to support demonstration
Discussion	Teachers use a range of different devices to encourage discussion; resources via interactive whiteboards are used to stimulate classroom discussion, or via laptops and handheld devices to stimulate discussions in smaller groups
Scaffolding	Teachers increasingly use the power of annotation on interactive whiteboard screens, commenting on individual learner documents, and offering cues in online discussions to scaffold learning
Questioning	Again, teachers use a range of devices, including material presented on interactive whiteboards, video clips followed by questions, and online discussion groups through which to pose and have questions posed, which they can create themselves, or encourage learners to, or gain these from external experts
Speculation	Teachers use digital resources via interactive whiteboards to ask learners to speculate about possibilities, but they also do this through the online medium
Consolidation	Teachers use handheld voting devices as well as online questions and quizzes, or access to online revision material, to support consolidation
Summarising	Teachers ask learners to summarise key points from lessons in plenary sessions, as well as asking them to create notes that are summaries of wider documents
Initiating and guiding exploration	Teachers use sequences of digital resources to take learners along learning pathways, and also provide notes and questions online that provide stimuli to initiate avenues for exploration
Evaluating learners' responses	Teachers use online quizzes so that learners can gain immediate feedback about their responses, but they also then look at these responses as well as materials that are sent to them by learners online to evaluate their progress

that, in Italy, support teachers work directly with both parents and professionals, while in England there is no certainty this is the case.

In terms of roles within certain subject lessons, Houssart (2012) described roles of TAs in mathematics lessons. Although roles were found to vary widely, some general approaches taken by the sample group were also found: "Many TAs pointed out that how they worked depended on the teacher and varied considerably even within the same school" (p. 394). The author reported teaching assistants could find their support roles changing when they moved to a different class or year group, and while many found they supported learners facing most challenges with mathematics, one worked with the most able in a class. From 23 interviews conducted, the author identified four broad ways TAs worked: with an individual withdrawn from the class; with the same small group of learners; moving around different groups of learners; and working as required by the teacher.

Using Digital Technologies

TAs do use a range of digital technologies to support learners, although this can vary across classrooms and across schools. In terms of using an online learning platform, Passey (2011e) explored how TAs in some primary schools supported learners using these facilities, and looked also at how TAs used online digital resources to support learners in primary classrooms. In this study, 20 TAs in 11 schools, across a single LA responding to a survey, provided details about uses of online digital resources and their perceptions of use. All TAs felt the online digital resources (*Espresso Education* in this case) supported their needs, reporting using the resources across a wide subject range, with lower levels of use in subjects with less curriculum time (modern foreign languages, music and art). High levels of use were reported in numeracy and literacy, and moderate levels of use in geography, citizenship, science, history and religious education. The TAs reported the key features they valued most: high presentational qualities; ease of navigation; maintaining learner focus and keeping them on-task; and maintaining an up-to-date and meaningful curriculum.

School Librarians

Taking a very broad definition of TAs, to include all those supporting teachers in school in providing or supporting learning activities, school librarians would be a group included. They not only increasingly use and provide access through digital technologies, but are concerned with future strategic implementation and directions. For example, Hay (2012) stated in the Australian context, "As a result of the Australian Government's Building the Education (BER) funding program (DEEWR, 2009), a process of re-envisioning school libraries has been experienced by many school communities in the past two to three years" (p. 29). The author highlighted how building and renovation of school libraries had stimulated discussion about ways they could best meet learner needs over the next century. Hay (2012) described this in terms of

increasing demand for digital citizenship education programs in schools, the needs of students, teachers, principals, and parents have "shifted," and teacher librarians are seeing the culmination of all these changes as an opportunity to rethink "what we do" in school libraries.

(p. 29)

The author went on to describe features of a widely-accessible technology-supported school library: "An ICentre: is a qualified team of information, technology, and learning experts; is a central facility where strategic and operational functionality is driven by an integrated team approach; provides programs and services to support 21st-century learners" (p. 29). The author concluded by arguing school librarians need to provide what is relevant, flexibly, 24 hours a day and 7 days a week, customised to schools and homes, where pedagogy is considered in terms of library policy and practice, providing for the needs of all stakeholders.

Digital technology systems are themselves being developed to support school librarian practices. Chen and Tsai (2012) in their study showed students using an augmented reality library information system gained to the same extent as those using traditional librarian instruction, with the new system supporting learners with field-dependent cognitive styles better.

In Summary

Uses of digital technologies and outcomes for learning mediated by TAs arise through a number of forms of mediational interactivity, summarised in Table 5.2.

Additionally, TAs use resources to develop caring thinking in learners, through discussions with individual or small groups of learners, especially when TAs support learners with emotional or social or behavioural needs. In those cases particularly, TAs can support caring thinking that is appreciative (of needs and concerns of others), active (asking them to participate in discussion), normative (providing examples of acceptable practice), effective (in terms of those found to be most positive), and empathetic (concerned with feelings and attitudes of others). Although uses of digital technologies by TAs are often concerned with subject or topic needs, they can also use resources focusing on other societal aspects—citizenship (the role and behaviour of individuals in society), work (giving examples of how subject or topic learning is used beyond the classroom in work situations), and recreation (highlighting resources to learners that might support their own interests outside lessons).

Parents and Guardians

Parents and guardians find digital technologies in their homes allow their children to increasingly access school and college work and resources online. Educational work completed at home, integrated by the teacher with school practices, tends to be rather different in primary (elementary) from that in secondary (high) schools. In primary schools parents are often encouraged to read to their children, listen to their children reading, to encourage their children to complete homework activities and have an overview of what they are doing. In secondary schools parents are often encouraged to take a more distant role; to encourage but not to be too involved, so their children

Table 5.2 Mediational interactions used by teaching assistants to support learners

Mediational interactivity	Digital technology involvement
Instruction	Teaching assistants have often used topic-specific resources and software to support individual needs and groups of learners, but are now increasingly using online resources to meet these purposes
Explanation and illustration	Online resources are increasingly being accessed by teaching assistants to provide sources of explanation and illustration, particularly to support subject topics in literacy and numeracy
Direction	Teaching assistants use online examples to direct the attention of learners to approaches they might take in their learning of subject matter
Demonstration	Online digital resources provide teaching assistants with examples that can be used to demonstrate particular techniques or strategies when learning about certain subject topics
Discussion	Discussion has always been a focal element in teaching assistant interactions. Online resources and topic-specific resources and software are used in order to enhance discussion or focus the discussion
Scaffolding	Scaffolding has been another focal element constructed by teaching assistants in supporting learners. They have often broken down learning challenges into steps, so that learners can move forward through staged approaches. Online digital resources and topic-specific resources and software are being used to support these approaches
Questioning	Teaching assistants encourage questioning by learners, in order to understand their needs as much as possible. Digital resources are sometimes used to encourage this questioning, but this is not observed as standard practice
Speculation	Teaching assistants do encourage learners to speculate, but their key roles are often focused on specific elements of learning, rather than using resources to stimulate speculation
Consolidation	Consolidation is often a key aim of interactions with teaching assistants. Digital resources often provide materials that allow learners to re-try and practice other examples of questions and problems, which enhances the range of consolidation opportunities for teaching assistants
Summarising	Summarising is often a key concern for teaching assistants when they are supporting writing or reading, for example. Increasing use is seen of texts that enable highlighting of key words and phrases for these purposes

Initiating and guiding exploration	Initiating and guiding exploration is often within the realm of the teacher rather than the teaching assistant, although some activities run by teaching assistants encourage learners to explore resource banks or internet resources to engage learners through areas of their interests
Evaluating learners' responses	Teaching assistants are focally concerned with evaluating learner responses. Using digital resources, often perceived as a neutral medium by learners, teaching assistants can gain valuable insights into a learner's responses to problems and questions. When curriculum-wide learner-centred software was used more commonly, it was often teaching assistants who explored and evaluated learner responses reported by the systems

become 'independent' learners. Actually, learners in this latter instance are being encouraged to be 'individual' learners rather than 'independent', and it can be argued their abilities to seek and gain support from parents and other adults, and the important opportunities this affords, are being unfortunately somewhat diminished. If parents are to support their children at home, it is important parents and guardians have access to 'artefacts' (resources they can use) and 'scaffolding' (ideas of how to use resources and develop learning outcomes) when they are not sure about subject or topic content (see Passey, 2011e).

The important role parents can play in supporting their children's learning, and in turn such support leading to higher attainments, are well documented in the research literature (see Bransford, Brown, & Cocking, 2000; Passey, 2011b). The impact of parental support on children's learning was summarised by Desforges and Abouchaar (2003) from their review of the literature, stating "parental involvement in the form of 'at-home good parenting' has a significant positive effect on children's achievement" (p. 4). They found for children in primary schools "the impact caused by different levels of parental involvement is much bigger than differences associated with variations in the quality of schools" (pp. 4–5). Harris and Goodall, in a later report to the then government department for education (DfES, 2007), stated: "Parental engagement is a powerful lever for raising achievement in schools. Where parents and teachers work together to improve learning, the gains in achievement are significant" (p. 5). They went on to make an important distinction: the greatest levels of influence and impact arise when parents support learning at home, rather than parents supporting events in a school, stating: "Where these activities are not directly connected to learning they have little impact on pupil achievement" (p. 5). Digital technologies supporting learning at home can clearly impact outcomes for learners.

But parents clearly influence what, when, how and why children use digital technologies at home. Valcke, Bonte, De Wever, and Rots (2010), in a survey of 533 parents of primary school children, found generally there was high internet access at home, with highest use by children when parents adopted more 'permissive' styles of interaction with their children, but parent uses of the internet and their educational backgrounds were also significant predictors of internet use by children at home. Similarly, Bourgonjon, Valcke, Soetaert, de Wever, and Schellens (2011) found parents' acceptance of games for learning was based largely around their views about learning opportunities they felt were provided in schools, whether they recognised games as being normally present in a learning setting, their beliefs about negative effects of gaming, their own experiences, their interests in innovation, and ideas about gender appropriateness.

How parents can positively influence their children has been the focus of a number of studies. Plowman, Stevenson, Stephen, and McPake (2012) analysed 14 case studies showing parents and guardians could support early learners with operational skills, extending learners' ideas about the world in which they live, encouraging learning in itself, and showing ways digital technologies could be commonly used. On the other hand, Eagle (2012), from a review of literature about uses of technologies with young children supported by their parents at home, argued the artefact itself has a bearing, particularly in cases where the parent associates this with certain practices; in the case of digital technologies this appears to reduce the role of the early learner in identifying learning goals or offering alternative ideas or explanations. In terms of ways to support parents and their positive involvement, Gil-Flores, Torres-Gordillo, and Perera-Rodríguez (2012) looked at the performance of 4,748 learners in Spain with their online experiences, and concluded digital reading performance would be enhanced by improving information seeking and searching activities at home.

Parental Concerns

While some parents wish to use digital technologies to support children's learning at home, they may at the same time be concerned about introducing uses of digital technologies to their children at a young age. Aubrey and Dahl (2008) recommended "ICT use by young children needs to be supervised and software available in the home or EYFS will need to be vetted for suitability as would be the case for any other book, toy or video" (p. 45). They argued young children's use of ICT should be observed, monitored and recorded, to ensure uses of digital technologies match children's developmental needs. They highlighted appropriate uses of digital technologies to support social interactions, cognitive development in specific areas, and links to teacher activities, as being particularly valuable. They went on to detail more specific uses of digital technologies with younger learners, stressing the roles of adults and parents in: mediating uses for social interaction; viewing and interacting when children watch television programmes; overseeing when children play educational games with other children; mediating in ways allowing children to maintain control of the operation of devices; and in ways supporting children's self-esteem.

Parents and guardians may have specific concerns about children's uses of online social media, but a study (Alloway, Horton, & Alloway, 2013) involving 104 15- to 17-year-old learners in a school in the UK showed that, when they used *Facebook* (but not *YouTube*) to check the status of friends for more than a year, this practice was associated with higher scores in tests of verbal ability, working memory, and spelling, as well as scores for social connectedness, compared to those using it for a shorter time period.

Parental Involvement and Learner Outcomes

Digital technologies over the past 15 years or so have been used in a range of ways in homes to support learning; some have been concerned with internet access to sites for research purposes, others with developing items published to a wide audience, others with games and competitive activities on a worldwide level, and others with links to school work and teachers—and this list is not exhaustive. Some studies have explored potential impacts arising from this range of home-based activities. Somekh et al. (2007), reporting on a national initiative involving 28 schools with high levels of ICT and with home links, reported a shift over four years resulting in levels of attainment in "mathematics, 64% to 75% compared to 74% to 73% for the comparator schools" (p. 8). These results related high levels of technologies to an enabling of learning activities to be undertaken in schools and in homes leading to statistically significant results for learners aged 7 to 11 years. Watson and Watson (2011) studied outcomes arising at home and in school for learners in a disadvantaged alternative school with limited access to resources, stating "CBI [computer-based instruction] technology was important in this learner-centered culture, playing the role of an instructional choice that provided students with self-paced learning for math and science" (p. 52). Digital technology resources can clearly provide opportunities for children to work in locations remote from classrooms and schools. But, the development of social interactions to support those activities is clearly an important contributory aspect highlighted in the literature.

Intergenerational Practices

In considering appropriate ways to support parental engagement with children's learning through digital technologies, approaches to intergenerational learning practices in the home have played important roles in the development of some practices (Passey, 2012c). Affordances and selected forms of topic-specific software, software involving and supporting parents, and online learner support, are all factors influencing involvement, interactions and outcomes when parents and guardians support, praise, discuss, question, or help learners to consolidate or to summarise.

Passey (2011d) detailed findings of a community-based project, providing computers and internet access to parents and their children within a socio-economically deprived area of England, using an intergenerational learning approach. The initiative enabled parents to provide computers and internet access to support their children and their children's learning. A focus of the project was on parental training and involvement; training programmes for parents were run regularly, to raise their ICT skills. Workshop sessions were offered, focusing on how parents could work with their children using online resources teachers would set for homework activities. Parents reported they particularly valued the benefits associated with homework for children, being able to be engaged and monitor what their children were doing in their learning. Although the quantitative element of this study did not deploy a randomised control model, tests used were age standardised. For matched results, for learners tested initially at 7 to 9 years of age and finally at 8 to 10 years of age, a paired sample t-test showed the difference between the start and end scores was highly statistically significant ($t=-8.58$, $p=0.000$). Overall, mathematics results shifted positively and strongly across this period of time, when schools focused on interventions to raise mathematics attainment, with a specific focus on homework activities involving mathematics practice using resources at home. Girls gained more over this period of time, and from multiple regression analyses, when predictive impacts on the final scores were considered, four factors together (having a project computer, gender, year group, and the baseline test score) accounted for 70% of the differences noted.

In Summary

Uses of digital technologies and outcomes for learning mediated by parents and guardians arise through a number of forms of mediational interactivity, summarised in Table 5.3.

Parents and guardians can play significant roles with their children in terms of longer-term engagement and thinking. Through ways parents and guardians talk about digital technologies, and ways they perceive those technologies being used, they can support their children in terms of caring thinking—appreciating the importance of uses or benefits, showing active engagement, providing normative role models, indicating what effect caring has with regard to use of

Table 5.3 Mediational interactions used by parents and guardians to support learners

Mediational interactivity	Digital technology involvement
Instruction	Parents and guardians are not generally involved in instructional practice, but may well highlight specific website resources or online resources that could be of benefit in particular topics or subject areas
Explanation and illustration	Using online resources, either produced within a school specifically or those accessed in more ad hoc ways via the internet, children can be involved in explaining and illustrating points, facts or understanding to their parents or guardians
Direction	Parents and guardians can take a hand in directing efforts, whether it be encouraging children to complete homework activities, or encouraging them to explore areas and to research topics online that could be of interest to them

Demonstration	Generally children demonstrate principles or practice to their guardians and parents more than guardians or parents demonstrating to their children. However, some parents are skilled in particular areas of practice (sometimes digital practice) or subjects or topics, and in these cases can readily discuss and demonstrate ideas or knowledge or concepts
Discussion	Parents and guardians play a key role in engaging and maintaining discussion with their children, whether this is when children are using digital technologies or not
Scaffolding	Some schools and providers are now increasingly supporting parents and guardians by providing scaffolding to help them engage with their children in particular ways
Questioning	Parents and guardians can engage positively with their children through questioning. When children are accessing, or have completed, activities that are digitally based, parents and guardians can support the learning resulting by questioning children so that their knowledge and understanding is being challenged and consolidated
Speculation	Parents and guardians may play a role in supporting speculation, if they ask their children 'what if' questions
Consolidation	When children have completed activities, discussion about these can support consolidation. Parents and guardians asking children to explain their answers and learning can help to consolidate that learning. Many parents do feel unsure of their own subject or topic knowledge, however, especially as this becomes more detailed as children get older, and the act of consolidation may then need to move more towards encouragement of teacher involvement
Summarising	Parents and guardians can play a key role in helping their children to pick out key points, and to summarise their learning. Suitable questions asked by parents and guardians can stimulate this form of thinking in their children
Initiating and guiding exploration	Parents and guardians can play a key role in initiating exploration, by suggesting or encouraging children to look at particular subject or topic areas, or to look at them in particular ways
Evaluating learners' responses	Although parents and guardians may not feel competent in evaluating their children's responses, encouragement and praise can themselves be important as means to evaluate responses

digital technologies, and showing empathy with regard to different users and outcomes. Similarly, they can play key roles in modelling thinking and behaviours encouraging children to maintain engagement with education and how they will engage with education in the future, how they will use digital technologies to be involved as active citizens, how they and others use the digital technologies for work, and for recreation.

Support Workers and Youth Workers

Uses of Digital Technologies

Passey and Davies (2010), in a study exploring uses of digital technologies across groups of support and youth workers, identified a number of ways digital technologies were used:

- Engaging and maintaining contact with young people (using mobile devices, or email).
- Providing courses or learning opportunities (creating presentations, undertaking research, or producing video clips).
- Creating records of achievement (creating online texts or CVs, or multimedia presentations through a learning platform, or developing e-portfolios).
- Matching interests with vacancies, voluntary activities or apprenticeships (linking database records with alerts sent out through a learning platform).
- Collecting and reporting opportunities of vacancies arising (linking website information from different sources, or inputting data into a single accessible database source).
- Collecting and reporting data about the status of young people (using databases to record information, selected and reported to other stakeholders).

But they concluded (Passey & Davies, 2010) that "Technologies currently in place are being used most commonly to offer two forms of support: communication between support workers and young people; and the provision of information to young people" (p. 77). In the latter case, Bimrose et al. (2010) explored ways websites were being used to support guidance in careers advice. They concluded: "The current use of internet-based technologies in service delivery for guidance is currently limited" (p. 35). They went on to say use of digital technologies as a resource was more commonly found than its use as either for communication or for developing materials. So, as they said, "Most participants used the internet routinely for researching information for their work role" (p. 35). But, more encouragingly, they also noted PAs were coaching young people in using websites, "some by simply providing the url for sites recommended as part of guidance to research and some by sitting next to young people during a guidance interview and coaching their usage" (p. 35). They identified the most commonly accessed and used internet resources, "CV writing; KUDOS; Jobs4U; UCAS; Unistats; job and work experience vacancies; and Area Prospectus" (p. 35). While the importance of interacting and mediating when digital technologies are used has been raised so often, the authors found "The use of technology as a medium for communication was more limited amongst the participant sample. Email was used to a limited extent with young people, though more heavily used to communicate with other PAs" (p. 35). The authors noted online discourse (email or texts) often only happened after discourse through more traditional routes had been established, and often for reminder purposes rather than anything more substantial. Duplication of services, safety concerns with contacting young people, and costs were all raised as issues, and led to reduced uses of communication facilities across the accessible range—from telephones to chat rooms.

Uses of Social Media

In spite of issues and concerns about social media, some developments and studies have indicated the positive potential digital technologies could afford in terms of communication using social media. Prinzjakowitsch and Seisenbacher (2010) described reasons for considering uses of social media by youth workers in Austria: "Social Software tools or Web 2.0 are a constantly growing part of the Internet. Especially for youngsters these tools have become a part of their daily life" (p. 21). On the basis that both quality and quantities of contacts between youth workers and young people who were at risk of being socially marginalised could be increased, Verein Wiener Jugendzentren (the Association of Viennese Youth Centres, VJZ) together with the Vienna University of Technology under-took an EU project in 2010, developing and using social network sites (SNS). Three youth centres were selected for the project, and all three provided volun-tary access to facilities including table games, board games and internet access on a drop-in basis. Fifteen young people were involved in the project, both boys and girls, between 13 and 19 years of age, all from families with a low socio-economic or migrant background, or both. Each young person was given a Netbook computer and mobile internet access. The young people were asked to complete two activities using the digital technologies: to create a Christmas card; and to create a multimedia CV using presentational software. The authors reported the activities were not successful, and "To a great extent this was due to the fact that both activities did not come from the youngsters themselves . . . Also, in both cases the abilities of the youngsters in working with standard software was overestimated" (p. 24). However, the authors reported the ICT facilities and skills developed were used in a range of ways by the young people, leading to positive outcomes: "Some youngsters started to intensively work with the Netbooks, in one case even building up some network and programming skills. Image editing software that was not used during the Christmas card activity was widely used to improve profile pictures" (p. 24). As the authors said, skills in accessing the internet were used extensively by the young people, and passed on to others visiting the centres. Even though the non-formal activities did not work in ways mediators had planned, nevertheless the aims of the project were fulfilled: "In general, the number and intensity of contacts between youngsters and youth workers increased both in quantity and in quality" (p. 25). An important point raised by the authors was: "Activities that came either directly or indirectly from the youngsters or met their immediate needs were more successful" (p. 24).

Youth Worker Uses

Some youth workers are developing uses of digital technologies to support both communications with young people and to support the development of specific aspects of learning. Bacon (2010) described her reasons for using digital technologies as a youth worker, saying "Social media platforms create dynamic, variable and constantly evolving environments to engage with young people and enable their participation in local issues/services" (p. 215). Her uses have focused on creative and content generation as well as on communication (Bacon, 2010), since "Online digital media offers new tools which enable young people to move from consumer to creators of content and the Internet gives access to a wealth of free content that can be used in work creatively with young people" (p. 215). She highlighted how different forms of digital technologies could support communication—social network site group discussions and chatting through instant messenger—while also indicating the need to consider safety and effectiveness, saying: "The opportunities for positive use of social media by practitioners working with young people are almost unlimited—providing practitioners think carefully about how to make their engagement with social media safe, sustainable and effective" (p. 215). She described three projects using a social media platform she had run: enabling young people to participate in local elections, exchange information, and enabling views of those at risk to be heard; enabling young parents to communicate across the area, exchange information, and enabling views to contribute to area policy and decision making; enabling a group of at risk young people to research, gather and record views of other young people from across the area, and to report more widely through a variety of digital media, including images, video clips and textual reports.

Youth Counsellors

In Denmark, youth counsellors support young people with specific emotional and social issues. Lund (2010) described uses and outcomes of an online facility (*Cyberhus*) used by counsellors with young people; this included peer forums, question and answer sessions, and one-to-one chat facilities. He described one form of counselling as follows: "Volunteers from relevant walks of life share their expertise about music, legal issues, sexuality, etc.—all under supervision of our full-time counselling coordinators" (p. 82). In terms of facilities enabling young people to interact directly, the author described these as "basic forums where anyone can post, as you would see on any number of websites, but of course monitored by our staff" (p. 82). In terms of uses and outcomes, the author went on to say: "what we can give, is a place to vent sorrows and frustrations, and maybe figure out what is needed to improve one's situation" (p. 84). Importantly, he further said: "It is precisely because the child or young person has control over the situation, that they have the courage to seek us out" (p. 84). He indicated the approach counsellors need to take must be "soft-spoken and one of encouragement" (p. 84). He stressed advice is taken by the young people due to how they see its merit, and how they respect it. As he said, "*Cyberhus*' counsellors are different from other adults around them, who will often hold some degree of power that is, or is seen as, oppressive" (p. 84). Important in this context too, of course, is the fact that the digital environment supports elements of anonymity, neutrality and distance.

In Summary

Uses of digital technologies and outcomes for learning mediated by support and youth workers arise through a number of forms of mediational interactivity, summarised in Table 5.4.

Table 5.4 Mediational interactions used by support and youth workers to support learners

Mediational interactivity	Digital technology involvement
Instruction	Mediators, support and youth workers are not widely using digital technologies to instruct. However, use of the internet as a provider of instructional material is being considered strongly in areas such as careers counselling
Explanation and illustration	Explanation and illustration is increasingly being provided through online resources, through video clips, for example. Currently, mediators, support and youth workers are not commonly engaging or interacting with young people in this form of interactivity directly
Direction	Mediators, support and youth workers are sometimes using an online medium, whether it be via text on a mobile telephone, or email, or chat room facilities, to direct learners, for example, to courses or voluntary activities that are available and felt to be of value
Demonstration	Demonstration is increasingly being provided through online resources such as video clips. Mediators, support and youth workers are not commonly engaging directly with young people using this form of interaction
Discussion	Discussion is seen as a major requirement in the support of learners by mediators, support and youth workers. Mobile and landline telephones have traditionally been used to support discussion, and more asynchronous discussion is now being used by this group through use of email or chat room facilities including *Facebook*
Scaffolding	Where mediators, support and youth workers use digital communication channels, they often use these in order to scaffold involvement for learners

(Continued overleaf)

Table 5.4 Continued

Mediational interactivity	Digital technology involvement
Questioning	Where mediators, support and youth workers use digital communication channels, they often engage with learners through appropriate forms of questioning
Speculation	Where mediators, support and youth workers use digital communication channels, they may encourage speculation by offering suggestions or possibilities for learners to explore or consider
Consolidation	Consolidation is not a form of interaction that is commonly identified with this group and their engagement with learners. When digital communication channels are used, confirmation and reassurance tends to be a pattern that is seen rather than consolidation
Summarising	Where mediators, support and youth workers use digital communication channels, they do ask learners sometimes to summarise key points or aspects concerned with job seeking, for example
Initiating and guiding exploration	Where mediators, support and youth workers use digital communication channels, they often use these media to point learners to specific web-sites, for example, that they can explore and are felt to be of likely interest to them
Evaluating learners' responses	Where mediators, support and youth workers use digital communication channels, they can use the responses from learners to evaluate aspects such as levels of communication skills, and use of appropriate language when seeking employment opportunities

Support and youth workers are generally concerned with the development of caring thinking as well as engagement in learning. Using digital communication channels and specific software to explore or model certain behavioural or developmental areas, these mediators can support an appreciation of caring thinking, offering ways learners might engage in active caring thinking (such as voluntary activities in homes of senior citizens, or animal welfare clinics), being able to point out normative approaches, as well as effective approaches, and showing empathy with others. Similarly, this group of mediators is concerned with longer-term learning needs of young people. They can use digital technologies to point young people towards educational opportunities, work opportunities, to signpost recreational activities, and to highlight ways young people can engage in active citizenship (for example, taking direct actions with online e-government activities such as voting and completing tax or revenue returns).

Counsellors

Mental Health Counsellors

Uses of digital technologies are now included in some preparatory courses for counsellors. As Hayes (2008) concluded from a study of uses of digital technologies (multimedia) in preparing counsellors of mental health for their practices, "Multimedia instruction has greatly increased in recent years and many educators are integrating this creative media into the delivery of instruction to enhance and simulate the lecture, didactic, and experiential approaches" (p. 251). The author went on to say: "Technology usage in counselor preparation has also increased and has provided educators with different methods of teaching students. Use of this medium should be seen as an ongoing effort to improve professional practices, teaching, services, and research" (p. 251). The suggestion here is that using digital technologies in the preparation of counsellors should affect uses when counsellors engage in professional practices with young people. The author described ways student counsellors and guidance counsellors used digital technologies in their everyday practice; student counsellors can work with young people as well as adults and families in the practice counselling clinics, and "Each room in the clinic is equipped with a desktop computer for student trainees to use with clients. Student trainees are also required to use a computerized, commercial program for writing clients' progress notes and treatment plans" (p. 248). Digital technologies were used also to record (videotape) sessions, and live supervision was undertaken by professionals using video technologies. Clients were informed of all these processes, and involvement followed carefully constructed ethical guidelines. Wall-mounted cameras fed into a central system the supervisor had access to, and communication between supervisor and student was maintained through an audio route using an ear piece the student wore during the session: "The ear device is plugged into the wall of the counseling room that links to the control room. This process allows the faculty supervisor the ability to communicate privately with the student during the counseling session" (p. 249).

In terms of using digital technologies in mental health counselling practice, the use of email to support appropriate interactions was considered by Hayes (2008), but Bradley, Hendricks, Lock, Whiting, and Parr (2011) conducted a focal study on this form of intervention. In their study they stated the critical importance of discussion about confidentiality through a digital technology medium, stating: "It is the counselor's responsibility to discuss confidentiality before engaging in e-mail communication with clients. For example, counselors must acknowledge that it is possible for third parties to gain access to e-mails" (p. 72). Indeed, the authors recommended use of this form of digital technology should be decided on the basis of a risk assessment of confidentiality. They also raised the issue of whether email might be judged as a more informal form of communication, and the impact this might have on communications at a professional level, between counsellor and client. The authors recommended counsellors discuss time commitment with clients, and "E-mail has become a method of informal communication. Therefore, when using e-mail to communicate with clients, counselors must be careful to insure that professional boundaries are maintained at all times" (p. 73). The authors in summary stressed,

"The AMHCA [American Mental Health Counselors Association] and ACA [American Counseling Association] ethical codes stipulate a number of obligations that arise when counselors decide to use e-mail to interact with clients" (p. 76). While uses of email were encouraged by outcomes identified through research, the authors stressed the need for caution also, stating counsellors must consider and address "issues of confidentiality, changes in the counseling relationship, and the need to ensure that clients are given avenues for immediate assistance in times of crisis before they provide their email address to clients" (p. 76).

It is worth mentioning here that some addiction counsellors are now finding they need to address issues of internet addiction. Acier and Kern (2011) reported suggestions from counsellors of those with internet addiction, measures such as moving computers into communal areas, encouraging controlled and balanced use, and engaging in other interests.

Health Counsellors

Digital technologies can clearly support timely and rapid communication between counsellors and clients, and this offers advantages for those with mental health issues. In terms of other health counsellors, Stephen et al. (2011) studied the development and practices of online support groups (OSGs) for counsellors of cancer patients. As they said, "Counsellor familiarity and engagement with technology-mediated communication represents an important factor in the ability to implement support programs to cancer patients" (p. 832). The authors described important issues emerging during early development of practices with counsellors, saying: "During the early phase of training, feelings of frustration and challenge were high, and disruptive events and anxieties were common. These barriers interfered, in early sessions, with counsellors feelings of being 'present' and effective" (p. 838). But, as happens in other professional practices, these counsellors started to look at advantages and ways affordances could support their work positively and actively. The authors reported: "OSG facilitators were challenged to bring emotional process and immediacy to online groups, and devised creative 'work-arounds' to overcome limitations of the modality" (p. 838). The authors concluded that "Internet counselling is an innovative and promising approach, and research is beginning to document benefits for clients and counsellors, and positive therapeutic processes and outcomes" (p. 839). While the challenges were clearly recognised, so too was the potential provided by this medium, with the authors stating: "This study shows that counsellors acculturated in face-to-face approaches can, with training and practice, adapt clinical skills to OSGs and offer an additional medium for support" (p. 839).

School Counsellors

The development of online support systems for school counsellors has identified similar issues, concerns and needs. As McAdams III and Wyatt (2010) said, "Diminished capabilities to ensure confidentiality, observe nonverbal cues, and provide effective crisis management were named in this study as just some of the potential and variable risks that are inherent with any application of TADP"

(p. 189). The authors found risks needed to be considered in very similar ways, saying: "the responsibility lies squarely with the individual practitioner to determine the specific nature and level of risks associated with each proposed TADP application and to carefully balance them against anticipated benefits" (p. 189). The need for an agreed understanding of the practices to be adopted by counsellors and clients, the need to continue to explore new practices of potential benefit, and the need to disseminate outcomes concerned with innovative practices were all raised as important recommendations for this counsellor group.

Taking such needs into consideration, Pierce (2012) argued that "Technology offers opportunities and efficiencies to the school counselors who support students, parents, and educators alike. But few counselors are taking advantage of these resources today" (p. 24). She stated digital technologies already exist to support situations where "School counselors assist students with a number of academic, social, and life goals" (p. 26). She identified three applications:

- *Middle School Confidential 1: Be Confident in Who You Are*—supporting transfers to middle school.
- *Hannah Rose Knows*—supporting the development of self-confidence and empathetic caring thinking for others.
- *Burston's favorites helps kids*—supporting self-expression by younger learners.

In terms of perceptions of quality of support offered by digital technology-based facilities compared to more traditional face-to-face forms, Conn, Roberts, and Powell (2009) found from their study with 76 school counselling interns that "the hybrid model of group supervision was positively related to attitudes toward technology in counselor education, future professional practice, and the overall supervisory experience" (p. 298). They found differences in approaches did not affect perceptions of supervision quality.

In Summary

Uses of digital technologies and outcomes for learning mediated by counsellors arise through a number of forms of mediational interactivity, summarised in Table 5.5.

Counsellors are often highly concerned with the development of caring thinking. Through digital technology media, they can highlight aspects of caring thinking for young people, showing their appreciation of certain responses, encouraging them to take part actively in caring thinking, providing ideas of normative practices, indicating effective practices, and showing and encouraging empathy. These practices can all be undertaken within what can be regarded by young people as a 'neutral' medium. However, it is not being advocated here that the role of face-to-face intervention and support should be diminished or replaced; rather, digital technologies are seen as providing additional support not otherwise provided for some young people, following initial face-to-face intervention. Counsellors are concerned through their interactions about a focus where possible on future welfare, including a focus on future education, work, recreation and needs for citizenship, all of which can be supported through appropriate uses of digital technologies.

Table 5.5 Mediational interactions used by counsellors to support learners

Mediational interactivity	Digital technology involvement
Instruction	Counsellors can use topic-specific resources and software to support instruction, but often this is done with on-hand mediation. Instruction is also provided through some website resources and online communication media
Explanation and illustration	Counsellors are using both website resources and online communication media to support explanation and illustration
Direction	Direction is often embedded within long-term concerns for counsellors, who thread direction through online communication using facilities such as email and chat rooms
Demonstration	Counsellors do use online resources to demonstrate points, issues and facts
Discussion	Increasingly the use of email or social media is being suggested for use in both the development of practice among professional counsellors, but also in their practice with young people they are supporting. Ethical and organisational needs have been highlighted as needing to be well accommodated in this growing practice
Scaffolding	In a threaded discussion, counsellors are able to scaffold ideas and longer-term concerns, identifying key points or interim goals for young people
Questioning	Questions are able to be raised by counsellors through email and social media, but the need to consider the number, order and depth of questions has been raised
Speculation	Speculation is not a form of interaction that is highlighted within the literature when counsellors use digital technologies
Consolidation	Consolidation is a form of interaction that counsellors can focus on by sending regular, short messages as texts on mobile devices or via email
Summarising	Counsellors can ask young people to summarise points or to pick out key issues for them at crucial stages of intervention
Initiating and guiding exploration	Exploration can be extended when counsellors can point young people to online and other resources, and can guide them through a series of details or routes that can lead towards an end goal
Evaluating learners' responses	Counsellors are being encouraged increasingly to consider the use of email and social media as a way to more regularly evaluate implications arising from young people's responses

Online Tutors

Online tutors are often not known personally to learners they support. This means they can work in ways and through technological environments regarded by learners as being highly 'neutral' (Passey, 2007). Often online tutors relate to learners by using digital technologies in particular ways, in the past using textual forms, perhaps via email or discussion forums, sometimes synchronously, but also asynchronously. The current literature about online tutoring focuses more on college and university practices of online tutors, rather than tutors involved with other learners. Jopling (2012), for example, reviewed practices used to support online tutoring mainly at university level.

Online Tutoring and Motivation

Xiao (2012) studied factors motivating students (in this case, university students) when online tutors supported distant language learning. The study sought to explore how online tutors might influence learner motivations, and the language context was English language learning for Chinese native-speakers. The author detailed the context: "China Central Radio and Television University (CCRTVU) is the mainstream distance education institution in China. . . . This study involved current students and graduates of the 3-year distance education Bachelor of Arts program in English at a metropolitan branch of CCRTVU" (p. 367). Evidence was gathered from both learners and tutors. Overall, the author found "teaching competence, personal characteristics, subject matter expertise, and tutor–student relationship were four tutor-related factors which affected students' learning motivation, reinforcing results of previous studies" (p. 365). The author found there were some differences in ways learners and tutors considered levels and forms of these factors, however. The author said he felt tutors believed their teaching qualities to be better than the reports shown by learners. He reported findings in terms of motivations arising from teaching competence, "which covers presentation skills, student engagement, use of technology, facilitation skills, and practical relevance, ... identified as a motivating factor almost unanimously by both cohorts (100% vs. 97%)" (p. 375). He reported ratings of individual aspects within this factor, however, differed so "only facilitation skills received higher rating from tutors than students, a result that may be related to the role of distance tutors. In distance education, tutors are not course producers" (p. 375). As the author said, with tutors not being course producers, tutors value facilitation; this could explain why learners rated presentation skills more highly, and hence was indicative of their different expectations. He also detailed motivations arising from personal characteristics, reporting "committed, approachable, empathetic, accepting, humble, and egalitarian—were also highly rated as a motivating factor by both students (93%) and tutors (91%)" (p. 375). The author stressed, however, that commitment and empathy were ranked differently by tutors and learners, and "As for the other characteristics, far more students than the tutors themselves took the view that a motivating tutor should be approachable (63% vs. 38%), accepting (38% vs. 25%), and egalitarian (13% vs. 0%)" (p. 376). The author argued that online tutors need to be entirely empathetic and sympathetic to the affective needs of learners, and tutors should recognise the tutor–learner relationship is an important factor affecting learning.

In terms of looking at a different and specific online tutoring context, Vasquez III, Forbush, Mason, Lockwood, and Gleed (2011) undertook a detailed mixed methods study looking at how online reading could be supported for at-risk students. The authors described the context of their study as "a preliminary investigation of the effects of live online reading tutoring on 4th grade students in a high minority, high 'poverty' school in Philadelphia, PA" (p. 16). The approach involved "Using a distance teleconferencing system, trained and supervised undergraduate students located at Utah State University delivered tutoring" (p. 16). The study gathered measures of reading fluency from three learners, as well as evidence from tutors, parents, learners and teachers. The learners were African-American, and the tutors were college undergraduates. Teachers identified the learners, selected on the basis of low scores on reading tests. Their results showed an improvement in performance, "Overall, supplemental reading instruction in an online format led to a marked increase in the participants' oral reading fluency" (p. 21). The numbers of correct words per minute shifted as a result of the intervention—for learner 1 from a mean of 26.25 to a mean of 41.50, for learner 2 from 50.75 to 58.45, and for learner 3 from 56.82 to 64.57. The authors stated:

> The implications for schools are also numerous. With a collaborative effort, universities are able to deliver reduced-cost tutoring to public school students. This tutoring is perhaps less expensive than it would cost to hire tutors locally and train them to deliver instruction.
>
> (p. 24)

While the authors recognised costs incurred by schools or parents for required digital technologies, they reported that, for parents

> in-home, online tutoring allows them greater flexibility and convenience in addressing their students' needs. Rather than taking their students to a central location to get tutoring, they can simply turn on their computer and tutoring is delivered to their home office.
>
> (p. 24)

The authors indicated parent and teacher engagement with their children's learning could be enhanced, "providing them access and weekly updates of student progress. In a typical online home tutoring session, tutors will debrief the parents at the end of the lesson to share data and inform the parents on how the tutoring session went" (p. 24). The authors highlighted issues for those exploring online tutoring:

- Monitoring learner behaviour at a distance may require local support and involvement from parents or teachers.
- Ensuring sound quality is good is essential.
- Learners may need some practice in speaking clearly and strongly.
- Tutors should become familiar with the online tutoring system affordances before using it with learners.
- How the facility accepts and shows documents or files needs to be trialled and known beforehand.

Other studies have looked at techniques online tutors have used or identified to gain maximum engagement and outcomes for learners. Sun and Rueda (2012), for example, in a study involving 203 undergraduate students in the United States, concluded online tutors supporting students taking online courses for the first time should consider particularly how to support their emotional engagement and offer strategies to enhance self-regulation. Junco, Heiberger, and Loken (2011) in a controlled study involving 125 college students showed that integrating use of Twitter increased engagement and average end of course grades at statistically significant levels. Kopp, Matteucci, and Tomasetto (2012) in a study of responses from 76 online tutors across 17 European countries showed experienced online tutors tended to identify specific cognitive exercises to engage learners in collaborative activity, and identified at early stages when to intervene in situations that might lead to social dysfunction. Kim (2013) concluded higher levels of participation in online discussions could be gained by sub-grouping a class-size group.

Online Tutoring for Secondary School Learners

Projects described above could clearly potentially support learners in remote and rural locations, especially where qualified teachers or tutors are not available to support certain subjects or topics. Passey (2007) described activities run by online tutors (teachers in some cases and bespoke online tutors in other cases) supporting secondary school students across two LAs in England working across rural and urban areas. He concluded: "The socialisation of learning is an aspect that is supported through a number of the Virtual Workspace facilities. Learning through discussion, through social engagement, and through an internal 'verbalisation' is likely to be supported by the facilities that are available" (p. 3). Specific involvement of online mentors in this early system was particularly important for some learners (even though, overall, the level of activity with online tutors was quite low). As the author said, "It is recognised by a range of learners (as by some teachers) that mentors have provided positive support not just with subject and topic endeavours, but also with social or emotional issues" (p. 5). Online tutors carefully handled social and emotional issues, preserving confidentiality; reports from teachers and schools indicated "mentors have supported at social and emotional levels in ways that would have been difficult through face-to-face situations" (p. 5). As the author said, trying to estimate the value of this support is difficult, but having such support during holiday times was clearly important for some learners. Across the two LAs, 9 online mentors were involved, working 5 days a week, for 12 hours a day, providing in total 140 hours of access per week. Online mentors reported "quiet and shy learners 'get a lot out of it'. It is felt that they can raise questions and opinions" (p. 22). But it was also reported that mentoring supported "learners who want to do well, but who have got into a 'behaviour' stereotype (they are excluded, or are out of class, for example). A learner in school can be 'someone else on line'" (p. 22). Additionally, it was reported that "the very physically disabled can interact more (disabilities are not known when someone interacts online)" (p. 22). The use of a reward system for learners was implemented in this environment, and "According to the mentors, incentives provide a big motivator for a lot of learners. However, to gain from these incentives, teachers need to set assignments so that they can gain points" (p. 22).

Private Online Tutoring

The facilities above consider online tutoring within a public or state system. However, it is becoming clear that private online tutoring is a growing and expanding business. Kozar (2012) looked at the ways online tools are being used in Russia to support private language learning. She stated: "Like many other industries, private tutoring is now being transformed by the growth of information and communication technologies (ICT). An increasing number of educational entrepreneurs in different countries are incorporating Internet tools in their professional practice" (p. 415). She described how companies employ private tutors in India to deliver online support for learners in mathematics and science in the US, and how online tutoring is also supporting after-school support in Korea, for example. The author in her study looked at the use of online audio and video facilities by private tutors to support English language learning in Russia (a country where only 50% of the population had internet access in 2012). She analysed the facilities provided by 100 private online tutoring services advertised publicly on the internet (in Russian and in English). She used three selection criteria to identify websites for analysis: offering audio or video lessons using freeware; not belonging to a formal educational institution; and advertising to Russian speakers. Her conclusions were clear: "The fact that there are hundreds of web sites offering private English lessons via synchronous VoIP tools to Russian learners suggests a growing acceptance of computer-mediated language learning among Russian students, in particular for Conversational English and English for Work" (p. 418). She also concluded that "private individuals are currently more active compared to previously established language teaching providers in adopting synchronous online tools for English language teaching" (p. 418) The author suggested this might mean more traditional language learning providers will be challenged in the future. She speculated that "In some countries and contexts, live online tutoring via freeware products might be used by schools or students desirous of language instruction but lacking specialist staff" (p. 419). Additionally, she argued that after-school 'cram' schools might be provided through this route in the future, as might adults needing to learn languages for work, or for personal interest reasons.

In Summary

Uses of digital technologies and outcomes for learning mediated by online tutors arise through a number of forms of mediational interactivity, summarised in Table 5.6.

In addition to supporting these forms of interaction, online mentors may also be concerned with considering and supporting aspects of caring thinking—pointing out elements to be appreciated, identifying active caring in thinking, offering ideas of normative criteria, effective outcomes and empathetic concerns. They may also, through their individual understandings and perspectives, offer learners wider contexts—ideas of longer-term interests and opportunities in education, links to aspects of citizenship, relationships to work, and to recreation and outside interests.

Table 5.6 Mediational interactions used by online tutors to support learners

Mediational interactivity	Digital technology involvement
Instruction	Online mentors often take the lead and instruct. They may well identify specific needs, and 'teach online'
Explanation and illustration	Explanation and illustration is a key element that is referred to commonly. Online mentors are often recognised as offering valuable 'alternative explanations'
Direction	Online mentors can direct a discussion, and can take forward a line of thinking by picking up ideas and phrases that learners expose
Demonstration	Demonstration can be provided, often in the form of web links, which allow learners to see demonstrations of concepts or ideas
Discussion	Discussion is key to all involvement and interactions, and the quality of outcome is often judged by the perceived qualities of discussion that the online mentor leads. Online facilities now allow tutors and learners to choose discussion media – text, audio or video
Scaffolding	Scaffolding is important. Online mentors need to pick up issues and challenges, and structure ways for learners to look at and explore these through appropriate scaffolded approaches
Questioning	Questioning is a key element, not just as a tool that online mentors can use, but also as a form of interaction that is encouraged of the learner by the mentor
Speculation	Speculation can play a part in discussions, but this is likely to depend largely on the topic or subject of the activity
Consolidation	Consolidation is an element that the online mentor needs to include at key points. How online mentors offer extension and consolidation activities for learners can influence learner interest and longer-term understanding and memorisation
Summarising	Summarising is an important element for the online mentor to consider. How online mentors draw out key findings and phrases from learners at key points is often judged as a sign of quality of the interaction
Initiating and guiding exploration	Initiating exploration and guiding it are key aspects that online mentors use in their armoury of tools to engage and focus learners on pertinent approaches and needs. These elements are often crucial at early stages of interactions between learners and online mentors
Evaluating learners' responses	Online mentors need to evaluate learner responses in an on-going way, picking up both issues and challenges, and points where learning and understanding are clear. Online mentors also need to feed back an assessment perspective for learners at regular intervals

Table 5.7 Mediational interactions involving digital technologies used by each group of mediators

Mediational interactivity	Teachers	Teaching assistants	Parents and guardians	Mediators, support workers and youth workers	Counsellors	Online tutors	Total
Instruction	√√√	√√		√	√	√√	9
Explanation and illustration	√√√	√√	√	√	√	√√√	11
Direction	√	√√	√	√√	√	√√	9
Demonstration	√√	√√	√	√	√√	√	9
Discussion	√√√	√√	√√√	√√√	√√	√√√	16
Scaffolding	√√	√√√	√	√√	√	√√	11
Questioning	√√	√√	√√	√√	√	√√	11
Speculation	√	√	√	√		√	5
Consolidation	√	√√√	√√		√	√	8
Summarising	√	√√	√√√	√	√	√√√	11
Initiating and guiding exploration	√√	√	√√	√√√	√√	√√√	13
Evaluating learners' responses	√√	√√√		√√	√	√√√	11
Total	**23**	**25**	**17**	**19**	**14**	**26**	

An Overview

While digital technologies are being used across the full range of mediator groups discussed in this chapter to support interactions with learners, different groups of mediators are applying them in more specific ways. The pattern currently seen is shown in Table 5.7, where wide or key use is shown by three ticks, general use by two ticks and occasional or irregular use by one tick.

From the pattern shown in Table 5.7 (and it must be recognised that 'ticks' awarded are based on views from across the literature sourced, but at the same time are subjective to a degree):

- Interactions where digital technologies are used most across all mediator groups are 'discussion' and 'initiating and guiding exploration'.
- Interactions where digital technologies are used least across all mediator groups are 'speculation' and 'consolidation'.
- Mediator groups using digital technologies most to support their interactions are 'online tutors' and 'teaching assistants'.
- Mediator groups using digital technologies least to support their interactions are 'counsellors' and 'parents and guardians'.

Chapter 6

Conclusions and Where Next
Balance, Balance, Balance

Introduction

This chapter offers a number of overviews, of how educational digital technologies can be considered when thinking about enhancing learning at an individual learner level, and at wider curriculum levels. Implications arising for the management of learning, policies of learning, and future research into this field are also considered.

Current concerns about uses of educational digital technologies by learners often focus on needs to maximise gains from present and past investment and resources. To ensure this happens, policy makers and managers are expected to focus their efforts in ways to fully benefit learners and learning. At the same time, economic concerns about future organisation and structures of education are being raised internationally, nationally and locally, and questions are raised in this context about the future nature of educational organisations and practices. Some schools, areas and countries are considering how alternative support mechanisms might offer more economically effective structures without subsequent organisational changes affecting learning outcomes.

Balancing Theoretical Perspectives

What is clear from research into this field is a general concern that educational digital technologies should support learning as effectively as possible, and that there is a clear understanding of how educational digital technologies support practices described by learning theories or concepts. If, however, theoretical or conceptual perspectives on education and learning are considered in a narrow sense (such as focusing on cognition alone without considering the importance of metacognition or megacognition), then this can clearly in itself be a major disadvantage, especially if it leads to an ideological approach dismissing or missing other important key aspects of learning. Ideological approaches may work for some learners for some time, but from experiences of past practices they are unlikely to work for all learners for all time. When educational policies rely upon an ideological focus, practitioners apply and use these concepts for some time, but subsequently gaps are identified, and these gaps then need to be accommodated for the longer-term benefit of learners in the wider and more specific sense.

Current theories of learning are often based on in-depth studies, providing valuable insights through qualitative and observational approaches, but only involving small numbers of learners. While outcomes of these studies can offer deep understanding, the width of observations means their generalisation beyond those small numbers cannot be absolutely guaranteed or known. While many researchers and practitioners use former studies when developing their own studies, and provide what is then considered as supportive evidence of the same 'theory', the fact that those observations have used the originating 'theoretical framework' as a construct for their own design and identification of features to observe, means other important or relevant features could have been missed.

There has been something of a trend in arguing distinctions between 'theories' in recent years – considering, for example, the differences and arguments for and against social constructivism versus social constructionism. Certainly it appears the 'theory of learning' is elusive – we do not have a single unifying theory. But, should we have one at all? Is it either a necessity or indeed feasible? What we do have are 'constructs' – perspectives on learning, from neurobiological, behavioural, cognitive, social constructivist, social constructionist, socio-cultural, and instructional perspectives, for example. This book has not sought to identify a single unifying theory, and indeed, rather than taking an approach to arguing a case for one construct rather than another, it has taken an approach integrating constructs or perspectives, or at least considering them as alternatives to explain the practices and rationale of a single learner's perspective and focus on learning. This is also an approach taken by van Merriënboer and Kirschner (2012), who, when considering roles of learning constructs and concepts for designing instruction, argued that "Complex learning involves integrating knowledge, skills, and attitudes; coordinating qualitatively different 'constituent skills', and often transferring of what is learned in the school or training setting to daily life and work settings" (p. 2). They went on to describe an integrative approach from a learning activity perspective, saying: "The current interest in complex learning is manifest in popular educational approaches that call themselves inquiry, guided discovery, project-based, case method, problem-based, design-based, and competency-based" (p. 2).

Balancing the Curriculum and Curriculum Opportunities

The importance of considering a balance of theoretical perspectives, constructs, or concepts of learning is highlighted even more when the needs of those managing learning are considered. The management of education (rather than learning per se) has traditionally (and largely) been focused on managing learning through institutions – whether these are kindergarten, schools, colleges, or universities. This focus is irrespective of countries, although alternative educational management to match different forms of provision is seen in some specific regions or areas of the world. Some reports suggest, however, that home-schooling as a practice outside institutional education management is increasing, and some countries provide for this at a policy level. The Australian Bureau of Statistics report (2010), for example, states children can be home-schooled, although "they must be enrolled as a student at a day school and be available when required for assessment against the regular school year curriculum"; but no figures of numbers of children involved in home-schooling are provided. A recent ABC News report (Townsend, 2012) suggested this figure could be in the order of 50,000. This is a larger proportion than those managed through distance provision, but is nevertheless quite small (some 1.43%).

But if home-schooling is increasing, then why is this trend happening? Certainly dislike and distrust of authority by a range of parents who home-school their children was raised in the ABC News report, but there appear also to be concerns with how education is matching future social and employment needs of children, and the fact that educational digital technologies are supporting alternatives are being seen as preferable for some children. While management of education has in the past often been concerned with supporting individuals in terms of a single 'vocation', employment patterns are increasingly not stable and new areas of employment and jobs continue to emerge. The US Department of Labor in 2012 projected that, between 2010 and 2020, the 10 occupations to be the fastest growing would be: personal care aides; home health aides; biomedical engineers; brick-masons, block-masons, stonemasons, and tile and marble setters; carpenters; veterinary technologists and technicians; reinforcing iron and rebar workers; physical therapist assistants; pipe-layers, plumbers, pipefitters, and steamfitters; and meeting, convention, and event planners. Even this detailed form of predictive analysis does not accommodate and show gains in 'new' jobs arising, initially in small numbers and perhaps increasingly over time, but it does show jobs that would have at one time been in relatively small number – such as care aides – are clearly seen to be in major positions and increasing in number. These forms of figures also do not indicate the importance of 'entrepreneurial' endeavour – the abilities and needs for increasing numbers of young people to be able to understand how to develop their own jobs and interests, where self-employment or social employment is more fitting to the economic and local landscape.

Clearly the way employment shifts are considered by and integrated into future-thinking practices of education is a focus for educationalists and policy makers not just at national, but also at local, levels. These concerns call for an adequate balance between the needs of future vocations and the needs of a core curriculum serving all. Additionally, however, two other major factors have emerged over the past few decades, highlighting the need to reconsider and review traditional approaches to educational management to support an educational provision matching current and future contexts as effectively as possible. First, individuals appear to be much more likely to be involved in a series of 'vocations' in their lives. The *Wall Street Journal* in 2010 reported a study to assess levels of job change across a range of US workers. From 10,000 interviews, workers had had 10.8 jobs on average over a period of 21 years. The author of the study noted these shifts needed to be considered in terms of both the age of the worker (more changes could be associated with younger workers), and this level of change might not persist over time, especially when recessionary factors are considered at certain points in time. Second, ICT and digital technologies now enable education to happen beyond the walls of institutions. The deployment of digital technologies to support learning beyond the school is clearly being evidenced. As indicated by Picciano and Seaman, from a survey in the US reported in 2007, it was estimated 700,000 students (some 1.46%) from across the entire population of 48,000,000 public school students in the US were enrolled in online or blended learning courses; they predicted the growth would continue for the foreseeable future. However, if these factors are indeed impinging on practices currently, then they certainly imply the need for lifelong learning approaches to education and training, where people of any age can update their skills or engage in new areas of skills.

Formal, Non-formal and Informal Environments

So, how does this help us to consider roles of educational digital technologies within management practices and models? Looking at forms of digital technologies being used, needs of different specific groups of learners, and supportive opportunities mediators can bring, there is now a need to consider three key curriculum elements: the formal (classroom) environments; the non-formal (after-school and society) clubs and activities; and the informal (in out-of-school, home and other location) opportunities chosen as and when desired by learners, parents and those mediating educational endeavours. These three different curriculum elements can be considered as a simple model (see Figure 6.1), indicating curriculum activities in each sector confer distinctive, different yet important and complementary skills, knowledge and attitudes – the formal curriculum offers a core range of subject needs; the informal curriculum provides opportunities for these to be developed in another context and with the support

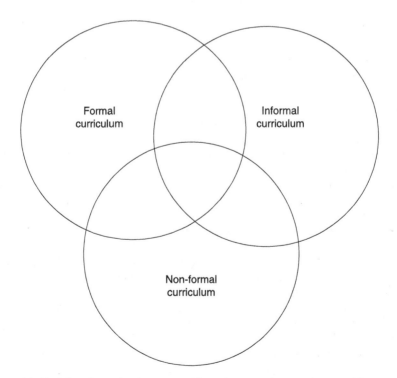

Figure 6.1 Model to show the three curriculum elements that consitute a wide curriculum

Table 6.1 The relationship between forms of educational technologies and specific curriculum elements

Form of educational digital technology	Formal curriculum element	Informal curriculum element	Non-formal curriculum element
Topic-specific software	√√√	√	
Curriculum-wide learner-centred software	√√√	√	
Curriculum-wide teacher-centred software	√√√		
Online resources supporting curriculum-wide needs	√√√	√	
Online resources supporting revision needs	√	√√√	√
Online learner support		√√√	√√√
Software involving and supporting parents		√√√	
Project and after-school club activities involving digital technologies			√√√

or involvement of parents, family or friends; and the non-formal curriculum provides opportunities for young people to work in teams and groups on authentic problems and products.

Referring to the taxonomy of educational digital technologies discussed in Chapter 3, it is possible to see how distinct categories work and fit with each of these three curriculum elements. This match is shown in Table 6.1, where the number of ticks indicates strength of match and fit according to evidence currently accessible and presented throughout this book.

The pattern indicated in Table 6.1 shows specific forms of educational digital technologies are associated with specific elements of the curriculum. While these three elements are often in place, links between them, shown by overlaps in Figure 6.1, are often less developed and used by schools and mediators (and responses from a practitioner group in a workshop session at an annual conference in the UK demonstrated this point clearly). Yet evidence from the literature presented in this book shows gains arise where contributions through overlaps occur as well as contributions through the three specific elements. Developing future blended models of education and learning will need to consider these potentials.

Blended Models of Education and Learning

Balancing the three key elements (in Figure 6.1) in different ways means different models of education and learning can now be conceived and considered. Different blended possibilities already exist, when we consider practices undertaken in different countries. For example, 'afternoon school' in Germany has traditionally been the responsibility of parents, with teachers providing work for pupils to complete at those times; but in some schools, teachers now use digital technologies to support learning at home and link it to lessons more strongly, involving uses of virtual learning environments (VLEs) to set work, gather work from learners, and to engage in online discussions while at home. Similarly, Schools of the Air now use VLEs, as does the Open University in the UK, which previously ran courses largely reliant upon self-directed learning from books, videos and television programmes, blended with a number of residential activities across a year. Some secondary schools in the Netherlands involve learners in the *Technasium* initiative where they routinely work on research questions to address real and commercial needs identified by businesses and services and discussed with local schools. The growth of virtual schools in the US demonstrates policy makers have considered alternative and blended models rather than attempting to adopt a single solution for all. Picciano and Seaman (2007) stated: "Twenty or more states currently operate their own virtual school. The largest virtual schools include the Utah Electronic High School, with around 35,000 enrollments in 2004–05, and the Florida Virtual School, which reported 33,000 enrollments that year" (p. 7).

Some studies have looked at current blended learning situations. Kember, McNaught, Chong, Lam, and Cheng (2010) in their study involved 595 students in 21 university courses in Hong Kong using online environments blended with face-to-face teaching, and found features enabling constructive dialogue and interaction in activities encouraged deep approaches to learning, as well as enhanced communication skills and understanding of content. Similarly, different examples of public versus private provision of education already exist in different countries. The EU (2011) reported spending on private tutoring in Greece was estimated at more than €950 million per year (equivalent to 20% of government expenditure on primary and secondary education), in Spain estimated at €450 million, in Italy €420 million, in Cyprus €111 million, in Romania €300 million, but it was much less popular in Sweden and Finland, where schools appear to satisfy expectations more. They reported the scale of tutoring had increased in France (to €2.2 billion per year and growing at an estimated 10% a year), in Germany it was up to €1.5 billion, in Austria €126 million, there were also indications of significant increases in the UK and Belgium, with low purchasing power of teachers' salaries driving an expansion of private tutoring in Eastern European countries. They noted demand for private tutoring comes mainly from parents of high-achievers, and is driven by parents' concerns learners do well in examinations and are able to be socially competitive.

Provision of education through online tutors is not a new concept, but is likely to be growing as digital technologies offer different options. As a *Telegraph* article states (Wall, 2012):

> E-tutoring has become increasingly popular over the past three years, with thousands of British families taking up the services. Worldwide, the industry is estimated to have grown from a standing start in just a few years to be worth £8 billion.

Paying for private tuition and supporting uses of digital technologies to provide this are certainly not now new concepts, but there is the clear suggestion these practices are becoming widespread across some communities.

The EU report (2011) argued that private tutoring both reflects and exacerbates social inequalities, as demand is concerned with maintaining competitive advantage of those already successful and privileged. Schools would expect to counter this trend, but clearly financial cutbacks can reduce ways educational institutions can provide learner support. The report suggested private tuition can limit a child's leisure time, so it is both psychologically and educationally undesirable. This picture does not invalidate the need to consider a three-element curriculum; indeed, it supports the notion all the more.

Longer-term Skills and Competencies

Curricula in schools and nationally have often focused on knowledge acquisition across a range of subject areas. The National Curriculum in England, for example, focuses on subject knowledge. The official website (Department for Education [DfE], 2012) states that, in primary schools, the statutory subjects are English, mathematics, science, design and technology, art and design, music, history, geography, and physical education. There are, additionally, non-statutory subjects, which are ICT, religious education, citizenship, and personal, social and health education (PHSE). For each subject there is a programme of study, identifying the content, and giving attainment target level descriptions. By comparison, in Northern Ireland, curriculum documents (Northern Ireland Curriculum, 2012) offer guidelines, and provide detail more within topic areas related to domains of future learning need – language and literacy; mathematics and numeracy; the arts; the world around us; physical education; religious education; and personal development and mutual understanding.

Although longer-term skills and competencies can be developed from these areas of knowledge, there is clearly now an arguably greater need for individuals to develop and use a wide range of technical and social skills for their future career needs. The balance of the elements of the curriculum shown in Figure 6.1 is clearly important in this respect. Evidence about outcomes arising from project and after-school club activities involving digital technologies indicates soft skills are developed through these opportunities, which learners can then link to a core or formal curriculum. To address such needs, some individuals now attend more than one school. In the UK, as a standard provision in some locations, some learners attend a secondary school for certain lessons, a further education college for specialist courses (often of a vocational nature, and involving practical or creative activity in authentic contexts), and have one-to-one support from a tutor or counsellor (see, for example, Passey et al., 2008). If learners do attend different institutions (or even if they do not), access to digital technologies and through these to resources including expert human resources, is likely to be fundamentally important to learners now and in the future. Digital technologies provide a range of features enhancing the educational process, but their management in a changing arena will be as important as the provision of the digital technologies themselves; management could mean the difference between supporting access and use, and limiting access and use. Similarly, as digital technologies are developed and other features become accessible, so management skills and understanding required will demand provision to support regular updating.

Vision and leadership are clearly important in this entire development. Valdez (2004) stated this succinctly, saying: "Knowledgeable and effective school leaders are extremely important in determining whether technology use will improve learning for all students. Many school administrators may be uncomfortable providing leadership in technology areas, however." The author went on to point to a time when perhaps more leaders become more uncertain over time, saying: "They may be uncertain about implementing effective technology leadership strategies in ways that will improve learning, or they may believe their own knowledge of technology is inadequate to make meaningful recommendations."

For those emerging blended models of education seen already and identified within this book, vision and leadership have been used in ways accounting for the past, accommodating the present, and considering important needs in the future. How future educational management needs will be provided, and how these will include adequate training and consideration of vision and leadership, is itself a clear need. In this context, a number of key elements concerned with digital technologies are arising, worthy of wider consideration, now and in the future.

New Spaces, Places and Processes

Digital technologies open up possibilities for using and exploiting new learning spaces. Online communication spaces, virtual worlds, online learning resource environments, mobile applications and learning platforms will all need to be managed as a part of blended models of education and learning in the future.

E-portfolios already provide opportunities for some learners to gather details of their achievements together at regular intervals, and systematically. Perry (2009), reviewing the deployment and uses of e-portfolios in vocational and education training settings in Australia, concluded:

> A good practice RPL [Recognition of Prior Learning] model includes facilitated self-assessment, links to units of competency and qualifications, evidence validation (not gathering and collection), use of a variety of evidence forms that corroborate the individual's competence and a conversational approach to assessing.
>
> (p. 1).

The author concluded that while uses of e-portfolios in the vocational and training sector were limited, practices demonstrated: "effective evidence capture and validation; by establishing linkages to existing forms of evidence, and by complimenting the conversational style of good RPL process through regular asynchronous dialogue" (p. 1).

Further development of e-portfolios to support different blended models of education and learning are likely to be a future as well as a current need. In particular, perhaps, the fact that an e-portfolio may, used and supported effectively, both enhance self-directed learning and enhance links to authentic learning situations, is an important aspect for future consideration. In terms of how e-portfolios might work most effectively in the future, issues have been raised about the assessment of work, how this is done, and by whom. In this context, Chang, Liang, and Chen (2013), in a study involving 72 senior high school students, found high levels of consistency between student self-assessment reports and peer assessments, student self-assessment and teacher assessments, and student self-assessments and end of course examination results.

Developing and considering different blended models of education and learning will require regular review and close consideration of curriculum, assessment and certification. Already, universities are regularly reviewing their curriculum, assessment and certification procedures in terms of different forms of online courses and blended courses offered. As Alade (2011) said of curriculum reform in Nigeria: "There has been the infusion of indigenous knowledge and technologies into the curriculum from such diverse fields as traditional arts and crafts, traditional cosmetics, traditional food systems and medicine, knowledge of the environment, and African civilization." As the author stated, curriculum reform introduced computer literacy and communication skills as core modules, but, at the same time, pedagogies encouraged were more learner-centred, problem based, and project driven.

To support blended models of education, data recording, reporting and flow will all be crucially important in terms of supporting all stakeholders – learners fundamentally, but also teachers, tutors, online tutors, other mediators, parents, and those concerned with monitoring and policy. Many countries are concerned that assessment outcomes are not just considered as standalone items for the individual student, but are considered in terms of shorter- and longer-term aims linked to school improvement. Visscher and Coe (2002), and Schildkamp, Rekers-Mombarg, and Harms (2012) have explored how different forms of performance feedback in a number of countries, and specifically in the Netherlands, can support school development, improvement and effectiveness.

Balancing Activities

If we consider the balance of activities needed, then recommendations of van Merriënboer and Kirschner (2012) are a useful place to start. They suggest there are four major components to be considered when creating any form of curriculum or course or series of learning activities:

- Learning tasks – ensuring skills, knowledge and attitudes are covered in sequential ways, moving from easy to difficult, in recurrent ways to consolidate and reintroduce ideas, using real-life tasks, reducing scaffolding with each subsequent task, and varying forms of practice.
- Supportive information to accompany them – bridging links between tasks, explaining how to approach problems and questions, offering strategies to consider, and showing how the domain (the 'big' picture) is organised.
- Procedural information to accompany them – what is needed before tasks can be attempted, what should be practised, how to undertake any routines needed, and any step-by-step instructions needed.
- Part-task practice – providing more practice tasks so learners can gain a level of automaticity in undertaking them, offering repetition, once a real-life task has been completed.

The authors go further to describe curriculum development through a series of processes, or steps. The 10 steps they suggest are: designing learning tasks (what learners should be able to do); developing assessment instruments (standards and qualities to be met); sequencing learning tasks (ordering the tasks to gain effective learning); designing supportive information (to support problem solving and reasoning); analysing cognitive strategies (strategies learners need to solve the problems or tasks); analysing mental models (describing the way a subject or topic is organised and grounded); designing procedural information (letting learners know how to proceed with tasks at relevant times); analysing cognitive rules (ways strategies and problem-solving tasks are linked); analysing prerequisite knowledge (knowledge learners need before they can link strategies and problem solving); and designing part-task practice (more practice if learners need to achieve automaticity in particular subject areas).

Balancing activities using digital technologies is just as much a need as it is for those using other forms of media or resource. Considering the taxonomy of activities available:

- Topic-specific resources and software provide opportunities for selection or design of learning tasks, linked to assessment instruments, tasks can be sequenced, supportive information can be provided around them, cognitive strategies for learners can be analysed, mental models can be considered (and are clearly vitally important as it might not be very easy for learners to recognise a 'big' picture through very specific topic resources), procedural information can be provided, cognitive rules can be analysed so learners understand how problems from one task relate to another, prerequisite knowledge can be considered, and part-task practice can be introduced if appropriate.

- Curriculum-wide software already selects pre-designed learning tasks, links them to assessment instruments, the system sequences them, but supportive information might need to be additionally provided around them, cognitive strategies for learners might need to be analysed outside and beyond the system, mental models for this form of digital technology are clearly vitally important as individual tasks presented by the system might not be easy for learners to recognise in terms of a 'big' picture, procedural information is usually provided as a part of the system, cognitive rules might well need to be analysed outside the system so learners understand how problems from one task relate to another, prerequisite knowledge is generally considered through pre-tests within the system, and part-task practice is usually a general component of this form of software.

- Teaching-wide software provides opportunities for selection or design of learning tasks, these can be linked to assessment instruments, tasks can be sequenced, supportive information can be provided around them, cognitive strategies for learners can be analysed, mental models can be considered and available video clips sometimes provide contexts and the 'big' picture, procedural information can be provided, cognitive rules can be analysed so learners understand how problems from one task relate to another, prerequisite knowledge can be considered in an on-going way, and part-task practice can be introduced as appropriate.

- Parent-involved software provides opportunities for the teacher to select or design learning tasks, these are often linked to assessment instruments when particular tasks are selected, tasks can be sequenced and integrated with other classroom tasks, supportive information can be provided around them and this may be needed for parents as well as for learners themselves, cognitive strategies for learners can be analysed and these might be of value to parents too, mental models can be considered and are vitally important for this form of digital technology as these resources do need to be contextualised in terms of the 'big' picture, procedural information can be provided and this might be needed for parents as well as learners, cognitive rules certainly need to be analysed so learners understand how problems from these tasks relate to others they might be doing in classrooms, prerequisite knowledge can be considered, and part-task practice is often introduced as an element of selected activities.

- Curriculum-supportive online resources enable selection for learning tasks, they can be linked to assessment instruments, sequenced, supportive information can be provided around them, cognitive strategies for learners can be analysed, mental models can be considered and video clips are often available to offer the 'big' picture for learners, procedural information can be provided, cognitive rules can be analysed so learners understand how problems from one task relate to another, prerequisite knowledge can be considered, and part-task practice can be introduced as appropriate.

- Online resources supporting revision do enable learner (or teacher-guided) selection of learning tasks, they are usually linked to assessment instruments, tasks are not generally sequenced by a teacher, supportive information might not always be provided around them, cognitive strategies for learners are not generally analysed and made known, mental models to provide the 'big' picture are not generally provided, procedural information is usually provided, cognitive rules are not generally analysed so learners understand how problems from one task relate to another, prerequisite knowledge may be considered within the system or by the learner or guided by the teacher, and part-task practice is usually a strong element of this form of resource.

- Online learner support provides opportunities for selection or design of learning tasks by mentors and tutors, these can be linked to assessment instruments by tutors, tasks can be sequenced and for the individual, supportive information can be provided, cognitive strategies for learners are often analysed and form an important component of this form of resource, mental models to offer the 'big' picture are not always so obviously provided, procedural information can be provided, cognitive rules are often analysed so learners understand how problems from one task relate to another, prerequisite knowledge is often considered, and part-task practice can be introduced if it is felt by the mentor to be appropriate.

- Project and after-school club activities can include opportunities for selection or design of learning tasks and are often real-life in nature, they can be linked to assessment instruments but are often integral to outcomes rather than being separated, tasks often need to be sequenced, supportive information is provided around them and is vital, cognitive strategies for learners are analysed by both learners themselves as well as by supporters, mental models are considered strongly and the real-life nature provides often a context in terms of the 'big' picture, procedural information is often provided and is vital, cognitive rules are analysed so learners understand how problems from one task relate to another, prerequisite knowledge is considered and often shared through strengths and weaknesses of individuals in teams, and part-task practice is introduced if it is appropriate for undertaking certain tasks requiring levels of automaticity.

The wide range of digital technologies and associated activities now accessible provides opportunities for teachers and mediators to design a balanced curriculum, accounting for the needs of: blended models of formal, informal and non-formal elements; balanced activities meeting learning purpose; access from different providers perhaps in different locations that might be both public and private; use of new spaces; longer-term skills and competencies; development of e-portfolios; assessment and certification; and data records and formative assessment. Some studies are now exploring ways a variety of different digital technologies can be integrated into practice and what results arise. Hur and Suh (2012), for example, explored how the interactive whiteboard, podcasts, and digital storytelling were integrated to support English language learning in a summer programme, identifying affordances and uses, and finding this combination led to significant improvements to vocabulary learning with a large effect size (Cohen's d=−2.720).

Balancing Research Approaches

Finally, researching current and future needs in this field is likely to become increasingly important and prominent for all stakeholders – to provide for practice based on outcomes with evidence, as well as on theoretical constructs and concepts identified at learning levels; to support curriculum based on models evidenced from trials and practice; to integrate with development based on researched constructs, and to have research built into implementation and adoption routes; and to support policy based on identification of key needs and factors.

A range of different forms of research are clearly needed, but essentially there is a need to understand more about certain groups of learners, as well as about certain ranges of educational digital technologies and their applications in the field of practice. In particular this book highlights a need for more examples and detail through studies exploring:

- Impacts of different categories of digital technologies on long-term memorisation and the development of social and societal aspects of learning.
- Uses, outcomes and impacts of project and after-school club activities involving digital technologies and software involving and supporting parents.
- School-based online learner support, both through public and private sources.
- Megacognitive and metacognitive outcomes and impacts of online resources supporting curriculum-wide needs.
- Outcomes and impacts for: learners with limited cognitive abilities or attributes engaged with online revision resources, online learner support,

and project and after-school club activities; learners with limited opportunities engaged with curriculum-wide teacher-centred software, software involving parents, and online resources used in classrooms; mainstream early learners; mainstream secondary or school or college age learners engaged with software involving parents; learners with physical disabilities or attributes engaged with online revision resources, online learner support, and project and after-school club activities; for learners not physically present in classrooms, those with challenging emotional features and attributes, and those where attitudes pose problems; for learners with challenging behavioural attributes engaged with online learner support and project and after-school club activities; for learners with challenging social attributes and abilities engaged with online learner support; for learners where geography poses problems engaged with curriculum-wide learner-centred software and project and after-school club activities.

- Ways parents and guardians, support workers and youth workers, counsellors and online tutors are interacting with learners across school sectors.
- How lifelong learning is being conceptualised and developed across school sectors.
- How intergenerational learning is being developed and used across school sectors.

There is clearly a need for a balance of methodological approaches. Our research foundation is rich, but generally at the extremes – there are findings allowing us to look at individual cases with individual learners, teachers and mediators and schools, and findings allowing us to look at national pictures. But these provide different perspectives, and our findings are not so rich in areas in between these extremes – there are limited wide research findings exploring areas between a case study and a national study at levels allowing us to explore fundamental needs of learners – who have individual characteristics and attributes. The value of educational digital technologies arises from its width of applicability to individuals – sufficient evidence to allow us to do this with ease or finesse is yet to be fully gained.

This Book:

This book offers a number of unique perspectives on a field of widening interest to those concerned with learning and education.

With growing concerns that digital technologies should be used effectively to support learning, and especially integrating effectively their uses in informal, non-formal and formal educational settings, this book draws together research, policy and practice evidence about uses of digital technologies and their influences on learning. Importantly, this book takes a number of novel perspectives – it analyses uses of digital technologies and their outcomes through detailed learning frameworks; it considers different groups of users, and how they can be individually supported through uses of digital technologies; and it looks at how those who support different categories of learners can apply uses of technologies to their support needs.

Readership:

This book is of relevance to three main audiences: those in the research community (exploring uses, outcomes and impacts of digital technologies on learning and across subject areas and age ranges); those in a variety of teaching communities (teaching ICT and digital technology courses at undergraduate and postgraduate levels); and those in the practitioner community (teaching using technologies in schools and colleges, as well as those supporting the vulnerable and those at risk).

The book focuses on aspects that have international appeal, discussing concerns and interests raised internationally. The evidence within the book takes evidence from wide international sources.

The Author:

Don Passey, BSc (Hons), PGCE, MA, MBCS, PhD

Professor Don Passey is a Professor of Technology Enhanced Learning in the Department of Educational Research at Lancaster University, where he co-directs the Centre for Technology Enhanced Learning. He has wide experience with developing and using evaluation and research methods to explore and analyse aspects of technological innovation, researching in primary and secondary school settings, focusing often on the management of implementation, and on those who find it hard to learn. He has written widely on aspects of leading edge ICT uses in home and formal settings.

He has undertaken commissioned studies for government departments, agencies, commercial and non-commercial groups, educational institutions and schools, to support both policy and practice. He was a consultant to a previous government department and agencies on a number of projects, and has worked on the development of innovative approaches to data management systems in schools and LAs. He has worked for commercial companies in the UK, Switzerland and Germany, for state pedagogical research institutions in France and Germany, for educational groups in Hong Kong, Bermuda and Peru, for LAs across England and Scotland, for RBCs, and for individual schools. He is vice-chair of the International Federation for Information Processing Working Group on Information Technology in Educational Management, was a member of the BCS Schools Expert Panel, and a member of an international Working Group on Elementary Education and ICT.

References

Abbott, C. (2007). *E-inclusion: Learning Difficulties and Digital Technologies – Report 15: Futurelab Series*. Bristol: Futurelab.

Abbott, C., Detheridge, T., & Detheridge, C. (2006). *Symbols, Literacy and Social Justice*. Leamington: Widgit.

Abdous, M., & Yoshimura, M. (2010). Learner outcomes and satisfaction: A comparison of live video-streamed instruction, satellite broadcast instruction, and face-to-face instruction. *Computers & Education, 55*, 733–741.

AbuSeileek, A. F. (2012). The effect of computer-assisted cooperative learning methods and group size on the EFL learners' achievement in communication skills. *Computers & Education, 58*, 231–239.

AbuSeileek, A. F., & Qatawneh, K. (2013). Effects of synchronous and asynchronous computer-mediated communication (CMC) oral conversations on English language learners' discourse functions. *Computers & Education, 62*, 181–190.

Acier, D., & Kern, L. (2011). Problematic Internet use: Perceptions of addiction counsellors. *Computers & Education, 56*, 983–989.

Agosto, D. E., Forte, A., & Magee, R. (2012). Cyberbullying and teens: What YA librarians can do to help. *Young Adult Library Services, 10* (2), 38–43.

Akpan, J. P., & Andre, T. (2000). Using a computer simulation before dissection to help students learn anatomy. *Journal of Computers in Mathematics and Science Teaching, 19* (3), 297–331.

Alade, I. W. (2011). Trends and issues on curriculum review in Nigeria and the need for paradigm shift in educational practice. *Journal of Emerging Trends in Educational Research and Policy Studies, 2* (5), 325–333.

Al-Bayati, M. A., & Hussein, K. Q. (2009). Effects of tutorial e-lessons for hearing impaired persons on motivation towards learning (general science topic as case study). *European Journal of Scientific Research, 38* (2), 189–198.

Alcoholado, C., Nussbaum, M., Tagle, A., Gomez, F., Denardin, F., Susaeta, H., Villalta, M., & Toyama, K. (2012). One mouse per child: Interpersonal computer for individual arithmetic practice. *Journal of Computer Assisted Learning, 28*, 295–309.

Alexander, R. J. (2008). *Towards Dialogic Teaching: Rethinking Classroom Talk* (4th ed.). York: Dialogos.

Alloway, T. P., Horton, J., & Alloway R. G. (2013). Social networking sites and cognitive abilities: Do they make you smarter? *Computers & Education, 63*, 10–16.

Anastasiades, P. S., Filippousis, G., Karvunis, L., Siakas, S., Tomazinakis, A., Giza, P., & Mastoraki, H. (2010). Interactive videoconferencing for collaborative learning at a distance in the school of 21st century: A case study in elementary schools in Greece. *Computers & Education, 54*, 321–339.

Andrews, R., & Haythornthwaite, C. (2007). Introduction to e-learning research. In R. Andrews & C. Haythornthwaite (Eds.), *The Sage Handbook of e-learning Research* (pp. 1–52). London: Sage.

Apostol, T. M. (1991). Teaching mathematics with computer animated videotapes. *PRIMUS, 1* (1), 29–44.

Ardaiz-Villanueva, O., Nicuesa-Chacón, X., Brene-Artazcoz, O., de Acedo Lizarraga, M. L. S., & de Acedo Baquedano, M. T. S. (2011). Evaluation of computer tools for idea generation and team formation in project-based learning. *Computers & Education, 56,* 700–711.

Association for Learning Technology (2012). *Evidence-based Policy Development in Learning Technology.* Accessible at: http://repository.alt.ac.uk/2213.

Aubrey, C., & Dahl, S. (2008). *A Review of the Evidence on the Use of ICT in the Early Years Foundation Stage.* Coventry: Becta.

Australia.gov.au (2012). *School of the Air.* Accessible at: http://australia.gov.au/aboutaustralia/australianstory/schooloftheair.

Australian Bureau of Statistics (2010). *4221.0 Schools, Australia, 2010.* Canberra: Commonwealth of Australia.

Bacon, K. (2010). Social media and vulnerable young people's participation. In J. Engelen, J. Dekelver & W. Van den Bosch (Eds.), *Social Media for Social Inclusion of Youth at Risk: Proceedings of the INCLUSO 2010 Conference* (pp. 215–219). Leuven: K.U. Leuven.

Bai, H., Pan, W., Hirumi, A., & Kebritchi, M. (2012). Assessing the effectiveness of a 3-D instructional game on improving mathematics achievement and motivation of middle school students. *British Journal of Educational Technology, 43* (6), 993–1003.

Ball, S., & Bogatz, G. A. (1970). *The First Year of Sesame Street: An Evaluation.* Princeton, NJ: Educational Testing Service.

Balshaw, M., & Farrell, P. (2002). *Teaching Assistants: Practical Strategies for Effective Classroom Support.* London: David Fulton Publishers.

Bangert-Drowns, R. L. (1993). The word processor as an instructional tool: A meta analysis of word processing in writing instruction. *Review of Educational Research, 63,* 69–93.

Banister, S. (2010). Integrating the iPod Touch in K–12 education: Visions and vices. *Computers in the Schools, 27* (2), 121–131.

Barak, M., Ashkar, T., & Dori, Y. J. (2011). Learning science via animated movies: Its effect on students' thinking and motivation. *Computers & Education, 56,* 839–846.

Barker, J., Smith, F., Morrow, V., Weller, S., Hey, V., & Harwin, J. (2003). *The Impact of Out of School Care: A Qualitative Study Examining the Views of Children, Families and Playworkers.* London: Department for Education and Skills.

Barn, R., & Barn, B. S. (2010). Tackling youth crime: exploring technological solution to enhance youth engagement and promote social inclusion. In J. Engelen, J. Dekelver, & W. Van den Bosch (Eds.), *Social Media for Social Inclusion of Youth at Risk: Proceedings of the INCLUSO 2010 Conference* (pp. 197–206). Leuven: K.U. Leuven.

Bartolini Bussi, M. G., & Mariotti, M. A. (2008). Semiotic mediation in the mathematics classroom. In L. D. English (Ed.), *Handbook of International Research in Mathematics Education* (2nd ed.). New York, NY: Routledge.

Bay, E., Bagceci, B., & Cetin, B. (2012). The effects of social constructivist approach on the learners' problem solving and metacognitive levels. *Journal of Social Sciences, 8* (3), 343–349.

Bayraktar, S. (2001). A meta-analysis of the effectiveness of computer-assisted instruction in science education. *Journal of Research on Technology in Education, 34* (2), 173–189.

Beauchamp, G., & Kennewell, S. (2010). Interactivity in the classroom and its impact on learning. *Computers & Education, 54,* 759–766.

Becta (2001). *The Secondary School of the Future – A Preliminary Report to the DfEE.* Coventry: Becta.

Becta (2003). *Primary Schools – ICT Standards. An Analysis of National Data from Ofsted and QCA.* Coventry: Becta.

Becta (2007). *Emerging Technologies for Learning Volume 2.* Coventry: Becta.

Bee, H. (1997). *Lifespan Development* (2nd ed.). New York, NY: Longman.

Beetham, H., & Sharpe, R. (2007). *Rethinking Pedagogy for a Digital Age: Designing and Delivering e-Learning.* London: Routledge.

Benitti, F. B. V. (2012). Exploring the educational potential of robotics in schools: A systematic review. *Computers & Education, 58,* 978–988.

Bennett, S., & Oliver, S. (2011). Talking back to theory: The missed opportunities in learning technology research. *Research in Learning Technology, 19* (3), 179–189.

Berger, M. (2010). Using CAS to solve a mathematics task: A deconstruction. *Computers & Education, 55,* 320–332.

Berger, P. L., & Luckmann, T. (1966). *The Social Construction of Reality: A Treatise in the Sociology of Knowledge.* Garden City, NY: Anchor Books.

Berns, A., Gonzalez-Pardo, A., & Camacho, D. (2013). Game-like language learning in 3-D virtual environments. *Computers & Education, 60,* 210–220.

Bertacchini, F., Bilotta, E., Pantano, P., & Tavernise, A. (2012). Motivating the learning of science topics in secondary school: A constructivist edutainment setting for studying Chaos. *Computers & Education, 59,* 1377–1386.

Bickel, W. K., Christensen, D. R., & Marsch, L. A. (2011). A review of computer-based interventions used in the assessment, treatment, and research of drug addiction. *Substance Use and Misuse, 46* (1), 4–9.

Bimrose, J., Barnes, S.-A., & Attwell, G. (2010). *An Investigation into the Skills Needed by Connexions Personal Advisers to Develop Internet-based Guidance: Full Report.* Reading: CfBT Education Trust.

Blasco-Arcas, L., Buil, I., Hernández-Ortega, B., & Sese, F. J. (2013). Using clickers in class: The role of interactivity, active collaborative learning and engagement in learning performance. *Computers & Education, 62,* 102–110.

Blok, H., Oostdam, R., Otter, M., & Overmaat, M. (2002). Computer-assisted instruction in support of beginning reading instruction: A review. *Review of Educational Research, 72* (1), 101–130.

Blood, E., Johnson, J. W., Ridenour, L., Simmons, K., & Crouch, S. (2011). Using an iPod Touch to teach social and self-management skills to an elementary student with emotional/behavioral disorders. *Education and Treatment of Children, 34* (3), 299–322.

Bloom, B. (1956). *Taxonomy of Educational Objectives.* New York, NY: Longman.

Bolliger, D. U., & Supanakorn, S. (2011). Learning styles and student perceptions of the use of interactive online tutorials. *British Journal of Educational Technology, 42* (3), 470–481.

Bork, P. M. (2010). Prospect of selective mutism intervention: Techno style. *The International Journal of Technology, Knowledge and Society, 6* (3), 37–42.

Bos, B. (2009). Technology with cognitive and mathematical fidelity: What it means for the math classroom. *Computers in the Schools, 26* (2), 107–114.

Bourgonjon, J., Valcke, M., Soetaert, R., de Wever, B., & Schellens, T. (2011). Parental acceptance of digital game-based learning. *Computers & Education, 57,* 1434–1444.

Boyle, C., Lynch, L., Lyon, A., & Williams, C. (2011). The use and feasibility of a CBT intervention. *Child and Adolescent Mental Health, 16* (3), 129–135.

Bradley, L. J., Hendricks, B., Lock, R., Whiting, P. P., & Parr, G. (2011). E-mail communication: Issues for mental health counselors. *Journal of Mental Health Counseling, 33* (1), 67–79.

Bransford, J. D., Brown, A. L., & Cocking, R. R. (2000). *How People Learn: Brain, Mind, Experience, and School.* Washington, DC: National Academy Press.

Bridgeman, B., Harvey, A., & Braswell, J. (1995). Effects of calculator use on scores on a test of mathematical reasoning. *Journal of Educational Measurement, 32* (4), 323–340.

Broma, C., Preuss, M., & Klement, D. (2011). Are educational computer micro-games engaging and effective for knowledge acquisition at high-schools? A quasi-experimental study. *Computers & Education, 57,* 1971–1988.

Brown, D. J., McHugh, D., Standen, P., Evett, L., Shopland, N., & Battersby, S. (2011). Designing location-based learning experiences for people with intellectual disabilities and additional sensory impairments. *Computers & Education, 56*, 11–20.

Bureau of Labor Statistics (2012). *Economic News Release, Employment Projections: 2010–2020 Summary.* Washington, DC: United States Department of Labor.

Cakir, O., & Simsek, N. (2010). A comparative analysis of the effects of computer and paper-based personalization on student achievement. *Computers & Education, 55*, 1524–1531.

Campigotto, R., McEwen, R., & Epp, C. D. (2013). Especially social: Exploring the use of an iOS application in special needs classrooms. *Computers & Education, 60*, 74–86.

Carbonaro, M., Szafron, D., Cutumisu, M., & Shaeffer, J. (2010). Computer-game construction: A gender neutral attractor to computing science. *Computers & Education, 55*, 1098–1111.

Carnahan, C. R., Basham, J. D., Christman, J., & Hollingshead, A. (2012). Overcoming challenges: Going mobile with your own video models. *Teaching Exceptional Children, 45* (2), 50–59.

Carnahan, C. R., Williamson, P. S., Hollingshead, A., & Israel, M. (2012). Using technology to support balanced literacy for students with significant disabilities. *Teaching Exceptional Children, 45* (1), 20–29.

Cavanaugh, C., Gillan, K., Kromrey, J., Hess, M., & Blomeyer, R. (2004). *The Effects of Distance Education on K–12 Student Outcomes: A Meta-analysis.* Naperville, IL: North Central Regional Educational Laboratory.

Cavendish, S., Underwood, J., Lawson, T., & Dowling, S. (1997). When and why do pupils learn from ILS? In J. Underwood & J. Brown (Eds.), *Integrated Learning Systems: Potential into Practice* (pp. 40–53). Oxford: Heinemann.

Chang, C.-C., Liang, C., & Chen, Y.-H. (2013). Is learner self-assessment reliable and valid in a Web-based portfolio environment for high school students? *Computers & Education, 60*, 325–334.

Charsky, D., & Ressler, W. (2011). "Games are made for fun": Lessons on the effects of concept maps in the classroom use of computer games. *Computers & Education, 56*, 604–615.

Chen, C.-M., & Sun, Y.-C. (2012). Assessing the effects of different multimedia materials on emotions and learning performance for visual and verbal style learners. *Computers & Education, 59*, 1273–1285.

Chen, C.-M., & Tsai, Y.-N. (2012). Interactive augmented reality system for enhancing library instruction in elementary schools. *Computers & Education, 59*, 638–652.

Chen, J.-M., Chen, M.-C., & Sun, Y. S. (2010). A novel approach for enhancing student reading comprehension and assisting teacher assessment of literacy. *Computers & Education, 55*, 1367–1382.

Chen, L.-H. (2010). Web-based learning programs: Use by learners with various cognitive styles. *Computers & Education, 54*, 1028–1035.

Chen, N.-S., Teng, D. C.-E., Lee, C.-H., & Kinshuk (2011). Augmenting paper-based reading activity with direct access to digital materials and scaffolded questioning. *Computers & Education, 57*, 1705–1715.

Chen, P.-S. D., Lambert, A. D., & Guidry, K. R. (2010). Engaging online learners: The impact of Web-based learning technology on college student engagement. *Computers & Education, 54*, 1222–1232.

Chen, S. (2010). The view of scientific inquiry conveyed by simulation-based virtual laboratories. *Computers & Education, 55*, 1123–1130.

Chen, Y. L., Liu, E. Z. F., Shih, R. C., Wu, C. T., & Yuan, S. M. (2011). Use of peer feedback to enhance elementary students' writing through blogging. *British Journal of Educational Technology, 42* (1), E1–E4.

Cheng, Y., & Ye, J. (2010). Exploring the social competence of students with autism spectrum conditions in a collaborative virtual learning environment – the pilot study. *Computers & Education*, 54, 1068–1077.

Cheng, Y., Chiang, H.-C., Ye, J., & Cheng, L.-h. (2010). Enhancing empathy instruction using a collaborative virtual learning environment for children with autistic spectrum conditions. *Computers & Education*, 55, 1449–1458.

Child, D. (1973) *Psychology and the Teacher.* London: Holt, Rinehart and Winston.

Chiu, C.-H., Wu, C.-Y., Hsieh, S.-J., Cheng, H.-W., & Huang, C.-K. (2013). Employing a structured interface to advance primary students' communicative competence in a text-based computer mediated environment. *Computers & Education*, 60, 347–356.

Christner, B., & Dieker, L. A. (2008). Tourette syndrome: A collaborative approach focused on empowering students, families, and teachers. *Teaching Exceptional Children*, 40 (5), 44–51.

Ciampa, K. (2012). ICANREAD: The effects of an online reading program on grade 1 students' engagement and comprehension strategy use. *Journal of Research on Technology in Education*, 45 (1), 27–59.

Classroom Assistant (n.d.). *Software and Technological Equipment.* Accessible at: http://www.classroom-assistant.net/software.html.

Cognition and Technology Group at Vanderbilt (CTGV) (1997). *The Jasper Project: Lessons in Curriculum, Instruction, Assessment, and Professional Development.* Mahwah, NJ: Lawrence Erlbaum Associates.

Conn, S. R., Roberts, R. L., & Powell, B. M. (2009). Attitudes and satisfaction with a hybrid model of counseling supervision. *Educational Technology and Society*, 12 (2), 298–306.

Connolly, T. M., Boyle, E. A., MacArthur, E., Hainey, T., & Boyle, J. M. (2012). A systematic literature review of empirical evidence on computer games and serious games. *Computers & Education*, 59, 661–686.

Conole, G. (2007). Describing learning activities: Tools and resources to guide practice. In H. Beetham & R. Sharpe (Eds.), *Rethinking Pedagogy for a Digital Age* (pp. 81–91). London: Routledge.

Conti-Ramsden, G., Durkin, K., & Walker, A. J. (2010). Computer anxiety: A comparison of adolescents with and without a history of specific language impairment (SLI). *Computers & Education*, 54, 136–145.

Coomey, M., & Stephenson, J. (2001). Online learning: It is all about dialogue, involvement, support and control—according to the research. In J. Stephenson (Ed.), *Teaching and Learning Online: Pedagogies for New Technologies* (pp. 37–52). London: Kogan Page.

Coutinho, C., & Mota, P. (2011). Web 2.0 technologies in music education in Portugal: Using podcasts for learning. *Computers in the Schools*, 28 (1), 56–74.

Cox, M., Abbott, C., Webb, M., Blakeley, B., Beauchamp, T., & Rhodes, V. (2003). *ICT and Attainment: A Review of the Research Literature. ICT in Schools Research and Evaluation Series No. 17.* Coventry/London: Becta/DfES.

Cranmer, S. (2010). Excluded young people's perspectives on how digital technologies support and challenge their lives? In J. Engelen, J. Dekelver, & W. Van den Bosch (Eds.), *Social Media for Social Inclusion of Youth at Risk: Proceedings of the INCLUSO 2010 Conference* (pp. 187–196). Leuven: K.U. Leuven.

Crawford, C. (1984). *The Art of Computer Game Design.* Berkeley, CA: Osborne/McGraw-Hill. Accessible at: http://www.scribd.com/doc/140200/Chris-Crawford-The-Art-of-Computer-Game-Design.

Crawford, R. (2010). Valuing technology in the music classroom: Results from a recent case study indicate why technology should be used in education. *Victorian Journal of Music Education*, 1, 29–35.

Cross, D., Monks, H., Hall, M., Shaw, T., Pintabona, Y., Erceg, E., Hamilton, G., Roberts, C., Waters, S., & Lester, L. (2011). Three-year results of the Friendly Schools whole-of-school intervention on children's bullying behaviour. *British Educational Research Journal, 37* (1), 105–129.

Çubukçu, Z. (2012). Teachers' evaluation of student-centered learning environments. *Education, 133* (1), 49–66.

Dalgarno, B., & Lee, M. J. W. (2010). What are the learning affordances of 3-D virtual environments? *British Journal of Educational Technology, 41* (1), 10–32.

Dangwal, R., & Sharma, K. (2013). Impact of HiWEL learning stations on women living in shelter homes. *British Journal of Educational Technology, 44* (1), E26–E30.

Daniel, D. B., & Woody, W. D. (2013). E-textbooks at what cost? Performance and use of electronic v. print texts. *Computers & Education, 62*, 18–23.

Davies, C. (2011). Digitally strategic: How young people respond to parental views about the use of technology for learning in the home. *Journal of Computer Assisted Learning, 27*, 324–335.

de Freitas, S., Harrison, I., Magoulas, G., Mee, A., Mohamad, F., Oliver, M., Papmarkos, G., & Poulovassilis, A. (2006). The development of a system for supporting the lifelong learner. *British Journal of Educational Technology, 37* (6), 867–880.

de Vicente Gutiérrez, F. J., & García, L. M. C. (2010). User modeling and user interfacing in a mobile online community for marginalized youth. In J. Engelen, J. Dekelver, & W. Van den Bosch (Eds.), *Social Media for Social Inclusion of Youth at Risk: Proceedings of the INCLUSO 2010 Conference* (pp. 49–58). Leuven: K.U. Leuven.

Delialioğlu, Ö. (2012). Student engagement in blended learning environments with lecture-based and problem-based instructional approaches. *Educational Technology and Society, 15* (3), 310–322.

Deng, L., & Yuen, A. H. K. (2011). Towards a framework for educational affordances of blogs. *Computers & Education, 56*, 441–451.

Department for Children, Schools and Families (2008). Statistical Volume: Education and Training Statistics for the United Kingdom: 2008 (Internet only). Accessible at: http://www.education.gov.uk/rsgateway/DB/VOL/v000823/v01-2008.pdf.

Department for Education (2012). *The School Curriculum.* Accessible at: http://www.education.gov.uk/schools/teachingandlearning/curriculum/primary?page=1.

Department for Education and Skills (2004). *A National Conversation about Personalised Learning.* Nottingham: Department for Education and Skills.

Department for Education and Skills (2005). *The National Curriculum.* Norwich: DfES.

Department for Education and Skills (2006). *Thinking Skills web-pages, on the National Curriculum pages.* Accessible at: http://www.nc.uk.net/LACcs_thinkskill.htlm.

Desforges, C., & Abouchaar, A. (2003). *The Impact of Parental Involvement, Parental Support and Family Education on Pupil Achievement and Adjustment: A Literature Review. Report Number 433.* London: Department of Education and Skills.

Devecchi, C., Dettori, F., Doveston, M., Sedgwick, P., & Jament, J. (2012). Inclusive class-rooms in Italy and England: The role of support teachers and teaching assistants. *European Journal of Special Needs Education, 27* (2), 171–184.

Dockrell, J. E., & Shield, B. (2012). Research note: The impact of sound-field systems on learning and attention in elementary school classrooms. *Journal of Speech, Language, and Hearing Research, 55*, 1163–1176.

Doyle, D. (2010). Immersed in learning: Supporting creative practice in virtual worlds. *Learning, Media and Technology, 35* (2), 99–110.

Doyle, T., & Arnedillo-Sánchez, I. (2011). Using multimedia to reveal the hidden code of everyday behaviour to children with autistic spectrum disorders (ASDs). *Computers & Education, 56*, 357–369.

Durkin, K., Conti-Ramsden, G., & Walker, A. J. (2011). Txt lang: Texting, textism use and literacy abilities in adolescents with and without specific language impairment. *Journal of Computer Assisted Learning, 27*, 49–57.

Eagle, S. (2012). Learning in the early years: Social interactions around picturebooks, puzzles and digital technologies. *Computers & Education, 59*, 38–49.

Edelson, S. M. (2012). *Learning Styles and Autism*. San Diego, CA: Autism Research Institute. Accessible at: http://www.autism.com/index.php/understanding_learning.

Ejiwale, J. A. (2012). Facilitating teaching and learning across STEM fields. *Journal of STEM Education: Innovations and Research, 13* (3), 87–94.

El Emary, I. M. M., & Hussein, K. Q. (2012). Analyzing the various aspects of e-learning modules for the hearing impaired students. *International Journal of Academic Research, 4* (3), 122–130.

Ellington, A. J. (2003). A meta-analysis of the effects of calculators on students' achievement and attitude levels in precollege mathematics classes. *Journal for Research in Mathematics Education, 34* (5), 433–463.

Ellis, R. A., Goodyear, P., Bliuc, A.-M., & Ellis, M. (2011). High school students' experiences of learning through research on the Internet. *Journal of Computer Assisted Learning, 27*, 503–515.

European Commission (2012). *Strategic Framework for Education and Training*. Accessible at: http://ec.europa.eu/education/lifelong-learning-policy/framework_en.htm.

European Commission Education and Training (2011). *News – Parents Spend Several Billion Euros a Year on Private Tuition for their Children, says Report*. Accessible at: http://ec.europa.eu/education/news/news2954_en.htm.

Fassbender, E., Richards, D., Bilgin, A., Thompson, W. F., & Heiden, W. (2012). VirSchool: The effect of background music and immersive display systems on memory for facts learned in an educational virtual environment. *Computers & Education, 58*, 490–500.

Feiler, A., & Watson, D. (2011). Involving children with learning and communication difficulties: The perspectives of teachers, speech and language therapists and teaching assistants. *British Journal of Learning Disabilities, 39* (2), 113–120.

Felvégi, E., & Matthew, K. I. (2012). eBooks and literacy in K–12 schools. *Computers in the Schools, 29* (1–2), 40–52.

Fernández-López, A., Rodríguez-Fórtiz, M. J., Rodríguez-Almendros, M. L., & Martínez-Segura, M. J. (2013). Mobile learning technology based on iOS devices to support students with special education needs. *Computers & Education, 61*, 77–90.

Fessakis, G., Gouli, E., & Mavroudi, E. (2013). Problem solving by 5–6 years old kindergarten children in a computer programming environment: A case study. *Computers & Education, 63*, 87–97.

Fisch, S. M. (2004). *Children's Learning from Educational Television: Sesame Street and Beyond*. Mahwah, NJ: Lawrence Erlbaum Associates.

Fisch, S. M., & Truglio, R. T. (2001). *"G" is for Growing: Thirty Years of Research on Children and Sesame Street*. Mahwah, NJ: Lawrence Erlbaum Associates.

Fischer Family Trust (2004). *Impact of E-Learning on GCSE Results of 105,617 Students, 2004*. Cardiff: Fischer Family Trust.

Fiske, S. T., & Taylor, S. E. (1991). *Social Cognition* (2nd ed.). New York, NY: McGraw Hill International Editions.

Fletcher-Flinn, C. M., & Gravatt, B. (1995). The efficacy of computer assisted instruction (CAI): A meta-analysis. *Journal of Educational Computing Research, 12* (3), 219–242.

Fox, G. (2001). *Supporting Children with Behaviour Difficulties: A Guide for Assistants in Schools*. London: David Fulton Publishers.

Fredrikson, M., & Tikkanen, R. (2010). Music making as a social integrative tool – design experiences with children. In J. Engelen, J. Dekelver, & W. Van den Bosch (Eds.), *Social Media for Social Inclusion of Youth at Risk: Proceedings of the INCLUSO 2010 Conference* (pp. 41–48). Leuven: K.U. Leuven.

Freire, A. P., Linhalis, F., Bianchini, S. L., Fortes, R. P. M., & Pimentel, M. da G. C. (2010). Revealing the whiteboard to blind students: An inclusive approach to provide mediation in synchronous e-learning activities. *Computers & Education, 54*, 866–876.

Gallardo-Virgen, J. A., & DeVillar, R. A. (2011). Sharing, talking, and learning in the elementary school science classroom: Benefits of innovative design and collaborative learning in computer-integrated settings. *Computers in the Schools, 28* (4), 278–290.

Gamage, V., Tretiakov, A., & Crump, B. (2011). Teacher perceptions of learning affordances of multi-user virtual environments. *Computers & Education, 57,* 2406–2413.

Garcia, L., Nussbaum, M., & Preiss, D. D. (2011). Is the use of information and communication technology related to performance in working memory tasks? Evidence from seventh-grade students. *Computers & Education, 57,* 2068–2076.

Gardner, H. (1991) *The Unschooled Mind: How Children Think, How Schools Should Teach.* New York, NY: Basic Books.

Gardner, J. (1997). ILS and under-achievers. In J. Underwood & J. Brown (Eds.), *Integrated Learning Systems: Potential into Practice* (pp. 88–102). Oxford: Heinemann.

Geer, R., & Sweeney, T.-A. (2012). Students' voices about learning with technology. *Journal of Social Sciences, 8* (2), 294–303.

Gibson, J. J. (1977). The theory of affordances. In R. Shaw & J. Bransford (Eds.), *Perceiving, Acting and Knowing* (pp. 67–82). New York, NY: Wiley.

Gil-Flores, J., Torres-Gordillo, J.-J., & Perera-Rodríguez, V.-H. (2012). The role of online reader experience in explaining students' performance in digital reading. *Computers & Education, 59,* 653–660.

GL Assessment (2002a). *Suffolk Reading Scale 2: Form A.* London: GL Assessment.

GL Assessment (2002b). *Suffolk Reading Scale 2: Form B.* London: GL Assessment.

GL Assessment (2004). *Progress in Maths 9.* London: GL Assessment.

Goldberg, A., Russell, M., & Cook, A. (2003). The effect of computers on student writing: A metaanalysis of studies from 1992 to 2002. *Journal of Technology, Learning, and Assessment, 2* (1), 3–51.

González, J. A., Jover, L., Cobo, E., & Muñoz, P. (2010). A web-based learning tool improves student performance in statistics: A randomized masked trial. *Computers & Education, 55,* 704–713.

Gu, X., Gu, F., & Laffey, J. M. (2011). Designing a mobile system for lifelong learning on the move. *Journal of Computer Assisted Learning, 27,* 204–215.

Gupta, G., & Sehgal, S. (2012). Comparative effectiveness of videotape and handout mode of instructions for teaching exercises: Skill retention in normal children. *Pediatric Rheumatology, 10* (1), 4–11.

Gyabak, K., & Godina, H. (2011). Digital storytelling in Bhutan: A qualitative examination of new media tools used to bridge the digital divide in a rural community school. *Computers & Education, 57,* 2236–2243.

Habib, L., Berget, G., Sandnes, F. E., Sanderson, N., Kahn, P., Fagernes, S., & Olcay, A. (2012). Dyslexic students in higher education and virtual learning environments: An exploratory study. *Journal of Computer Assisted Learning, 28,* 574–584.

Haché, A., & Cullen, J. (2009). *JRC Scientific and Technical Reports: ICT and Youth at Risk – How ICT-driven Initiatives can Contribute to their Socio-economic Inclusion and How to Measure it.* Seville: JRC IPTS.

Haché, A., Dekelver, J., Montandon, L., Playfoot, J., Aagaard, M., & Elmer, S. (2010). *JRC Scientific and Technical Notes: Research and Policy Brief on ICT for Inclusion of Youth at Risk – Using ICT to Reengage and Foster the Socio-economic Inclusion of Youth at Risk of Social Inclusion, Marginalized Young People and Intermediaries Working With Them.* Luxembourg: Office for Official Publications of the European Communities.

Hansen, N., Koudenburg, N., Hiersemann, R., Tellegen, P. J., Kocsev, M., & Postmes, T. (2012). Laptop usage affects abstract reasoning of children in the developing world. *Computers & Education, 59,* 989–1000.

Hanson, E., Magnusson, L., & Sennemark, E. (2011). Blended learning networks supported by information and communication technology: An intervention for knowledge transformation within family care of older people. *The Gerontologist, 51* (4), 561–570.

Hansson, H. (n.d.). *Evaluation of Interactive Whiteboards: Smartboard – Vinstagårdsskolan and Activboard – Kvickenstorpsskolan*. Stockholm: Kompetensfonden.

Harcourt, D. (2012). Learner engagement: Has the child been lost in translation? *Australasian Journal of Early Childhood, 37* (3), 71–78.

Harris, A., & Goodall, J. (2007). *Engaging Parents in Raising Achievement: Do Parents Know They Matter? Research Report DCSF-RW004*. London: DCSF.

Harrison, C. (1997). The use of ILS among pupils for whom English is a second language. In J. Underwood & J. Brown (Eds.), *Integrated Learning Systems: Potential into Practice* (pp. 127–135). Oxford: Heinemann.

Harrison, C., Comber, C., Fisher, T., Haw, K., Lewin, C., Lunzer, E., McFarlane, A., Mavers, D., Scrimshaw, P., Somekh, B., & Watling, R. (2002). *ICT in schools. Research and Evaluation Series No. 7: The Impact of Information and Communication Technologies on Pupil Learning and Attainment*. London: DfES.

Hartas, D. (2011). Young people's participation: Is disaffection another way of having a voice? *Educational Psychology in Practice, 27* (2), 103–115.

Hathorn, L. G., & Rawson, K. A. (2012). The roles of embedded monitoring requests and questions in improving mental models of computer-based scientific text. *Computers & Education, 59*, 1021–1031.

Hauptman, H., & Cohen, A. (2011). The synergetic effect of learning styles on the interaction between virtual environments and the enhancement of spatial thinking. *Computers & Education, 57*, 2106–2117.

Hay, L. (2012). Experience the "shift": Build an iCentre. *Teacher Librarian, 39* (5), 29–35.

Hayes, B. G. (2008). The use of multimedia instruction in counselor education: A creative teaching strategy. *Journal of Creativity in Mental Health, 3* (3), 243–253.

Hedberg, J. G. (2011). Towards a disruptive pedagogy: Changing classroom practice with technologies and digital content. *Educational Media International, 48* (1), 1–16.

Hendry, D. G., Woelfer, J. P., Harper, R., Bauer, T., Fitzer, B., & Champage, M. (2011). How to integrate digital media into a drop-in for homeless young people for deepening relationships between youth and adults. *Children and Youth Services Review, 33* (5), 774–782.

Hennessy, S. (2011). The role of digital artefacts on the interactive whiteboard in supporting classroom dialogue. *Journal of Computer Assisted Learning, 27*, 463–489.

Higgins, S., Mercier, E., Burd, L., & Joyce-Gibbons, A. (2012). Multi-touch tables and collaborative learning. *British Journal of Educational Technology, 43* (6), 1041–1054.

Higginson, C. (2001). Online tutoring e-book. Nottingham: OTiS (Online Skills Tutoring Project). Accessible at: http://www.nottingham.ac.uk/nmp/sonet/resources/otis/t8-02.pdf.

Hohlfeld, T. N., Ritzhaupt, A. D., & Barron, A. E. (2010). Connecting schools, community, and family with ICT: Four-year trends related to school level and SES of public schools in Florida. *Computers & Education, 55*, 391–405.

Hollingworth, S., Mansaray, A., Allen, K., & Rose, A. (2011). Parents' perspectives on technology and children's learning in the home: Social class and the role of the habitus. *Journal of Computer Assisted Learning, 27*, 347–360.

Holmes, W. (2011). Using game-based learning to support struggling readers at home. *Learning, Media and Technology, 36* (1), 5–19.

Houssart, J. (2012). Teaching assistants' roles in daily mathematics lessons. *Educational Research, 54* (4), 391–403.

Hoyles, C., & Noss, R. (2003). What can digital technologies take from and bring to research in mathematics education? In J. Bishop, K. Clements, C. Keitel, J. Kilpatrick, & F. Leung (Eds.), *Second International Handbook of Mathematics Education (Part 1)* (pp. 323–349). Dordrecht, the Netherlands: Kluwer Academic.

Huang, Y.-M., Lin, Y.-T., & Cheng, S.-C. (2010). Effectiveness of a mobile plant learning system in a science curriculum in Taiwanese elementary education. *Computers & Education, 54*, 47–58.

Hunter, W. J., Jardine, G., Rilstone, P., & Weisgerber, R. (n.d.). The effects of using word processors: A hard look at the research. *The Writing Notebook*, *8* (1), 42–46.

Huppert J., Lomask, S. M., & Lazarowitz, R. (2002). Computer simulations in the high school: students' cognitive stages, science process skills and academic achievement in microbiology. *International Journal of Science Education*, *24* (8), 803–821.

Hur, J. W., & Suh, S. (2012). Making learning active with interactive whiteboards, podcasts, and digital storytelling in ELL classrooms. *Computers in the Schools*, *29* (4), 320–338.

Hussein, K. Q., Abo-Darwish, M., & Al-Atiat, K. (2010). Evaluating an e-dictionary for hearing impaired persons through case study (the effective role of speech visualization multimedia). *European Journal of Scientific Research*, *41* (4), 646–652.

Huston, A. C., Anderson, D. R., Wright, J. C., Linebarger, D. L., & Schmitt, K. L. (2001). Sesame Street viewers as adolescents: The recontact study. In S. M. Fisch & R. T. Trugio (Eds.), *"G" Is for Growing: Thirty Years of Research on Children and Sesame Street* (pp. 131–143). Hillsdale, NJ: Lawrence Erlbaum Associates.

Hwang, W.-Y., Chen, N.-S., Shadiev, R., & Li, J.-S. (2011). Effects of reviewing annotations and homework solutions on math learning achievement. *British Journal of Educational Technology*, *42* (6), 1016–1028.

Ibañez, F., Playfoot, J., Fabregat, M. A., Costa, M., & Torres, S. (2010). Gaming technology platform as a support tool for anti social behavior prevention in young people at risk to be marginalized. In J. Engelen, J. Dekelver, & W. Van den Bosch (Eds.), *Social Media for Social Inclusion of Youth at Risk: Proceedings of the INCLUSO 2010 Conference* (pp. 29–40). Leuven: K.U. Leuven.

Infogroup/ORC International (2010). *Harnessing Technology School Survey: 2010*. Coventry: Becta.

iPads for Learning (n.d.). *Royal Children's Hospital Education Institute: Case Studies*. Victoria, Australia: Department of Education and Early Childhood Development.

Isiksal, M., & Askar, P. (2005). The effect of spreadsheet and dynamic geometry software on the achievement and self-efficacy of 7th grade students. *Educational Research*, *47* (3), 333–350.

Ismail, I., & Azizan, S. N. (2012). Distance learners' needs on interactivity in SMS-based learning system. *Asian Social Science*, *8* (11), 119–128.

Janssens, E., Brijs, E., & Van den Branden, J. (2010). Inclusion and children with medical needs: The Bednet case. In J. Engelen, J. Dekelver, & W. Van den Bosch (Eds.), *Social Media for Social Inclusion of Youth at Risk: Proceedings of the INCLUSO 2010 Conference* (pp. 179–186). Leuven: K.U. Leuven.

Jenks, M. S., & Springer, J. M. (2002). A view of the research on the efficacy of CAI. *Electronic Journal for the Integration of Technology in Education*, *1* (2). Accessible at: http://ejite.isu.edu/Volume1No2/Jenks.htm.

Jewitt, C., & Parashar, U. (2011). Technology and learning at home: Findings from the evaluation of the Home Access Programme pilot. *Journal of Computer Assisted Learning*, *27*, 303–313.

Joffe, V. L., & Black, E. (2012). Social, emotional, and behavioral functioning of secondary school students with low academic and language performance: Perspectives from students, teachers, and parents. *Language, Speech and Hearing Services in Schools*, *43* (4), 461–473.

Jones, C. (2004). Networks and learning: Communities, practices and the metaphor of networks. *Alt-J*, *12* (1), 81–93. DOI: 10.1080/0968776042000211548.

Jones, C., & Czerniewicz, L. (2011). Editorial: Theory in learning technology. *Research in Learning Technology*, *19* (3), 173–177.

Jones, M. E., Antonenko, P. D., & Greenwood, C. M. (2012). The impact of collaborative and individualized student response system strategies on learner motivation, metacognition, and knowledge transfer. *Journal of Computer Assisted Learning*, *28*, 477–487.

Jones, T., & Cuthrell, K. (2011). YouTube: Educational potentials and pitfalls. *Computers in the Schools*, *28* (1), 75–85.

Jopling, M. (2012). 1:1 online tuition: A review of the literature from a pedagogical perspective. *Journal of Computer Assisted Learning, 28*, 310–321.

Joshi, A., Pan, A., Murakami M., & Narayanan, S. (2010). Role of computers in educating young children: U.S. and Japanese teachers' perspectives. *Computers in the Schools, 27* (1), 5–19.

Junco, R., Heiberger, G., & Loken, E. (2011). The effect of Twitter on college student engagement and grades. *Journal of Computer Assisted Learning, 27*, 119–132.

Kane, T. J. (2004). Extracting evaluation lessons from four recent out of school time program evaluations. *The Evaluation Exchange, 10* (1), 1–4.

Karemaker, A., Pitchford, N. J., & O'Malley, C. (2010). Enhanced recognition of written words and enjoyment of reading in struggling beginner readers through whole-word multimedia software. *Computers & Education, 54*, 199–208.

Kaveh, Z. (2012). Integration and impact of educational media (technologies) in the teaching-learning process: A case study in Iran. *Middle East Journal of Family Medicine, 10* (7), 30–38.

Ke, F. (2013). Computer-game-based tutoring of mathematics. *Computers & Education, 60*, 448–457.

Kebritchi, M., Hirumi, A., & Bai, H. (2010). The effects of modern mathematics computer games on mathematics achievement and class motivation. *Computers & Education, 55*, 427–443.

Kelly, S. M., & Wolffe, K. E. (2012). Internet use by transition-aged youths with visual impairments in the United States: Assessing the impact of postsecondary predictors. *Journal of Visual Impairment and Blindness, 106* (10), 597–608.

Kember, D., McNaught, C., Chong, F. C. Y., Lam, P., & Cheng, K. F. (2010). Understanding the ways in which design features of educational websites impact upon student learning outcomes in blended learning environments. *Computers & Education, 55*, 1183–1192.

Kennedy, M. J., & Swain-Bradway, J. (2012). Rationale and recommended practices for using homegrown video to support school-wide positive behavioral interventions and supports. *Beyond Behavior, 21* (2), 20–28.

Kılıçkaya, F., & Krajka, J. (2012). Can the use of web-based comic strip creation tool facilitate EFL learners' grammar and sentence writing? *British Journal of Educational Technology, 43* (6), E161–E165.

Kim, H. J., & Pedersen, S. (2011). Advancing young adolescents' hypothesis-development performance in a computer-supported and problem-based learning environment. *Computers & Education, 57*, 1780–1789.

Kim, J. (2013). Influence of group size on students' participation in online discussion forums. *Computers & Education, 62*, 123–129.

Kim, J.-M., & Lee, W.-G. (2011). Assistance and possibilities: Analysis of learning-related factors affecting the online learning satisfaction of underprivileged students. *Computers & Education, 57*, 2395–2405.

Kim, P., & Olaciregui, C. (2008). The effects of a concept map-based information display in an electronic portfolio system on information processing and retention in a fifth-grade science class covering the Earth's atmosphere. *British Journal of Educational Technology, 39* (4), 700–714.

Kim, P., Hagashi, T., Carillo, L., Gonzales, I., Makany, T., Lee, B., & Gàrate, A. (2011). Socioeconomic strata, mobile technology, and education: A comparative analysis. *Educational Technology Research and Development, 59* (4), 465–486.

Kirschner, P. A. (2002). Can we support CSCL? Educational, social and technological affordances for learning. In P. A. Kirschner (Ed.), *Three worlds of CSCL: Can we support CSCL?* Heerlen, the Netherlands: Open University of the Netherlands.

Kleemans, T., Segers, E., Droop, M., & Wentink, H. (2011). WebQuests in special primary education: Learning in a web-based environment. *British Journal of Educational Technology, 42* (5), 801–810.

Ko, C.-C., Chiang, C.-H., Lin, Y.-L., & Chen, M.-C. (2011). An individualized e-reading system developed based on multirepresentations approach. *Educational Technology and Society, 14* (4), 88–98.

Kolikant, Y. B.-D., & Broza, O. (2010). The effect of using a video clip presenting a contextual story on low-achieving students' mathematical discourse. *Educational Studies in Mathematics, 76* (1), 23–47.

Kollöffel, B. (2012). Exploring the relation between visualizer–verbalizer cognitive styles and performance with visual or verbal learning material. *Computers & Education, 58,* 697–706.

Kopp, B., Matteucci, M. C., & Tomasetto, C. (2012). E-tutorial support for collaborative online learning: An explorative study on experienced and inexperienced e-tutors. *Computers & Education, 58,* 12–20.

Korallo, L., Foreman, N., Boyd-Davis, S., Moar, M., & Coulson, M. (2012). Do challenge, task experience or computer familiarity influence the learning of historical chronology from virtual environments in 8–9 year old children? *Computers & Education, 58,* 1106–1116.

Korat, O. (2010). Reading electronic books as a support for vocabulary, story comprehension and word reading in kindergarten and first grade. *Computers & Education, 55,* 24–31.

Kozar, O. (2012). Use of synchronous online tools in private English language teaching in Russia. *Distance Education, 33* (3), 415–420.

Kühl, T., Scheiter, K., Gerjets, P., & Gemballa, S. (2011). Can differences in learning strategies explain the benefits of learning from static and dynamic visualizations? *Computers & Education, 56,* 176–187.

Kulkarni, M. V. (2012). A study on secondary school teachers' attitude towards using new technologies in education. *Indian Streams Research Journal, 2* (8), 1–6.

Kurth, R. (1987). Using word processing to enhance revision strategies during student writing activities. *Educational Technology, 27* (1), 13–19.

Laborde, C. (2007). The role and uses of technologies in mathematics classrooms: Between challenge and modus vivendi. *Canadian Journal of Science, Mathematics and Technology Education, 7* (1), 68–92.

Lane, A. E., & Ziviani, J. M. (2010). Factors influencing skilled use of the computer mouse by school-aged children. *Computers & Education, 55,* 1112–1122.

Larkin, K. (2011). You use! I use! We use! Questioning the orthodoxy of one-to-one computing in primary schools. *Journal of Research on Technology in Education, 44* (2), 101–120.

Laurillard, D. (2001). *Rethinking University Teaching: A Framework for the Effective Use of Educational Technology* (2nd ed.). London: Routledge.

Lave, J., & Wenger, E. (1991). *Situated Learning: Legitimate Peripheral Participation.* New York, NY: Cambridge University Press.

Lavin, A. M., Korte, L., & Davies, T. L. (2010). The impact of classroom technology on student behaviour. *Journal of Technology Research, 2,* 1–13.

Laxman, K. (2010). A conceptual framework mapping the application of information search strategies to well and ill-structured problem solving. *Computers & Education, 55,* 513–526.

Lee, J. A., & McDougall, D. E. (2010). Secondary school teachers' conceptions and their teaching practices using graphing calculators. *International Journal of Mathematical Education in Science and Technology, 41* (7), 857–872.

Lei, J. (2010). Quantity versus quality: A new approach to examine the relationship between technology use and student outcomes. *British Journal of Educational Technology, 41* (3), 455–472.

Leman, J., Trappers, A., Brandon, E., & Ruppol, X. (2008). Migration related socio-cultural changes and e-learning in a European globalising society. *Studies in Philosophy and Education, 27* (4), 237–251.

Leppisaari, I., & Lee, O. (2012). Modeling digital natives' international collaboration: Finnish-Korean experiences of environmental education. *Journal of Educational Technology and Society, 15* (2), 244–256.

Levesque, D. A., Johnson, J. L., Welch, C. A., Prochaska, J. M., & Fernandez, A. C. (2012). Computer-tailored intervention for juvenile offenders. *Journal of Social Work Practice in the Addictions*, *12* (4), 391–411.

Levy, M. S. (2011). Migrant laptops: Extending the academic day for the children of farm workers and their credit recovery via laptops. *Computers in the Schools*, *28* (2), 140–157.

Levy, S. T., & Lahav, O. (2012). Enabling people who are blind to experience science inquiry learning through sound-based mediation. *Journal of Computer Assisted Learning*, *28*, 499–513.

Lewin, C. (2004). Access and use of technologies in the home in the UK: Implications for the curriculum. *Curriculum Journal*, *15* (2), 139–154.

Lewis, A. (1997). ILS and pupils with special educational needs. In J. Underwood & J. Brown (Eds.), *Integrated learning systems: Potential into practice* (pp. 103–117). Oxford: Heinemann.

Li, Y., & Ranieri, M. (2013). Educational and social correlates of the digital divide for rural and urban children: A study on primary school students in a provincial city of China. *Computers & Education*, *60*, 197–209.

Liao, Y.-K. C. (1998). Effects of hypermedia versus traditional instruction on students' achievement: A meta-analysis. *Journal of Research on Computing in Education*, *30* (4), 341–360.

Liao, Y.-K. C. (2007). Effects of computer-assisted instruction on students' achievement in Taiwan: A meta-analysis. *Computers & Education*, *48* (2), 216–233.

Lidström, H., Granlund, M., & Hemmingsson, H. (2012). Use of ICT in school: A comparison between students with and without physical disabilities. *European Journal of Special Needs Education*, *27* (1), 21–34.

Lin, H.-s., Hong, Z.-R., & Lawrenz, F. (2012). Promoting and scaffolding argumentation through reflective asynchronous discussions. *Computers & Education*, *59*, 378–384.

Lin, L., & Bigenho, C. (2011). Note-taking and memory in different media environments. *Computers in the Schools*, *28* (3), 200–216.

Lin, L., & Atkinson, R. K. (2011). Using animations and visual cueing to support learning of scientific concepts and processes. *Computers & Education*, *56*, 650–658.

Lines, P. M. (2001). *Homeschooling: Educating Children Under the Supervision of Parents*. Eugene, OR: ERIC Clearinghouse on Educational Management.

Linn, M. C., & His, S. (2000). *Computers, Teachers, Peers: Science Learning Partners*. Mahwah, NJ: Erlbaum.

Lipman, M. (1995). Caring as thinking. *Inquiry: Critical Thinking across the Disciplines*, *15* (1), 1–13.

Liu, C.-C., & Hong, Y.-C. (2007). Providing hearing-impaired students with learning care after classes through smart phones and the GPRS network. *British Journal of Educational Technology*, *38* (4), 727–741.

Liu, C.-C., & Milrad, M. (2010). Guest editorial – one-to-one learning in the mobile and ubiquitous computing age. *Educational Technology and Society*, *13* (4), 1–3.

Liu, C.-C., Chung, C. W., Chen, N.-S., & Liu, B.-J. (2009). Analysis of peer interaction in learning activities with personal handhelds and shared displays. *Educational Technology and Society*, *12* (3), 127–142.

Liu, P.-L. (2011). A study on the use of computerized concept mapping to assist ESL learners' writing. *Computers & Education*, *57*, 2548–2558.

Liu, T.-C., Kinshuk, Lin, Y.-C., & Wang, S.-C. (2012). Can verbalisers learn as well as visualisers in simulation-based CAL with predominantly visual representations? Preliminary evidence from a pilot study. *British Journal of Educational Technology*, *43* (6), 965–980.

Livingstone, S. (2012). Critical reflections on the benefits of ICT in education. *Oxford Review of Education*, *38* (1), 9–24.

Looi, C.-K., Zhang, B., Chen, W., Seow, P., Chia, G., Norris, C., & Soloway, E. (2011). 1:1 mobile inquiry learning experience for primary science students: A study of learning effectiveness. *Journal of Computer Assisted Learning*, *27*, 269–287.

López, O. S. (2010). The digital learning classroom: Improving English language learners' academic success in mathematics and reading using interactive whiteboard technology. *Computers & Education, 54*, 901–915.

Lorenzo, G., Pomares, J., & Lledó, A. (2013). Inclusion of immersive virtual learning environments and visual control systems to support the learning of students with Asperger syndrome. *Computers & Education, 62*, 88–101.

Luckin, R. (2010). *Re-Designing Learning Contexts: Technology-Rich, Learner-Centred Ecologies.* London: Routledge.

Luckin, R., Bligh, B. Manches, A., Ainsworth, S., Crook, C., & Noss, R. (2012). *Decoding Learning: The Proof, Promise and Potential of Digital Education.* London: Nesta.

Lund, K. (2010). Cyberhus: Experiences and lessons from online counselling. In J. Engelen, J. Dekelver, & W. Van den Bosch (Eds.), *Social Media for Social Inclusion of Youth at Risk: Proceedings of the INCLUSO 2010 Conference* (pp. 81–88). Leuven: K.U. Leuven.

Luu, K., & Freeman, J. G. (2011). An analysis of the relationship between information and communication technology (ICT) and scientific literacy in Canada and Australia. *Computers & Education, 56*, 1072–1082.

MacArthur, C. A. (2009). Reflections on research on writing and technology for struggling writers. *Learning Disabilities Research and Practice, 24* (2), 93–103.

Maher, D. (2011). Using the multimodal affordances of the interactive whiteboard to support students' understanding of texts. *Learning, Media and Technology, 36* (3), 235–250.

Manches, A., O'Malley, C., & Benford, S. (2010). The role of physical representations in solving number problems: A comparison of young children's use of physical and virtual materials. *Computers & Education, 54*, 622–640.

Mason, L., Tornatora, M. C., & Pluchino, P. (2013). Do fourth graders integrate text and picture in processing and learning from an illustrated science text? Evidence from eye-movement patterns. *Computers & Education, 60*, 95–109.

McAdams III, C. R., & Wyatt, K. L. (2010). The regulation of technology-assisted distance counseling and supervision in the United States: An analysis of current extent, trends, and implications. *Counselor Education and Supervision, 49* (3), 179–192.

McDonald, S., & Howell, J. (2012). Watching, creating and achieving: Creative technologies as a conduit for learning in the early years. *British Journal of Educational Technology, 43* (4), 641–651.

McDougall, A., Murnane, J., Jones, A., & Reynolds, N. (2010). *Researching IT in Education.* London: Routledge.

McFarlane, A. (1997a). The effectiveness of ILS. In J. Underwood & J. Brown (Eds.), *Integrated Learning Systems: Potential into Practice* (pp. 15–29). Oxford: Heinemann Educational Publishers.

McFarlane, A. (1997). *Information Technology and Authentic Learning: Realising the Potential of Computers in the Primary Classroom.* London: Routledge.

McLoughlin, C., & Reid, N. (2002). Seachange: design of online quiz questions to foster deep learning. In A. Williamson, C. Gunn, A. Young, & T. Clear (Eds.), *Winds of Change in the Sea of Learning: Proceedings of the 19th Annual Conference of the Australasian Society for Computers in Learning in Tertiary Education* (pp. 843–846). Auckland.

McMahon, G. (2009). Critical thinking and ICT integration in a Western Australian secondary school. *Educational Technology and Society, 12* (4), 269–281.

Meluso, A., Zheng, M., Spires, H. A., & Lester, J. (2012). Enhancing 5th graders' science content knowledge and self-efficacy through game-based learning. *Computers & Education, 59*, 497–504.

The Metiri Group (2006). *Technology in Schools: What the Research Says.* Cisco Systems.

Meyer, E., Abrami, P. C., Wadea, C. A., Aslan, O., & Deault, L. (2010). Improving literacy and metacognition with electronic portfolios: Teaching and learning with ePEARL. *Computers & Education, 55*, 84–91.

Migliorino, P. (2011). Digital technologies can unite but also divide: Cald communities in the digital age. *Aplis, 24* (3), 107–110.

Miller, D. J., & Robertson, D. P. (2011). Educational benefits of using game consoles in a primary classroom: A randomised controlled trial. *British Journal of Educational Technology, 42* (5), 850–864.

Miller, L. M., Chang, C.-I., Wang, S., Beier, M. E., & Klisch, Y. (2011). Learning and motivational impacts of a multimedia science game. *Computers & Education, 57,* 1425–1433.

Milligan, C., & Passey, D. (2011). *Ageing and the Use of the Internet – Current Engagement and Future Needs: State-of-the-Art Report.* Oxford: The Nominet Trust.

Ministerium für Schule und Weiterbildung des Landes Nordrhein-Westfalen (2009). *Das Schulwesen in Nordrhein-Westfalen aus quantitaver Sicht 2008/09: Statistische Übersich 369.* Düsseldorf, NRW: Ministerium für Schule und Weiterbildung des Landes Nordrhein-Westfalen.

Mintz, J. (2013). Additional key factors mediating the use of a mobile technology tool designed to develop social and life skills in children with Autism Spectrum Disorders: Evaluation of the 2nd HANDS prototype. *Computers & Education, 63,* 17–27.

Mintz, J., Branch, C., March, C., & Lerman, S. (2012). Key factors mediating the use of a mobile technology tool designed to develop social and life skills in children with Autistic Spectrum Disorders. *Computers & Education, 58,* 53–62.

Mishra, P., & Koehler, M. J. (2006). Technological pedagogical content knowledge: A framework for teacher knowledge. *Teachers College Record, 108* (6), 1017–1054.

Montero, F., López-Jaquero, V., Navarro, E., & Sánchez, E. (2011). Computer-aided relearning activity patterns for people with acquired brain injury. *Computers & Education, 57,* 1149–1159.

Moseley, D., Baumfield, V., Elliott, J., Higgins, S., Miller, J., & Newton, D. P. (2005). *Frameworks for Thinking: A Handbook for Teachers and Learning.* Cambridge: Cambridge University Press.

Moss, G., Jewitt, C., Levaãiç, R., Armstrong, V., Cardini, A., & Castle, F. (2007). *The Interactive Whiteboards, Pedagogy and Pupil Performance Evaluation: An Evaluation of the Schools Whiteboard Expansion (SWE) Project: London Challenge.* London: Institute of Education, University of London and DfES.

Murphy, D., Walker, R., & Webb, G. (2001). *Online Learning and Teaching with Technology: Case Studies, Experience, and Practice.* London: Routledge.

Murphy, E., Rodríguez-Manzanares, M. A., & Barbour, M. (2011). Asynchronous and synchronous online teaching: Perspectives of Canadian high school distance education teachers. *British Journal of Educational Technology, 42* (4), 583–591.

Nakamura, S. (2012). Investment and return: Wiki engagement in a "remedial" ESL writing course. *Journal of Research on Technology in Education, 44* (4), 273–291.

National Council for Educational Technology (1994). *Integrated Learning Systems – A Report of the Pilot Evaluation of ILS in the UK.* Coventry: NCET.

National Institute of Child Health and Human Development (2000). *Report of the National Reading Panel – Teaching Children to Read: An Evidence-based Assessment of the Scientific Research Literature on Reading and its Implications for Reading Instruction: Reports of the Subgroups (NIH Publication No. 00-4754).* Washington, DC: U.S. Government Printing Office.

The New Media Consortium (2010). *Horizon Report 2010: K-12 Edition.* Austin, TX: The New Media Consortium.

Newby, T. J., Stepich, D. A., Lehman, J. D., & Russell, J. D. (2006). *Educational Technology for Teaching and Learning* (3rd ed.). Upper Saddle River, NJ: Merrill/Prentice-Hall.

Northern Ireland Curriculum (2012). *Areas of Learning at Key Stages 1 and 2.* Accessible at: http://www.nicurriculum.org.uk/key_stages_1_and_2/areas_of_learning/.

O'Bannon, B. W., Lubke, J. K., Beard, J. L., & Britt, V. G. (2011). Using podcasts to replace lecture: Effects on student achievement. *Computers & Education, 57,* 1885–1892.

Ofcom (2012). *Communications Market Report*. London: Ofcom. Accessible at: http://stake-holders.ofcom.org.uk/binaries/research/cmr/cmr12/CMR_UK_2012.pdf.

Owusu, K. A., Monney, K. A., Appiah, J. Y., & Wilmot, E. M. (2010). Effects of computer-assisted instruction on performance of senior high school biology students in Ghana. *Computers & Education*, *55*, 904–910.

Özmen, H. (2011). Effect of animation enhanced conceptual change texts on 6th grade students' understanding of the particulate nature of matter and transformation during phase changes. *Computers & Education*, *57*, 1114–1126.

Oztok, M., Zingaro, D., Brett, C., & Hewitt, J. (2013). Exploring asynchronous and synchronous tool use in online courses. *Computers & Education*, *60*, 87–94.

Öztürk, E., & Özmen, S. K. (2011). An investigation of the problematic Internet use of teacher candidates based on personality types, shyness and demographic factors. *Educational Sciences: Theory and Practice*, *11* (4), 1799–1808.

Palaigeorgiou, G., Triantafyllakos, G., & Tsinakos, A. (2011). What if undergraduate students designed their own web learning environment? Exploring students' web 2.0 mentality through participatory design. *Journal of Computer Assisted Learning*, *27* (2), 146–159.

Panoutsopoulos, H., & Sampson, D. G. (2012). A study on exploiting commercial digital games into school context. *Journal of Educational Technology and Society*, *15* (1), 15–27.

Papastergiou, M., Gerodimos, V., & Antoniou, P. (2011). Multimedia blogging in physical education: Effects on student knowledge and ICT self-efficacy. *Computers & Education*, *57*, 1998–2010.

Pask, G. (1975). *Conversation, Cognition, and Learning*. New York, NY: Elsevier.

Passey, D. (1997). Supporting learning in isolated environments. In J. Underwood & J. Brown (Eds.), *Integrated Learning Systems: Potential into Practice* (pp. 156–165). Oxford: Heinemann.

Passey, D. (2006a). Technology enhancing learning: Analysing uses of information and communication technologies by primary and secondary school pupils with learning frameworks. *The Curriculum Journal*, *17* (2), 139–166.

Passey, D. (2006b). Digital video technologies enhancing learning for pupils at risk and those who are hard to reach. In M. Childs (Ed.), *Developing Innovative Video Resources for Students Everywhere: Proceedings of the DIVERSE 2006 Conference*, held in Glasgow, Scotland, pp. 156–168.

Passey, D. (2007). *Virtual Workspace: An Independent Evaluative Review*. Wolverhampton: Wolverhampton City Council and Worcestershire County Council.

Passey, D. (2010). Mobile learning in school contexts: Can teachers alone make it happen? *IEEE Transactions on Learning Technologies: Special Issue on Mobile and Ubiquitous Technologies for Learning*, *3* (1), 68–81.

Passey, D. (2011a). *Independent Evaluation of the Uses of Espresso Online Digital Resources in Primary Schools: Final Report – Summary*. Lancaster: Lancaster University. Accessible at: http://eprints.lancs.ac.uk/40904.

Passey, D. (2011b). Technologies involving parents and guardians with their children's learning. In A. Méndez-Vilas (Ed.), *Education in a Technological World: Communicating Current and Emerging Research and Technological Efforts* (pp. 467–477). Badajoz, Spain: Formatex Research Center.

Passey, D. (2011c). Learning mathematics using digital resources: Impacts on learning and teaching for 11 to 14 year old pupils. In A. Oldknow & C. Knights (Eds.), *Mathematics Education with Digital Technology* (pp. 46–60). London: Continuum International Publishing.

Passey, D. (2011d). *Independent Evaluation of the Aston Pride Phase 3 Computers in the Home Project (2009 to 2011): Final Report – March 2011*. Lancaster: Lancaster University.

Passey, D. (2011e). Implementing learning platforms into schools: An architecture for wider involvement in learning. *Learning, Media and Technology*, *36* (4), 367–397.

Passey, D. (2012a). Educational technologies and mathematics: Signature pedagogies and learner impacts. *Computers in the Schools, 29* (01–02), 6–39.

Passey, D. (2012b). *Independent Evaluation of the Little Big Planet 2 Project in Wolverhampton's Local Education Partnership Schools: Outcomes and Impacts – Final Report*. Lancaster: Lancaster University.

Passey, D. (2012c). *Educational Transformation with Open and Social Technologies in the Non-Formal School Curriculum: An Analysis of Three Case Studies in the United Kingdom*. Paper presented at the OST 2012 conference, Tallinn, Estonia, on August 3, 2012. Accessible at: http://ifip-ost12.tlu.ee/wp-content/uploads/2012/06/passey.pdf.

Passey, D., & Davies, P. (2010). *Technology to Support Young People 16 to 18 Years of Age who are not in Employment, Education or Training (NEET): A Local Authority Landscape Review*. Coventry: Becta.

Passey, D., Davies, P., & Rogers, C. (2010). *Independent Evaluation of the Intervention Study in Sunderland Local Authority (LA) with Young People who are not in Employment, Education or Training (NEET): Final Report, March 2010*. Coventry: Becta.

Passey, D., & Gillen, J. (2009). *BBC News School Report 2008/2009: Independent Evaluation*. London: BBC.

Passey, D., & Rogers, C., with Machell, J., & McHugh, G. (2004). *The Motivational Effect of ICT on Pupils: A Department for Education and Skills Research Project 4RP/2002/050-3*. Nottingham: DfES.

Passey, D., Williams, S., & Rogers, C. (2008). *Assessing the Potential of e-Learning to Support Re-Engagement amongst Young People with Not in Education, Employment or Training (NEET) Status: An Independent Research and Evaluation Study. Overview Report: April 2008*. Coventry: Becta.

Pearson, P. D., Ferdig, R. E., Blomeyer Jr., R. L., & Moran, J. (2005). *The Effects of Technology on Reading Performance in the Middle-School Grades: A Meta-Analysis with Recommendations for Policy*. Naperville, IL: Learning Point Associates/North Central Regional Educational Laboratory (NCREL).

Penglase, M., & Arnold, S. (1996). The graphics calculator in mathematics education: A critical review of recent research. *Mathematics Education Research Journal, 8* (1), 58–90.

Pennington, R. (1998). *A Study to Determine the Effect of Instruction in Effective Use of a Calculator on Test Scores of Middle School Students*. Unpublished master's thesis, Salem-Teikyo University.

Perry, W. (2009). *E-portfolios for RPL Assessment: Key Findings on Current Engagement in the VET Sector*. Canberra: Australian Government Department of Education, Employment and Workplace Relations.

Piaget, J. (1972). *The Psychology of the Child*. New York, NY: Basic Books.

Picciano, A. G., & Seaman, J. (2007). *K-12 Online Learning: A Survey of U.S. School District Administrators*. Needham, MA: Sloan-C.

Pierce, M. (2012). Take a human touch, then add guidance. *T H E Journal, 39* (5), 24–26.

Pilli, O., & Aksu, M. (2013). The effects of computer-assisted instruction on the achievement, attitudes and retention of fourth grade mathematics students in North Cyprus. *Computers & Education, 62*, 62–71.

Plowman, L., McPake, J., & Stephen, C. (2008). Just picking it up? Young children learning with technology at home. *Cambridge Journal of Education, 38* (3), 303–319.

Plowman, L., Stevenson, O., Stephen, C., & McPake, J. (2012). Preschool children's learning with technology at home. *Computers & Education, 59*, 30–37.

Ponce, H. R., López, M. J., & Mayer, R. E. (2012). Instructional effectiveness of a computer-supported program for teaching reading comprehension strategies. *Computers & Education, 59*, 1170–1183.

Potocki, A., Ecalle, J., & Magnan, A. (2013). Effects of computer-assisted comprehension training in less skilled comprehenders in second grade: A one-year follow-up study. *Computers & Education, 63*, 131–140.

Powell, D., & Dixon, M. (2011). Does SMS text messaging help or harm adults' knowledge of standard spelling? *Journal of Computer Assisted Learning, 27,* 58–66.

Prensky, D. (2001). Digital natives, digital immigrants. *On the Horizon, 9* (5), 1–6.

Presseisen, B. Z. (2001). Thinking skills: Meanings and models revisited. In A. L. Costa (Ed.), *Developing Minds: A Resource Book for Teaching Thinking* (3rd ed.) (pp. 47–53). Alexandria, VA: ASCD Publications.

Prinzjakowitsch, W., & Seisenbacher, G. (2010). Social software tools in open youth work. In J. Engelen, J. Dekelver, & W. Van den Bosch (Eds.), *Social Media for Social Inclusion of Youth at Risk: Proceedings of the INCLUSO 2010 Conference* (pp. 21–28). Leuven: K.U. Leuven.

Questacon (2012). *School of the Air.* Canberra: Commonwealth of Australia.

Ratcliff, C. C., & Anderson, S. E. (2011). Reviving the turtle: Exploring the use of logo with students with mild disabilities. *Computers in the Schools, 28* (3), 241–255.

Rauh, J. (2011). Online education as a toll good: An examination of the South Carolina virtual school program. *Computers & Education, 57,* 1583–1594.

Reed, H. C., Drijvers, P., & Kirschner, P. A. (2010). Effects of attitudes and behaviours on learning mathematics with computer tools. *Computers & Education, 55,* 1–15.

Reilly, J., Gallagher-Lepak, S., & Killion, C. (2012). "Me and my computer": Emotional factors in online learning. *Nursing Education Perspectives, 33* (2), 100–105.

Richardson, J. T. E. (2012). Face-to-face versus online tuition: Preference, performance and pass rates in white and ethnic minority students. *British Journal of Educational Technology, 43* (1), 17–27.

Rienties, B., Giesbers, B., Tempelaar, D., Lygo-Baker, S., Segers, M., & Gijselaers, W. (2012). The role of scaffolding and motivation in CSCL. *Computers & Education, 59,* 893–906.

Robertson, J. (2011). The educational affordances of blogs for self-directed learning. *Computers & Education, 57,* 1628–1644.

Robertson, J. (2012). Making games in the classroom: Benefits and gender concerns. *Computers & Education, 59,* 385–398.

Robinson, C., & Sebba, J. (2010). Personalising learning through the use of technology. *Computers & Education, 54,* 767–775.

Roblyer, M. D., Castine, W. H., & King, F. J. (1988). Assessing the impact of computer-based instruction: A review of recent research. *Computers in the Schools, 5* (3–4), 41–68.

Rodrigues, S. (1997). Able students working in ILS environments. In J. Underwood & J. Brown (Eds.), *Integrated Learning Systems: Potential into Practice* (pp. 118–126). Oxford: Heinemann.

Rodríguez, C. D., Filler, J., & Higgins, K. (2012). Using primary language support via computer to improve reading comprehension skills of first-grade English language learners. *Computers in the Schools, 29* (3), 253–267.

Rosas, R., Nussbaum, M., Cumsille, P., Marianov, V., Correa, M., Flores, P., Grau, V., Lagos, F., López, X., López, V., Rodriguez, P., & Salinas, M. (2003). Beyond Nintendo: Design and assessment of educational video games for first and second grade students. *Computers & Education, 40,* 71–94.

Roschelle, J., Penuel, W. R., Yarnall, L., Shechtman, N., & Tatar, D. (2005). Handheld tools that "Informate" assessment of student learning in science: A requirements analysis. *Journal of Computer Assisted Learning, 21* (3), 190–203.

Rosen, Y., & Beck-Hill, D. (2012). Intertwining digital content and a one-to-one laptop environment in teaching and learning: Lessons from the Time To Know program. *Journal of Research on Technology in Education, 44* (3), 225–241.

Rosen, Y., & Salomon, G. (2007). The differential learning achievements of constructivist technology-intensive learning environments as compared with traditional ones: A meta-analysis. *Journal of Educational Computing Research, 36* (1), 1–14.

Rubin-Vaughan, A., Pepler, D., Brown, S., & Craig, W. (2011). Quest for the golden rule: An effective social skills promotion and bullying prevention program. *Computers & Education, 56,* 166–175.

Rutten, N., van Joolingen, W. R., & van der Veen, J. T. (2012). The learning effects of computer simulations in science education. *Computers & Education*, *58*, 136–153.

Saçkes, M., Trundle, K. C., & Bell, R. L. (2011). Young children's computer skills development from kindergarten to third grade. *Computers & Education*, *57*, 1698–1704.

Salam, S. N. A., Yahaya, W. A. J. W., & Ali, A. M. (2010). Embedded social learning in a persuasive technology: Building up child confidence to dental treatment. *The International Journal of Science in Society*, *1* (4), 173–183.

Salmon, G. (2000). *E-moderating: The Key to Teaching and Learning Online*. London: Kogan Page.

Samur, Y. (2012). Redundancy effect on retention of vocabulary words using multimedia presentation. *British Journal of Educational Technology*, *43* (6), E166–E170.

Sánchez, J., & Sáenz, M. (2010). Metro navigation for the blind. *Computers & Education*, *55*, 970–981.

Sandberg, J., Maris, M., & de Geus, K. (2011). Mobile English learning: An evidence-based study with fifth graders. *Computers & Education*, *57*, 1334–1347.

Santoro, L. E. & Bishop, M. J. (2010). Selecting software with caution: An empirical evaluation of popular beginning reading software for children with early literacy difficulties. *Computers in the Schools*, *27* (2), 99–120.

Savage, R. S., Erten, O., Abrami, P., Hipps, G., Comaskey, E., & van Lierop, D. (2010). ABRACADABRA in the hands of teachers: The effectiveness of a web-based literacy intervention in grade 1 language arts programs. *Computers & Education*, *55*, 911–922.

Savill-Smith, C., & Kent, P. (2003). *The Use of Palmtop Computers for Learning: A Review of the Literature*. London: Learning and Skills Development Agency.

Scardamalia, M., & Bereiter, C. (1994). Computer support for knowledge-building communities. *The Journal of the Learning Sciences*, *3* (3), 265–283.

Schachter, J., & Fagnano, C. (1999). Does computer technology improve student learning and achievement? How, when, and under what conditions? *Journal of Educational Computing Research*, *20* (4), 329–343.

Schildkamp, K., Rekers-Mombarg, L. T. M., & Harms, T. J. (2012). Student group differences in examination results and utilization for policy and school development. *School Effectiveness and School Improvement: An International Journal of Research, Policy and Practice*, *23* (2), 229–255.

Schinke, S. P., Fang, L., Cole, K. C., & Cohen-Cutler, S. (2011). Preventing substance use among Black and Hispanic adolescent girls: Results from a computer-delivered, mother-daughter intervention approach. *Substance Use and Misuse*, *46* (1), 35–45.

Schönborn, K. J., Bivall, P., & Tibell, L. A. E. (2011). Exploring relationships between students' interaction and learning with a haptic virtual biomolecular model. *Computers & Education*, *57*, 2095–2105.

Schuller, T. (2009). *Crime and Lifelong Learning: IFLL Thematic Paper 5*. Leicester: National Institute of Adult Continuing Education.

Scrimshaw, P. (1997). *Preparing for the Information Age: Synoptic Report of the Education Departments' Superhighways Initiative*. Cardiff, Belfast, Edinburgh, London: Welsh Office, Department of Education for Northern Ireland, The Scottish Office, Department for Education and Employment.

Searle, J. (1995). *The Construction of Social Reality*. New York, NY: The Free Press.

Selwyn, N. (2011). *Schools and Schooling in the Digital Age: A Critical Analysis*. London: Routledge.

Selwyn, N., Banaji, S., Hadjithoma-Garstka, C., & Clark, W. (2011). Providing a platform for parents? Exploring the nature of parental engagement with school Learning Platforms. *Journal of Computer Assisted Learning*, *27*, 314–323.

Shahriar, A., Pathan, H., Mari, M. A., & Umrani, T. (2011). The extent of satisfaction on the key factors that affect learner motivation. *International Journal of Academic Research in Business and Social Sciences*, *1* (3), 96–108.

Shamir, A., & Shlafer, I. (2011). E-books effectiveness in promoting phonological awareness and concept about print: A comparison between children at risk for learning disabilities and typically developing kindergarteners. *Computers & Education, 57*, 1989–1997.

Sharpe, R., Beetham, H., & de Freitas, S. (2010). *Rethinking Learning for a Digital Age: How Learners are Shaping their Own Experiences*. London: Routledge.

Sheng, Z., Sheng, Y., & Anderson, C. J. (2011). Dropping out of school among ELL students: Implications to schools and teacher education. *The Clearing House, 84* (3), 98–103.

Shieh, R. S. (2012). The impact of Technology-Enabled Active Learning (TEAL) implementation on student learning and teachers' teaching in a high school context. *Computers & Education, 59*, 206–214.

Shumate, E. D., & Wills, H. P. (2010). Classroom-based functional analysis and intervention for disruptive and off-task behaviors. *Education and Treatment of Children, 33* (1), 23–48.

Shurnow, L. (2001). *Academic Effects of After School Programs*. ERIC Digest ED458010.

Silva, H., Pinho, R., Lopes, L., Nogueira, A. J. A., & Silveira, P. (2011). Illustrated plant identification keys: An interactive tool to learn botany. *Computers & Education, 56*, 969–973.

Simon, S., Johnson, S., Cavell, S., & Parsons, T. (2012). Promoting argumentation in primary science contexts: An analysis of students' interactions in formal and informal learning environments. *Journal of Computer Assisted Learning, 28*, 440–453.

Sissons, P., & Jones, K. (2012). *Lost in Transition? The Changing Labour Market and Young People not in Employment, Education or Training*. London: The Work Foundation.

Siu, K. W. M., & Lam, M. S. (2012). Public computer assisted learning facilities for children with visual impairment: Universal design for inclusive learning. *Journal of Early Childhood Education, 40*, 295–303.

Skinner, B. F. (1935). Two types of conditioned reflex and a pseudo type. *Journal of General Psychology, 12*, 66–77.

Skouras, A. S. (2006). Coordinating formal and informal aspects of mathematics in a computer based learning environment. *International Journal of Mathematical Education in Science and Technology, 37* (8), 947–964.

Slof, B., Erkens, G., Kirschner, P. A., & Helms-Lorenz, M. (2013). The effects of inspecting and constructing part-task-specific visualizations on team and individual learning. *Computers & Education, 60*, 221–233.

Slykhuis, D., & Park, J. C. (2006). The efficacy of online MBL activities. *Journal of Interactive Online Learning, 5* (1), 14–31.

Smith, H. J., Higgins, S., Wall, K., & Miller, J. (2005). Interactive whiteboards: Boon or bandwagon? A critical review of the literature. *Journal of Computer Assisted Learning, 21* (2), 91.

Snoddon, K. (2010). Technology as a learning tool for ASL literacy. *Sign Language Studies, 10* (2), 197–213.

Snodin, N. S. (2013). The effects of blended learning with a CMS on the development of autonomous learning: A case study of different degrees of autonomy achieved by individual learners. *Computers & Education, 61*, 209–216.

Soe, K., Koki, S., & Chang, J. M. (2000). *Effect of Computer-Assisted Instruction (CAI) on Reading Achievement: A Meta-Analysis*. Honolulu, HI: Pacific Resources for Education and Learning.

Somekh, B., Underwood, J., Convery, A., Dillon, G., Jarvis, J., Lewin, C., Mavers, D., Saxon, D., Sing, S., Steadman, S., Twining, P., & Woodrow, D. (2007). *Evaluation of the ICT Test Bed Project Final Report June 2007*. Coventry: Becta.

Spanjers, I. A. E., van Gog, T., & van Merriënboer, J. J. G. (2010). A theoretical analysis of how segmentation of dynamic visualizations optimizes students' learning. *Educational Psychology Review, 22* (4), 411–423.

Spanjers, I. A. E., van Gog, T., Wouters, P., & van Merriënboer, J. J. G. (2012). Explaining the segmentation effect in learning from animations: The role of pausing and temporal cueing. *Computers & Education, 59*, 274–280.

Standen, P. J., Camma, C., Battersby, S., Brown, D. J., & Harrison, M. (2011). An evaluation of the Wii Nunchuk as an alternative assistive device for people with intellectual and physical disabilities using switch controlled software. *Computers & Education*, *56*, 2–10.

Starbek, P., Erjavec, M. S., & Peklaj, C. (2010). Teaching genetics with multimedia results in better acquisition of knowledge and improvement in comprehension. *Journal of Computer Assisted Learning*, *26*, 214–224.

Stephen, J. E., Christie, G., Flood, K., Golant, M., Rahn, M., Rennie, H., Speca, M., Taylor-Brown, J., & Turner, J. (2011). Facilitating online support groups for cancer patients: The learning experience of psycho-oncology clinicians. *Psycho-Oncology*, *20* (8), 832–840.

Stephenson, J., & Carter, M. (2011). The use of multisensory environments in schools for students with severe disabilities: Perceptions from teachers. *Journal of Developmental and Physical Disabilities*, *23*, 339–357.

STEPS (2007). *Study of the Impact of Technology in Primary Schools*. Luxembourg: European Commission.

Stewart II, J. F., Choi, J., & Mallery, C. (2010). A multilevel analysis of distance learning achievement: Are college students with disabilities making the grade? *Journal of Rehabilitation*, *76* (2), 27–39.

Suleman, Q. (2011). Role of educational technology at primary school level In District Karak (Khyber Pukhtunkhwa) Pakistan. *International Journal of Academic Research in Business and Social Sciences*, *1* (3), 85–95.

Sun, J. C.-Y., & Rueda, R. (2012). Situational interest, computer self-efficacy and self-regulation: Their impact on student engagement in distance education. *British Journal of Educational Technology*, *43* (2), 191–204.

Sung, H.-Y., & Hwang, G.-J. (2013). A collaborative game-based learning approach to improving students' learning performance in science courses. *Computers & Education*, *63*, 43–51.

Tamim, R. M., Bernard, R. M., Borokhovsi, E., Abrami, P. C., & Schmid, R. F. (2011). What forty years of research says about the impact of technology on learning: A second-order meta-analysis and validation study. *Review of Educational Research*, *81* (1), 4–28.

Tan, C.-K. (2012). Effects of the application of graphing calculator on students' probability achievement. *Computers & Education*, *58*, 1117–1126.

Tan, T.-H., Lin, M.-S., Chu, Y.-L., & Liu, T.-Y. (2012). Educational affordances of a ubiquitous learning environment in a natural science course. *Journal of Educational Technology and Society*, *15* (2), 206–219.

Thomas, K., & Orthober, C. (2011). Using text-messaging in the secondary classroom. *American Secondary Education*, *39* (2), 55–76.

Timmerman, C. E., & Kruepke, K. A. (2006). Computer-assisted instruction, media richness, and college student performance. *Communication Education*, *55* (1), 73–104.

Timmers, C. F., van den Broek, J. B., & van den Berg, S. M. (2013). Motivational beliefs, student effort, and feedback behaviour in computer-based formative assessment. *Computers & Education*, *60*, 25–31.

Tong, V. C. H. (2012). Using asynchronous electronic surveys to help in-class revision: A case study. *British Journal of Educational Technology*, *43* (3), 465–473.

Torff, B., & Tirotta, R. (2010). Interactive whiteboards produce small gains in elementary students' self-reported motivation in mathematics. *Computers & Education*, *54*, 379–383.

Torgerson, C. J., & Elbourne, D. (2002). A systematic review and meta-analysis of the effectiveness of information and communication technology (ICT) on the teaching of spelling. *Journal of Research in Reading*, *25* (2), 129–143.

Townsend, I. (2012). Thousands of parents illegally home schooling. ABC News. Accessible at: http://www.abc.net.au/news/2012-01-28/thousands-of-parents-illegally-home-schooling/3798008.

Trundle, K. C., & Bell, R. L. (2010). The use of a computer simulation to promote conceptual change: A quasi-experimental study. *Computers & Education, 54*, 1078–1088.

Tsuei, M. (2012). Using synchronous peer tutoring system to promote elementary students' learning in mathematics. *Computers & Education, 58*, 1171–1182.

Tucker, S. (2009). Perceptions and reflections on the role of the teaching assistant in the classroom environment. *Pastoral Care in Education, 27* (4), 291–300.

Twining, P., & McCormick, R. (1999) *Learning Schools Programme: Developing Teachers' Information Communication Technology Competence In The Support Of Learning*. Milton Keynes: Open University.

Ucar, S., & Trundle, K. C. (2011). Conducting guided inquiry in science classes using authentic, archived, web-based data. *Computers & Education, 57*, 1571–1582.

Underwood, J. (2009). *The Impact of Digital Technology: A Review of the Evidence of the Impact of Digital Technologies on Formal Education*. Coventry: Becta.

Underwood, J., & Brown, J. (1997). *Integrated Learning Systems: Potential into Practice*. Oxford: Heinemann.

Underwood, J., Ault, A., Banyard, P., Bird, K., Dillon, G., Hayes, M., Selwood, I., Somekh, B., & Twining, P. (2005). *The Impact of Broadband in Schools*. Coventry: Becta.

Underwood, J., Cavendish, S., Dowling, S., & Lawson, T. (1997). A study of sustainable learning gains in UK schools. In J. Underwood & J. Brown (Eds.), *Integrated Learning Systems: Potential into Practice* (pp. 54–66). Oxford: Heinemann.

US Department of Education, Institute of Education Sciences, National Center for Education Evaluation and Regional Assistance (2003). *Identifying and Implementing Educational Practices Supported by Rigorous Evidence: A User Friendly Guide*. Washington, DC: The Council for Excellence in Government.

Valcke, M., Bonte, S., De Wever, B., & Rots, I. (2010). Internet parenting styles and the impact on Internet use of primary school children. *Computers & Education, 55*, 454–464.

Valdez, G. (2004). *Critical Issue: Technology Leadership: Enhancing Positive Educational Change*. Washington, DC: North Central Regional Educational Laboratory. Accessible at: http://www.ncrel.org/sdrs/areas/issues/educatrs/leadrshp/le700.htm.

Valentine, G., Marsh, J., & Pattie, C. (2005). *Children and Young People's Home Use of ICT for Educational Purposes: The Impact on Attainment at Key Stages 1–4. Research Report RR672*. Nottingham: Department for Education and Skills.

Van Acker, R. (2007). Antisocial, aggressive, and violent behavior in children and adolescents within alternative education settings: Prevention and intervention. *Preventing School Failure, 51* (2), 5–12.

van Merriënboer, J. J. G., & Kirschner, P. A. (2012). *Ten Steps to Complex Learning: A Systematic Approach to Four-Component Instructional Design* (2nd ed.). New York, NY: Routledge.

Vandewater, E. A., & Bickham, D. S. (2004). The impact of educational television on young children's reading in the context of family stress. *Applied Developmental Psychology, 25*, 717–728.

Vasquez III, E., Forbush, D. E., Mason, L. L., Lockwood, A. R., & Gleed, L. (2011). Delivery and evaluation of synchronous online reading tutoring to students at-risk of reading failure. *Rural Special Education Quarterly, 30* (3), 16–26.

Vaughn, M. G., Wexler, J., Beaver, K. M., Perron, B. E., Roberts, G., & Fu, Q. (2011). Psychiatric correlates of behavioral indicators of school disengagement in the United States. *Psychiatric Quarterly, 82*, 191–206.

Vekiri, I. (2010a). Boys' and girls' ICT beliefs: Do teachers matter? *Computers & Education, 55*, 16–23.

Vekiri, I. (2010b). Socioeconomic differences in elementary students' ICT beliefs and out-of-school experiences. *Computers & Education, 54*, 941–950.

Vernadakis, N., Gioftsidou, A., Antoniou, P., Ioannidis, D., & Giannousi, M. (2012). The impact of Nintendo Wii to physical education students' balance compared to the traditional approaches. *Computers & Education, 59*, 196–205.

Verpoorten, D., Westera, W., & Specht, M. (2012). Using reflection triggers while learning in an online course. *British Journal of Educational Technology, 43* (6), 1030–1040.

Visscher, A. J., & Coe, R. (2002). *School Improvement through Performance Feedback.* Lisse, the Netherlands: Swets and Zeitlinger.

von Marées, N., & Petermann, F. (2012). Cyberbullying: An increasing challenge for schools. *School Psychology International, 33* (5), 467–476.

Vygotsky, L. S. (1978). *Mind in Society: The Development of the Higher Psychological Processes.* Cambridge, MA: Harvard University Press.

Wall, E. (2012). Parents spend £6bn a year on private tuition. *The Telegraph*, November 2.

Wang, P.-Y., Vaughn, B. K., & Liu, M. (2011). The impact of animation interactivity on novices' learning of introductory statistics. *Computers & Education, 56*, 300–311.

Watson, D. M. (1993). *The ImpaCT Report: An Evaluation of the Impact of Information Technology on Children's Achievement in Primary and Secondary Schools.* London: Department of Education and King's College London.

Watson, S. L., & Watson, W. R. (2011). The role of technology and computer-based instruction in a disadvantaged alternative school's culture of learning. *Computers in the Schools, 28* (1), 39–55.

Watson, W. R., Mong, C. J., & Harris, C. A. (2011). A case study of the in-class use of a video game for teaching high school history. *Computers & Education, 56*, 466–474.

Waxman, H. C., Lin, M.-F., & Michko, G. M. (2003). *A Meta-Analysis of the Effectiveness of Teaching and Learning with Technology on Student Outcomes.* Naperville, IL: Learning Point Associates.

Wecker, C. (2012). Slide presentations as speech suppressors: When and why learners miss oral information. *Computers & Education, 59*, 260–273.

Wei, F.-H., & Chen, G.-D. (2006). Collaborative mentor support in a learning context using a ubiquitous discussion forum to facilitate knowledge sharing for lifelong learning. *British Journal of Educational Technology, 37* (6), 917–935.

Wengenroth, L., Hege, I., Förderreuther, K., Riu, E., Mandl, H., Kujath, P., & Radon, K. (2010). Promoting occupational health in secondary schools through virtual patients. *Computers & Education, 55*, 1443–1448.

Wenglinsky, H. (1998). *Policy Information Report: Does It Compute? The Relationship Between Educational Technology and Student Achievement in Mathematics.* Princeton, NJ: Policy Information Center.

Wichers, M., Simons, C. J. P., Kramer, I. M. A., Hartmann, J. A., Lothmann, C., Myin-Germeys, I., van Bemmel, A. L., Peeters, F., Delespaul, P., & van Os, J. (2011). Momentary assessment technology as a tool to help patients with depression help themselves. *Acta Psychiatrica Scandinavia, 124*, 262–272.

Wiest, L. R. (2001). The role of computers in mathematics teaching and learning. *Computers in the Schools, 17* (1), 41–55.

Wiliam, D. (2010). The role of formative assessment in effective learning environments. In OECD (Ed.), *The Nature of Learning: Using Research to Inspire Practice.* Accessible at: http://www.keepeek.com/Digital-Asset-Management/oecd/education/the-nature-of-learning/the-role-of-formative-assessment-in-effective-learning-environments_9789264086487-8-en.

Wilson, K., Boyd, C., Chen, L., & Jamal, S. (2011). Improving student performance in a first-year geography course: Examining the importance of computer-assisted formative assessment. *Computers & Education, 57*, 1493–1500.

Windle, J., & Miller, J. (2012). Approaches to teaching low literacy refugee-background students. *Australian Journal of Language and Literacy, 35* (3), 317–333.

Wishart, J. G. (1993). The development of learning difficulties in children with Down's syndrome. *Journal of Intellectual Disability Research, 37* (4), 389–403.

Wishart, J., & Triggs, P. (2010). MuseumScouts: Exploring how schools, museums and interactive technologies can work together to support learning. *Computers & Education, 54*, 669–678.

Wood, C., Jackson, E., Hart, L., Plester, B., & Wilde, L. (2011). The effect of text messaging on 9- and 10-year-old children's reading, spelling and phonological processing skills. *Journal of Computer Assisted Learning, 27*, 28–36.

Wood, C., Pillinger, C., & Jackson, E. (2010). Understanding the nature and impact of young readers' literacy interactions with talking books and during adult reading support. *Computers & Education, 54*, 190–198.

Wood, D. (1998). *The UK ILS Evaluations Final Report*. Coventry: Becta.

Woody, W. D., Daniel, D. B., & Baker, C. A. (2010). E-books or textbooks: Students prefer textbooks. *Computers & Education, 55*, 945–948.

Wouters, P., & van Oostendorp, H. (2013). A meta-analytic review of the role of instructional support in game-based learning. *Computers & Education, 60*, 412–425.

Wright, J. C., Huston, A. C., Murphy, K. C., St. Peters, M., Pinon, M., Scantlin, R., & Kotler, J. (2001). The relations of early television viewing to school readiness and vocabulary of low-income children: The Early Window Project. *Child Development, 72* (5), 1347–1366.

Wrzesien, M., & Raya, M. A. (2010). Learning in serious virtual worlds: Evaluation of learning effectiveness and appeal to students in the E-Junior project. *Computers & Education, 55*, 178–187.

Wu, H.-K., Lee, S. W.-Y., Chang, H.-Y., & Liang, J.-C. (2013). Current status, opportunities and challenges of augmented reality in education. *Computers & Education, 62*, 41–49.

Wu, H.-L., & Pedersen, S. (2011). Integrating computer- and teacher-based scaffolds in science inquiry. *Computers & Education, 57*, 2352–2363.

Xiao, J. (2012). Tutors' influence on distance language students' learning motivation: voices from learners and tutors. *Distance Education, 33* (3), 365–380.

Yang, F.-Y., Chang, C.-Y., Chien, W.-R., Chien, Y.-T., & Tseng, Y.-H. (2013). Tracking learners' visual attention during a multimedia presentation in a real classroom. *Computers & Education, 62*, 208–220.

Yang, H.-J., & Lay, Y.-L. (2005). Implementation and evaluation of computer-aided Mandarin phonemes training system for hearing-impaired students. *British Journal of Educational Technology, 36* (3), 537–551.

Yang, H.-J., Lay, Y.-L., Liou, Y.-C., Tsao, W.-Y., & Lin, C.-K. (2007). Development and evaluation of computer-aided music-learning system for the hearing impaired. *Journal of Computer Assisted Learning, 23*, 466–476.

Yang, Y., Zhang, L., Zeng, J., Pang, X., Lai, F., & Rozelle, S. (2013). Computers and the academic performance of elementary school-aged girls in China's poor communities. *Computers & Education, 60*, 335–346.

Yang, Y.-F. (2010). Students' reflection on online self-correction and peer review to improve writing. *Computers & Education, 55*, 1202–1210.

Yang, Y.-T. C., & Wu, W.-C. I. (2012). Digital storytelling for enhancing student academic achievement, critical thinking, and learning motivation: A year-long experimental study. *Computers & Education, 59*, 339–352.

Yılmaz, R., & Kılıç-Çakmak, E. (2012). Educational interface agents as social models to influence learner achievement, attitude and retention of learning. *Computers & Education, 59*, 828–838.

Yu, A. Y., Tian, S. W., Vogel, D., & Kwok, R. C.-W. (2010). Can learning be virtually boosted? An investigation of online social networking impacts. *Computers & Education, 55*, 1494–1503.

Zacharis, N. Z. (2011). The effect of learning style on preference for web-based courses and learning outcomes. *British Journal of Educational Technology, 42* (5), 790–800.

Zavarella, C. A., & Ignash, J. M. (2009). Instructional delivery in developmental mathematics: Impact on retention. *Journal of Developmental Education, 32* (3), 2–13.

Zhang, B., Looi, C.-K., Seowa, P., Chia, G., Wong, L.-H., Chen, W., So, H.-J., Soloway, E., & Norris, C. (2010). Deconstructing and reconstructing: Transforming primary science learning via a mobilized curriculum. *Computers & Education, 55,* 1504–1523.

Zhang, M., & Quintana, C. (2012). Scaffolding strategies for supporting middle school students' online inquiry processes. *Computers & Education, 58,* 181–196.

Zhao, Y. (2003). Recent developments in technology and language learning: A literature review and meta-analysis. *CALICO Journal, 21* (1), 7–27.

Zhu, C. (2012). Student satisfaction, performance, and knowledge construction in online collaborative learning. *Educational Technology and Society, 15* (1), 127–136.

Zhuzhu, W., & Xin, L. (2010). Chinese schools modern distance education project in rural areas. *British Journal of Educational Technology, 41* (4), 612–613.

Index